The Sacraments in Biblical Perspective

INTERPRETATION

Resources for the Use of Scripture in the Church

INTERPRETATION

RESOURCES FOR THE USE OF SCRIPTURE IN THE CHURCH

Patrick D. Miller, *Series Editor*
Ellen F. Davis, *Associate Editor*
Richard B. Hays, *Associate Editor*
James L. Mays, *Consulting Editor*

OTHER AVAILABLE BOOKS IN THE SERIES

Robert W. Jenson, *Canon and Creed*
Patrick D. Miller, *The Ten Commandments*

RONALD P. BYARS

The Sacraments in Biblical Perspective

INTERPRETATION *Resources for the Use of Scripture in the Church*

WESTMINSTER
JOHN KNOX PRESS
LOUISVILLE · KENTUCKY

© 2011 Ronald P. Byars

First edition
Published by Westminster John Knox Press
Louisville, Kentucky

11 12 13 14 15 16 17 18 19 20—10 9 8 7 6 5 4 3 2 1

Scripture quotations from the New Revised Standard Version of the Bible are copyright © 1989 by the Division of Christian Education of the National Council of the Churches of Christ in the U.S.A. and are used by permission.

Grateful acknowledgment is made to the following for permission to quote from copyrighted material:

Susan Palo Cherwien, "O Blessed Spring," © 1993 Susan Palo Cherwien, admin. Augsburg Fortress.
Susan Briehl, "By Your Hand You Feed Your People," © 2002 GIA Publications, Inc.
Herman G. Stuempfle, "No Sign to Us You Give," © 1997 GIA Publications, Inc.
Susan Dunstan, "Crashing Waters at Creation," © 1991 GIA Publications, Inc.
David A. Hoekema, "You Are Our God; We Are Your People." Reprinted with permission. Text by David A. Hoekema. © 1985 Faith Alive Christian Resources
Richard Leach, "The Empty-Handed Fisherman," © 1994, Selah Publishing Co., Inc.
Taize Community, "Eat This Bread, Drink This Cup," © 1984 Les Presses de Taizé France; GIA Publications, Inc.

Book design by Drew Stevens
Cover design by designpointinc.com

Library of Congress Cataloging-in-Publication Data

Byars, Ronald P.
The sacraments in biblical perspective / Ronald P. Byars.—1st ed.
    p. cm.—(Interpretation)
  Includes bibliographical references (p.   ) and indexes.
  ISBN 978-0-664-23518-5 (alk. paper)
  1. Baptism—Biblical teaching. 2. Lord's Supper—Biblical teaching. 3. Sacraments—Biblical teaching. I. Title.
  BS2545.B36B93 2011
  234'.16—dc23

                                                                    2011023745

Westminster John Knox Press advocates the responsible use of our natural resources. The text paper of this book is made from 30% postconsumer waste.

This book is dedicated to
Susan Rhodes Byars, Baptism day April 17

and to

Stephen Rhodes Byars, Baptism day May 8
Lisa Kendeigh Blackadar, Baptism day April 25

Matthew Mason Byars, Baptism day May 19
Melissa Popewiny Byars, Baptism day April 27

Jonas Mason Byars, Baptism day December 27

Grace Robbins Byars, Baptism day May 30

Audrey Ione Byars, Baptism day June 10

Benjamin Rhodes Byars, Baptism day January 5

CONTENTS

SERIES FOREWORD

This series of volumes supplements Interpretation: A Bible Commentary for Teaching and Preaching. The commentary series offers an exposition of the books of the Bible written for those who teach, preach, and study the Bible in the community of faith. This new series is addressed to the same audience and serves a similar purpose, providing additional resources for the interpretation of Scripture, but now dealing with features, themes, and issues significant for the whole rather than with individual books.

The Bible is composed of separate books. Its composition naturally has led its interpreters to address particular books. But there are other ways to approach the interpretation of the Bible that respond to other characteristics and features of the Scriptures. These other entries to the task of interpretation provide contexts, overviews, and perspectives that complement the book-by-book approach and discern dimensions of the Scriptures that the commentary design may not adequately explore.

The Bible as used in the Christian community is not only a collection of books but also itself a book that has a unity and coherence important to its meaning. Some volumes in this new series will deal with this canonical wholeness and seek to provide a wider context for the interpretation of individual books as well as a comprehensive theological perspective that reading single books does not provide.

Other volumes in the series will examine particular texts, like the Ten Commandments, the Lord's Prayer, and the Sermon on the Mount, texts that have played such an important role in the faith and life of the Christian community that they constitute orienting foci for the understanding and use of Scripture.

A further concern of the series will be to consider important and often difficult topics, addressed at many different places in the books of the canon, that are of recurrent interest and concern to the church in its dependence on Scripture for faith and life. So the series will include volumes dealing with such topics as eschatology, women, wealth, and violence.

The books of the Bible are constituted from a variety of kinds of literature such as narrative, laws, hymns and prayers, letters, parables, miracle stories. To recognize and discern the contribution and importance of all these different kinds of material enriches and enlightens the use of Scripture. Volumes in the series will provide help in the interpretation of Scripture's literary forms and genres.

The liturgy and practices of the gathered church are anchored in Scripture, as with the sacraments observed and the creeds recited. So another entry to the task of discerning the meaning and significance of biblical texts explored in this series is the relation between the liturgy of the church and the Scriptures.

Finally, there is certain ancient literature, such as the Apocrypha and the noncanonical gospels, that constitutes an important context to the interpretation of Scripture itself. Consequently, this series will provide volumes that offer guidance in understanding such writings and explore their significance for the interpretation of the Protestant canon.

The volumes in this second series of Interpretation deal with these important entries into the interpretation of the Bible. Together with the commentaries, they compose a library of resources for those who interpret Scripture as members of the community of faith. Each of them can be used independently for its own significant addition to the resources for the study of Scripture. But all of them intersect the commentaries in various ways and provide an important context for their use. The authors of these volumes are biblical scholars and theologians who are committed to the service of interpreting the Scriptures in and for the church. The editors and authors hope that the addition of this series to the commentaries will provide a major contribution to the vitality and richness of biblical interpretation in the church.

The Editors

PREFACE

It is my conviction that we who are in so-called mainline churches are in the midst of a profound process of relearning our place in the world. The process of leaving behind our semiestablished identity, and finding a place in the world that is likely to be less prominent, is painful but also promising. The Constantinian era is over, and Christendom needs to be defined quite differently than it has been, and that is not necessarily a bad thing. The challenge for the historic Protestant churches and churches that derive from them is to learn to understand ourselves in ways that do not necessarily set us *against* the dominant culture(s), but that do require us to *distinguish* ourselves from the culture(s) in which we are immersed 24/7. That is a difficult challenge, and to meet it successfully will be immensely aided as we rediscover the joy of Scripture, along with embodied and relational worship, as it is so beautifully enabled by a strong sacramental life.

Like many of the intended readers of this volume, the bulk of my career has been spent in pastoral ministry in congregations, and for all that time it has been my delight to be a lectionary preacher. The delight—along with a certain amount of agony—has come with the privilege and opportunity to engage a specific biblical text in some depth every week, and to do so looking and listening for God's word for me and for the congregation in that time and place. The process is difficult, and risky, and with no guarantees, but it can also be immensely encouraging and refreshing. Without a doubt, the prospect of returning to this task again every week has sustained me through all sorts of ecclesiastical and pastoral weather!

As a theological educator, I focused chiefly on teaching students about worship, a discipline that, like preaching, provides the opportunity to bring together what may at first seem to be quite different things: historical study, theological reflection, ritual studies, congregational studies, practical theology, reflection on contemporary culture(s), and, of course, the Bible. Daunting though that assignment invariably is, I welcomed it, as someone whose life and hope are so deeply nurtured by the church at worship, especially by its sacramental life.

So when Patrick Miller invited me to write a book on the sacraments that would involve careful reflection on biblical texts, it seemed the perfect opportunity to combine the preacher's attention to Scripture with the liturgical theologian's attention to sacramental theology and practice. It was also a challenge to write a kind of book that may not be readily available, namely, a study of the sacraments that works primarily from specific biblical texts. In the process of writing I have discovered how very wide is the range of texts that help to interpret baptism and Eucharist, including many from the Old Testament and also some texts from the New Testament that do not at first glance appear to have a sacramental interest.

A sincere thanks to the editors of this series for the opportunity to participate in it—especially to Patrick D. Miller, who has supervised the effort, and to Professor Ellen Davis of Duke Divinity School, who has provided careful, painstaking editorial critiques and guidance, To the extent that the book is successful and useful to the church, she deserves a great deal of credit. I would also like to thank Marianne Blickenstaff for her attentive reading of the manuscript.

The book is dedicated to my wife, two sons, two daughters-in-law, and four grandchildren, all of whom help me to see more clearly the beauty of this world as the theater of God's glory (as Calvin liked to put it).

Introduction

The Challenge of the Sacraments

While the churches derived from the Reformation are likely to hold a high view of the sacraments, at least officially, wide swaths of Protestantism show evidence of being uncomfortable with them, or indifferent to them, or even embarrassed by them. The Swiss Reformed theologian, J. J. von Allmen, has suggested that churches influenced by prolonged exposure to the Enlightenment have "never known quite what to do about the sacraments," and are "challenged more strongly by the sacraments than by anything else" (von Allmen, *Worship: Its Theology and Practice*, 148). For many church people, worship is primarily about preaching and music, while baptism and the Lord's Supper are occasional alterations of the conventional Sunday protocols. Why should this be, when Martin Luther, John Calvin, and John Wesley all held in common a commitment to weekly Communion alongside the reading and preaching of the Word?

One reason is that the Reformers and their immediate successors found themselves on the cusp of a watershed in the history of Western culture. Some of the seeds of the eighteenth-century Enlightenment (or age of reason) were already in place at the time of the Renaissance and the Reformation of the sixteenth century. The Enlightenment took a more radical form in France than it did in Great Britain, but wherever it took hold, it reshaped the way people perceived the world.

1

Beginning with intellectuals and then spreading to the general population, the Enlightenment created what the sociologist Peter Berger has called a new "plausibility structure" (*The Heretical Imperative*) replacing the fixed presumptions about plausibility that had been in place throughout the medieval period. Every society tends to perceive reality in terms specific to that culture. What societies have in common is that none are likely to realize how closely their sense of the plausible is bound to a specific time and place. Whole societies presume that the tools with which they examine and describe reality are the same tools every society must necessarily use for that purpose. If other societies construe reality differently, it must mean that they are either ignorant or hopelessly prejudiced. (If only these others would open their eyes!) It is easy to forget that even so basic a matter as to agree about what makes an argument, belief, or point of view plausible shifts over time as culture changes. In the era that Western society was not too proud to call the "Enlightenment," reason was defined in ways that set it against faith. Reason was understood as autonomous, self-regulating, and always the same for everyone everywhere, whereas faith was a kind of blind submission to authority or perhaps to wishful thinking.

However, it is more credible to argue that reason is not immune to the influence of self-interest, whether personal or communal. Reason is quite as susceptible to distortion as any other intellectual tool, and can be made to serve any master. It can serve faith as well as it can serve agnosticism or atheism or indifference. However that may be, the plausibility structure that has been in place at least since the eighteenth century, if not earlier, continues to exert a profound influence on contemporary people, and it is in tension with the plausibility structure of the Bible.

The God of the Philosophers

Western societies, from the Enlightenment on, took for granted that, if there were a God, that God was not likely to be involved with the world, except perhaps by influencing human thoughts and feelings. For some Christians, a way to salvage at least some of the biblical stories was to interpret them psychologically rather than either historically or theologically. Secular thinkers often found the idea of God to be a useful one, both as a way of explaining the origin of things and to support certain rules of morality, but the God of the philosophers had little in common with the God of Scripture. The enlightened Thomas Jefferson, for example, admired Jesus, the rabbi. Jefferson created an edited version of the Gospels, which he called *The Life and Morals of Jesus of Nazareth*, removing everything that suggested that God's power might be manifested in the world: No incarnation, no healings, no multiplication of loaves and fishes, no cross, and certainly no resurrection.

If von Allmen is right that the sacraments pose a challenge to the churches as they have adapted to an Enlightenment-shaped culture, why is that so? One aspect of that challenge stems from the fact that Thomas Jefferson's rejection of those things in the gospel that testify to anything that is beyond ordinary, everyday experience highlights the discomfort we have all learned to feel with phenomena that cannot be rationally dissected and explained. Baptism, for example, is celebrated in the name of the Triune God. What could be more uncomfortable in a rationalist age than the Holy Trinity? The Lord's Supper is understood to be a down payment on the *basileia*, the reign/kingdom of God, when God will gather those from east and west, north and south, to eat and drink together. While even a hard-core rationalist might be able to imagine a disembodied soul flying off into some sort of heaven, it is much more difficult to rationalize a new heaven and earth, a cosmic redemption, a universal consummation characterized by reconciliation and justice.

Adapting to the Reigning Plausibility Structure

In adapting to the power of the age of reason, the churches found over the decades and centuries that they were more likely to hold on to their constituents and maintain some social influence by soft-pedaling hard-core Christian doctrine and paying a certain amount of deference to rationalist conventionalities. In the modern (Enlightenment-shaped) world, it has proven easier to project the Christian faith as an ethical or moral system than as a theological system. Of course, it is absolutely true that the biblical faith has

3

profound implications for ethics and morality, but it is also true that they are rooted in an alternative way of understanding and experiencing reality. In other words, Christian reflection on ethical and moral issues will always be rooted in theology, that is, a particular view of God, God's character, and God's disposition toward the world and toward us.

Learning to discern God's character and God's ways requires an immersion in Scripture and the story it tells, from creation to incarnation, Jesus' ministry, his cross and resurrection, ascension, and promise of the coming reign/kingdom of God. The biblical story provides and sustains an alternative plausibility structure to all the other plausibility structures as they take shape in various times and places, sometimes in ways more or less compatible with Scripture, sometimes in radical discontinuity.

The sacraments are intimately related to the affirmation that God is able to act in the world. In baptism God reaches out to claim us, incorporate us into God's covenant people, draw us out of death into life, and pour out the Spirit upon us along with the whole church. In the Eucharist, the Spirit manifests Christ among us, Christ crucified and risen, his presence serving as a foretaste of the reign/kingdom that will be the consummation of all things. The sacraments defy the rationalism that imagines that the deepest reality can be reduced to the capacity of the human intellect. They testify to the conviction that the knowledge of God involves the mind, indeed—but not only the mind.

Given the impact upon us all of what the conventional standards of the age of reason permit us to conceive as plausible, it is not surprising that the church has often attempted to adapt to the dominant culture by muting its testimony, by smoothing out that which is angular and resistant to tidy explanations. To affirm that God created the world and set it in motion has proved acceptable, and to affirm that God is either the sponsor of or the cheerleader for ethical living serves to assign to God some ongoing usefulness. This is particularly helpful when there are clearly defined enemies against whom it is desirable to invoke God's moral repugnance. Within this conventional framework the sacraments may have a place, but it is likely to be a marginal place, perhaps only to serve as occasional and nostalgic reminders of generous principles that might yet be salvaged from what remains of biblical faith.

4

Evangelicals, Too

One might expect that those churches that have rejected many of the adaptations that the so-called mainstream churches have made in order to fit into the world as shaped by the Enlightenment would be able to claim that they, in contrast to the mainstream, do not experience the sacraments as a challenge. However, one is likely to find that those who describe themselves as evangelical, conservative, or even as fundamentalist are as likely, and even more likely, to have marginalized the sacraments. Why should this be so? One reason may be that many churches on the so-called evangelical side have grown out of and been shaped by nineteenth-century revivalism, with its intense focus on human actions. When the accent falls so heavily on "decisions for Christ" and on maintaining a proper inward disposition, such an ethos is shaped by rationalism in another guise. Another reason may be, I suspect, because these churches, while offering to provide refuge for those who seek a more certain voice, embody many of the same presumptions and prejudices that have affected historic mainstream Protestantism: suspicion of ritual, growing in part out of a misunderstanding of the Reformation conflict with medieval Catholicism; a conviction that worship is basically an inward and interior act; and a sense that the spiritual and the material are incompatible. These churches, like the others, "are challenged more strongly by the sacraments than by anything else."

In 1832, Ralph Waldo Emerson asked the officers of his Unitarian church to do away with the Lord's Supper, which he refused any longer to administer. He wrote, "The use of the elements, however suitable to the people and the modes of thought in the East, where it originated, is foreign and unsuited to affect us. . . . We are not accustomed to express our thoughts or emotions by symbolical actions" (*A Documentary History of Religion in America*, 291).

Emerson pursued the logic of the reigning Enlightenment's "plausibility structure" in a way that was quite consistent with its underlying foundations. The presumption was that as people reach a certain level of sophistication, they will no longer need to use material things and symbolic actions as a crutch. In other words, those who are capable of conceptualizing spiritual truths can worship in their minds and hearts, without any need for real water, bread, or wine, which, in their stubborn materiality, serve the primitive needs of those who have not yet grown to intellectual (or spiritual) maturity.

Do We Outgrow the Need for Ritual?

Is it true that, as people become more educated, and presumably less superstitious and more sophisticated, they outgrow the need for ritual? When a man in our neighborhood went missing, yellow ribbons began to appear on trees for blocks around. Every few months the daily news reports the accidental death of a carful of high school students, and at the site of the tragedy one begins to see candles, flowers, handmade signs, teddy bears, ribbons with school colors. Children go to birthday parties, and though the celebrations have often become elaborate and expensive, the ritual remains: cutting the cake, blowing out candles, singing "Happy birthday to you!" Before the football game, the flag is presented, and someone sings the national anthem, and people take off their hats and hold their hands over their hearts. At the military funeral, taps will be played, and a flag will be carefully folded following a specific protocol, and presented to the nearest survivor. On Veterans Day, the president will present a wreath at the Tomb of the Unknown Soldier, and on Memorial Day family members leave flowers on graves. At official functions, faculties put on their academic regalia and follow the faculty marshal, who will be carrying a mace or other symbol in a grand procession. All these rituals have become hallowed to the extent that to fail to keep them, or to be careless about them, arouses public disapproval. In our society we are both drawn to ritual and suspicious of it. Ritual is not, in fact, to be so easily dismissed as only a primitive instinct, even though the reigning plausibility structure has made us uneasy and self-conscious about it.

Human beings are not merely brains with legs. Human beings are thinking creatures, indeed, and yet we bring much more to our encounter with the environment—both the material and the spiritual environment—than our intellects. One's whole being is consciously and unconsciously, intentionally and unintentionally, tuned in to experience that includes the cognitive but is not limited to it. Ritual is a medium by which the whole self may become engaged in interaction with the whole of our environment. Even when we

6

imagine that we have outgrown ritual and banished it from our lives, we incorporate ritual, often unrecognized, into our necessary routines. If you doubt it, try suggesting to a child that Christmas presents be opened at a different time this year than they were last year, or to your mother that she serve her guests pork chops rather than turkey for Thanksgiving dinner, or to the preacher that he or she omit the sermon today! The fact that we are living in the twilight of the age of reason means that we are still feeling the effects of that centuries-long era in which mind and body have been broken apart. But ritual is basic to human life, not something primitive to be left behind as we learn to live more and more into our heads.

The Spiritual/Material Dichotomy

The officers of Emerson's Unitarian church were not willing to go along with his recommendation to suspend celebrating the Lord's Supper, which led to his resignation as pastor. Although later Unitarians certainly agreed with Emerson and eagerly followed in the direction he had desired to lead, the decision makers in his congregation in 1832 were not yet ready to go so far, if only because they were uneasy about such a radical break with tradition.

Even those Christians who retained an attachment to orthodox doctrine had not been unaffected by the influence of Enlightenment rationalism. The more extreme wing of the Puritan movement, influenced by various forms of pietism, heightened the credibility of those who saw a sharp division between the material and the spiritual. Sometimes quoting John 4:24 ("God is spirit, and those who worship him must worship in spirit and in truth"), many of our forebears interpreted "spirit" to exclude material things. If spirit and matter are incompatible, then how might the church worship "in spirit and in truth"? The answer seemed to be that spiritual worship was worship of an internalized sort, effected by the mind and heart. It was not that these ancestors of ours ceased to make use of sacraments, but that they seemed, for example, to link the integrity of the Lord's Supper with the inner dispositions of the worshipers. It is quite understandable that the view of worship as a primarily interior affair would create a situation in which it was difficult to consider the sacraments to matter much, except that there was no escaping that Scripture points to Jesus telling his disciples, "Do this

7

in remembrance of me" (Luke 22:19) and "Go therefore and make disciples of all nations, baptizing them . . ." (Matt. 28:19). Given the dominical mandate, the church would follow orders, even if uneasily.

The view that spirit and matter are incompatible is, of course, much older than Puritanism or pietism. As early as the first century of the Christian era, groups of gnostics (from the Greek *gnosis*, "knowledge") had a much more sharply developed belief in the incompatibility of the spiritual and the physical. Gnostics competed with others to influence the mainstream of Christian thinking. In the long run, they lost. Gospels written by gnostics failed to win the approbation and support of the church and did not find their way into the canon. However, even though the gnostics lost, their basic dualism has resurfaced in various forms periodically. Certainly, it would be unfair to call the Puritans gnostics, but it is possible to discern a similarity that did not end with them but trickled down to us with the help of revivalism, and persists to this day.

Feeling or Doing?

It is not uncommon, even now, to hear the opinion expressed that it does not matter what we do in worship as long as our hearts and minds are properly disposed. Such a view has come to be so conventional that it has the ring of authority. After all, who could quarrel with the idea that the best worship flows from the passion of heart and mind? And yet, the question arises, How does one command and control the heart and the mind? Are we to stay away from church if we awaken on Sunday morning with heart and mind far from a worshipful state? Should we stay home, and not unlock the church doors and turn on the lights, if that is our responsibility? Should we stay home, and not hand out the bulletins, not sing the alto solo, not accompany the singing, not read the Scripture, not preach the sermon, not sit among those who are, presumably, in a proper disposition for worship, for fear that we might contaminate them? If worship is all a matter of heart and mind, should we be on the lookout for those whose hearts and minds seem not to be engaged, and turn them out so that the integrity of the assembly's worship will not be compromised?

8

The notion that truly spiritual worship begins with the heart and mind in an integrated state of adoration simply does not square with a great deal of human experience. It is possible to go to church just because that is the pattern of one's life, the discipline by which one shapes one's week, and to keep the discipline even if one is angry, or disappointed, or close to despair, or distracted, or possessed by a numbing state of indifference. It is possible that, when we have nothing but our presence to bring to worship, others will hold us up, and that some other week we will participate in upholding others who have nothing to bring but their physical presence. And it is possible that the very *doing* of worship—the actions observed, the postures assumed, the assembly's voice or one's own speaking or singing, the sound and sight of water, movement toward the altar/ table, the smell and taste of bread and wine—will subtly alter the temper of the heart and the mind. In other words, the rite can influence the interior disposition. The rite may come first, with heart and mind following where it leads. Just as acts of kindness and the pursuit of justice do not always faithfully reflect the complexity of our feelings, but are nevertheless things that we do and disciplines we undertake, worship is first of all not a matter of how we feel but of what we do, and has an authenticity even when we do it without being able to manifest what would seem to be the proper feelings.

"Just a" Symbol

A good deal of gnosticism remains in the churches today, even among those who have never heard the word. It is a misreading of Jesus' words to think of "spirit and truth" (John 4:23) as in opposition to the ordinary material world. The Christian gospel does, after all, begin with God's incarnation in Jesus Christ: "And the Word became flesh and lived among us . . ." (John 1:14). If God is spirit, and if "the Word" that was from the beginning is understood to be the manifestation of God's personal presence, and if "flesh" is understood to be mortal human being, then it makes no sense to construe spirit as incompatible with the physical. Classical orthodox Christianity, rooted in incarnational theology, has refused to separate spirit and flesh as though spirit is uniformly good and flesh uniformly evil. Indeed, the New Testament itself speaks of *"evil*

9

spirits" (e.g., Luke 7:21), and refers in a positive way to "flesh," mortality, physical reality.

> Without any doubt, the mystery of our religion is great:
> He was revealed in flesh,
>> vindicated in spirit,
> seen by angels,
>> proclaimed among Gentiles,
> believed in throughout the world,
>> taken up in glory.
>>> (1 Tim. 3:16)

Spirit may become manifest in and through persons who are physically present to us, and, indeed, in certain uses of material things such as water, bread, and wine.

While Puritanism as an organized movement has mostly died out, the Enlightenment sensibilities that it inadvertently served to empower have not disappeared. It is not uncommon to sense a certain unease about sacraments when someone is heard to say about baptism, for example, or the Lord's Supper: "It's justasymbol." (These words are so familiar that I cannot resist the temptation to write them the way they sound when spoken aloud!) The water and the rite are justasymbol, the bread and the cup are justasymbol. By modifying the word "symbol" with the word "just," the word "symbol" is reduced, diminished, stripped of any power. When the word "justa" is combined with "symbol," we find ourselves entering the world of Emerson. It is as though anything tagged with the word "symbol" is entirely arbitrary, a mere emblem of something else, like the wildcat logo on the University of Kentucky T-shirt.

Paul Tillich insisted that "the symbol participates in the reality which is symbolized" (Tillich, *The Dynamics of Faith*, 42). One might test his hypothesis with an experiment best conducted in the imagination. For example, in every congregation may be found one or more persons who are highly revered. Maybe in your congregation it will be the woman who always used to be found in the kitchen preparing food for the homeless or for a family meal to follow a funeral. The same woman may have served as treasurer of the congregation, talented in preparing and interpreting financial statements. She visited the sick, taught Sunday school, never became involved in intramural quarrels, and always had a good word for everyone. Now, imagine that you are standing in front of the

10

congregation at her funeral service. You are holding a large photo of her. What if you were to tear the photo into pieces, and scatter the pieces on the floor? What kind of reaction might you expect? It was, after all, just a piece of photographic paper with an image imprinted on it. Or was it? The photo (symbol, one might say) is, in the minds of the observers, intimately linked with the beloved person. One might even say, to use Tillich's elevated language, that the symbol participates in the reality of who she was. Outrage, hurt, and bewilderment would seem to be both predictable and understandable, were you to deface the photograph.

In your imagination, try another experiment to test Tillich's hypothesis. Place yourself on the steps of your local courthouse, holding the national flag and a box of matches. Set the flag on fire, and take note of the public reaction. Do you expect people to be angry? Shocked? The national flag, after all, is only a piece of colorfully printed cloth. Or does it, like the photo, somehow participate in the reality it represents? Are people shocked at the burning of colored cloth, or at the insult to the people, history, and institutions to which it is intimately related?

Suppose that a painter, working in your church building, needs a place to clean his brushes and notices in the sanctuary something that would serve the purpose. If he were to use the baptismal font for his very practical and necessary task, what would the reaction of the congregation be? Is the font simply another object, a useful artifact, or does it in some way require the sort of respect appropriate to the Christ with whom we are united in baptism?

Tillich is right. A true symbol is more than just an arbitrary sign. A true symbol is intimately related to what it represents. Most of the human race, throughout history and today, has an intuitive understanding of the connectedness and power of a symbol, and would not be tempted to say "just a" symbol. The power of the reigning plausibility structure as it has been established by Enlightenment rationalism has overcome our natural ability to discern the reality in the symbol. For us, symbol and reality have been broken apart. In our churches we continue to do what Christ, as recorded in Scripture, has told us to do. We baptize, and we celebrate the Lord's Supper. However, for many, the devaluation of "symbol" has led to uncertainty about the value of a sacrament, a suspicion of ritual acts, and self-doubt drawn from the fear that "doing this" is not enough, but requires an inward spiritual effort we are not sure we can summon in adequate proportions. This may be one reason the contemporary church continues to be "challenged more strongly by the sacraments than by anything else."

The Intersection of Two Cultural Eras

We are standing now, once again, at the intersection of two major cultural eras. The reigning plausibility structure of the Middle Ages, after passing through the furnace of Reformation and Renaissance, was reshaped in the age of reason, and in its evolved form it has served as the dominant cultural force even into the twenty-first century. But the dominance of the Enlightenment has been severely challenged. The actual plausibility of the reigning plausibility structure is not as airtight as it used to be. It is becoming evident that, beginning with the insights of physicists Albert Einstein and Niels Bohr in the mid-twentieth century, the Enlightenment paradigm is no longer adequate, and we find ourselves at the beginning of a new era. It may be decades before historians find a name for the new era, but now it is common to describe it quite simply as postmodern. In other words, what one could take for granted in the Enlightenment (modern) era, one can no longer take for granted in the contemporary (postmodern) era. The postmodern paradigm is far less fixed in a machinelike model of reality than the modern paradigm and is far more open to that which is not so easily imagined, predicted, or explained. It is then less likely to be closed to the Bible's characterization of God, which provides the paradigm for a scripturally based plausibility structure.

Although we find ourselves living in the overlap between two eras, in which the old plausibility structure still exercises considerable strength, its power is waning. The challenge in the emerging era will be to rediscover the treasure that has been devalued and hidden away for the past several centuries. In rediscovering the treasure that is the church's sacramental life, we may find the resources to resist the persistent tendency to draw sharp distinctions between flesh and spirit, body and soul. We shall worry less about taking the pulse of our inner feelings on a specific occasion and focus more on doing—on practices and disciplines that shape and give form to our faith, even as our emotional landscapes shift from day to day and moment to moment. Worship in both Word and sacrament will not be an affair for the head only or the heart only, but for the whole embodied person. It will not look exactly like what has come to be called "traditional" worship, nor exactly like what has come to be called "contemporary" worship. It will be boldly biblical, incarnational, and Trinitarian.

Biblical, because the God worshiped in the Christian assembly is not a generic deity, but the God whose character and disposition toward us is revealed in the simplicity and the complexity of the biblical story, unfolded in the several "languages" of historical narrative, personal and communal piety, parable, commandment, and promise. While every generation has a language of its own in which to express what we have heard in the biblical testimony, our contemporary speech cannot do without the languages of the Bible. We must still borrow from the languages that direct us to grace and judgment, praise and lament, death and resurrection, Christ's priestly intercession for us, and the consummation yet to come. Even when we find other words with which to express its message, the Bible, with its several "languages," remains, in a sense, unsubstitutable.

Incarnational, because the God worshiped in the Christian assembly has been made manifest to us in a human person, Jesus of Nazareth, who lived, died, and was raised in the midst of the messiness of political, religious, and economic conflicts as well as in the midst of personal and communal desperation, neediness, and tragedy. It was in the complexity of a beautiful, unjust, gentle, and violent world that God drew near to us, healing, judging, and blessing, as intimately related to us as the waters with which we wash and the food on our tables. Our God is neither generic deity nor philosophical abstraction, distant and removed from the contradictions of life as we actually live it, but rather the God who challenges Pharaoh, the God who speaks through prophets, the incarnate God, crucified, risen, and ascended. It is this God whom we trust to stand among us in our assemblies in both Word and sacrament.

Trinitarian, because we can know nothing at all about you, O God, despite ever so much speculation, unless you reveal yourself to us, and you have so revealed yourself as Father, Son, and Holy Spirit. This self-revelation is the content of the Bible, Old Testament and New. The God who is above all things has bent down to

13

join us in our three-dimensional life, and by the Holy Spirit, has become the divine interpreter.

> Our unbelief is sure to err
> And scan Your work in vain;
> You are Your own interpreter,
> And You will make it plain.
> ("O God, in a Mysterious Way,"
> *The Presbyterian Hymnal,* #270)

Worship that is sensitive to a postmodern era with sensibilities quite different from the modern period will be unapologetically biblical, incarnational, Trinitarian, and unapologetically sacramental, as we look for God's Word and promised presence in and through the sacraments, as well as in and through the Word proclaimed.

The "Second Naiveté"

The church has adapted to the reigning plausibility structures in every culture it has encountered, sometimes more successfully, sometimes less. As the churches of the twenty-first century begin to move more deeply into the postmodern era, it may be that the challenge of the sacraments will prove to be the most helpful of all the challenges the church might expect to encounter. The challenge of the sacraments may prove helpful in reintroducing us to the classical theology and piety of the church catholic as we are able to encounter them from within our own postmodern and ecumenical context.

While the age of reason was a time for throwing overboard, the postmodern era may be one of recovering much of value that has been lost or marginalized—recovering not as though we could return to the sixteenth century or the twelfth or the first, or as though we had not passed through and been altered by our collective experience in the Enlightenment era, but recovering that which has become newly accessible to us now that it is clear that neither history nor theological reflection has reached its endpoint in the age of reason. Paul Ricoeur has written about the experience of a "second naiveté" (Ricoeur, *The Symbolism of Evil,* 351), the possibility of recovering the value and meaning of a symbol by revisiting it with the help of a fresh interpretive vision.

14

Our first encounters with the Trinity, the resurrection, "real presence," Noah's flood, the ascension may have the character of a naive encounter, received uncritically, just as a child first meets an image, symbol, or idea that has been reduced to its simplest form in order to make it fit her or his capacities. As we bring to that image, symbol, or idea a broader experience, our first naiveté may evolve into skepticism. This may not be the path that everyone takes, but the journey from naiveté to skepticism is a familiar one in many lives. However, if Ricoeur is right, and I believe he is, the story need not end there. It is possible to revisit the image, symbol, or idea and ponder it, reflect on it, walk around it in order to view it from various angles and discover that it is much larger, much more profound than one might have thought either in the first, naive encounter, or in the skeptical mode. The capacity to reengage the image, symbol, or idea is, I believe, what Ricoeur means by a second naiveté.

Many Christians have discovered the power and possibility of a second naiveté when we encounter Scripture again after having experienced and absorbed the initial shock of being introduced to the various critical methods with which scholars study the Bible. All is not lost, after all! The image, symbol, or idea may be much larger, much roomier, than we had imagined in the first encounter, thrilling as that may have been, and much more spacious and hospitable than it had seemed to be when a necessary skepticism had seemed to narrow it. So it is with the church's proclamation, its teaching, and its sacramental life. If the age of reason marked the zenith of skepticism, the postmodern era opens to us the possibility of becoming skeptical of our skepticism, of reappropriating a faith we had feared might no longer be open to us, an equally thrilling recovery, made possible not by clinging to an undisciplined naiveté, but by an eyes-wide-open *second* naiveté.

The Sacramental Moment

It is a blessing that the church still remains the steward of the sacraments and the challenge they pose. However marginalized they may be, however uncertain some may feel about them, if we encounter them honestly, the sacraments lead us to serious reflection on the very heart of the gospel. Who is God? What is God's disposition toward us? Where are we headed? Are we headed there all alone? The challenge of the sacraments opens to us the possibility of recovering the energy of a robust faith that will serve the church well in this in-between era during which we segue from one major cultural paradigm to another.

The very peculiarity of sacramental rites may offer the church opportunities to engage in conversation with those who are struck by their peculiarity. Whether encountering a sacrament for the first time or after many times, it is natural to ask, "What does this mean?" To some extent, when the rite itself accompanies exposure to the preaching of the gospel over time, the rite begins to interpret itself. That self-interpretation may be intuited rather than reasoned out. Nevertheless, asking questions and probing for answers has a place too. "What does this mean?" It is a supremely important question, because how it is answered leads us into the heart of the gospel story.

However, neither baptism nor Eucharist means just one thing. It is in the very nature of a rite to compress multiple associations into a few words and actions. To take those associations apart and interpret them meaningfully requires us to linger over them, even though that lingering will require more time than the actual performing of the rites themselves.

Exploring the several meanings of baptism or the Eucharist leads us to the Bible, where we discover that there is no extended, detailed treatment of either sacrament collected in a single text or even a single book. Rather, the New Testament traditions about baptism and Eucharist, though shaped primarily in relation to Jesus, have also been informed by a variety of texts in the Old Testament relating to water, bread, wine, drenching, washing, eating, and drinking. The purpose of this book is to consider and reflect upon texts from both the Old and the New Testaments that provide an angle of vision that may help us to ponder the multidimensional characteristics of both baptism and Eucharist.

Rite First, Then Interpreting the Rite

Scholars hold various opinions about the origins of baptism (Collins, "The Origins of Christian Baptism"). Some believe that Christian baptism evolved from Jewish proselyte baptism. However, no documentary evidence for proselyte baptism exists earlier than the second century, leaving open the possibility that proselyte baptism might have been, ironically, an imitation of Christian baptism! Christian baptism likely developed most specifically from the ministry of John the Baptizer, but what are the origins of his baptizing in the Jordan? Washing rituals existed in various religions, including Judaism and Jewish sects such as the Qumran community (e.g., see in the book of Leviticus the many directions about washing to remove ritual uncleanness, as in chaps. 6, 11, and 13–17). However historians might manage to trace the origins of Christian baptism, it seems as though it was not a ritual conceived by priests or theologians with the purpose of expressing a precise doctrine or set of doctrines. More likely, the ritual came into being "on the ground," so to speak, unaccompanied by a carefully defined explanation.

Baptism certainly did not spring out of nowhere, but rather owes a debt to some sort of precedent or precedents. Whatever those precedents may have been, they began to be reshaped first in John's ministry and then in the community forming around Jesus. Surely even from the beginning, baptism in Jesus' community had a shared meaning, although that meaning may not have taken the form of exact definitions. Like all ritual, meaning may be discerned in the doing of it as much as or more than in talking about it.

The Gospel of Matthew concludes with the Great Commission, in which Jesus sends his representatives out to make disciples, baptizing and teaching. In the book of Acts and various New Testament letters, it is evident that the church was baptizing, and the several references to baptism help us to understand some of the ways early Christians understood what it meant. However, the references to baptism take for granted that Christians know how it is done and for whom, and typically lift up only one or two aspects of it as a way of making a point about some other matter of interest to the writer.

Students of the New Testament know a little more about the origins of the Eucharist, which is rooted in meal traditions from the Old Testament, meal traditions in the Roman Empire and first-century Jewish practice, and meal traditions specific to Jesus' ministry. These reach a focal point at the Last Supper but do not end there, since postresurrection meal traditions are crucial to understanding its development. Nevertheless, like baptism, the fact of the eucharistic meal comes first, with various interpretations of its meaning appearing in various Christian communities even in the New Testament period.

17

When Christians debate whether baptism means this or the Eucharist means that, in contrast to some other meaning, important issues are often at stake. In some instances, however, understanding baptism or Eucharist may not be a matter of deciding between this meaning or that one; rather, more than one interpretation may be faithful. Just as the Bible holds together both grace and obligation, without choosing one over the other or even resolving the perceived tension between the two, interpreting the meaning of baptism or Eucharist may bring into juxtaposition several meanings, each of which serves the church's need to discern why the sacraments matter to us, and how God may be working in and through them. Some communities may accent one meaning rather than another, and cultural contexts may play a role in deciding where the accents will be placed. Exploring meanings, with the help of Scripture, is not primarily a matter of settling arguments but of nurturing a healthy and discerning piety, rooted both in disciplined reflection and in disciplined practice.

Preaching on Sacramental Themes

Many of the texts addressed in this book appear, in whole or in part, in the Revised Common Lectionary, thus offering an opportunity for those who preach to unwrap various perspectives on baptism or Eucharist one at a time over the course of the liturgical year. Those who do not use the lectionary may choose texts relevant to the sacraments with some regularity, as they see fit, perhaps especially on days when one or both sacraments are being celebrated. Also, those who have preached over a course of several years notice that, even when preaching from a text the second or third time, the sermons will not be identical. One reason for that is that the preacher brings to the text different concerns and sensibilities each time, depending on what is happening in the preacher's own life as well as in the church and in the world. If the preacher brings to the process of listening to the text an attentiveness to sacramental issues as well, she or he will find that very often one can discern a baptismal or eucharistic connection that can legitimately be drawn out of a text; the text may not immediately appear to have anything to do with the sacraments, but may indeed prove even more profound when pondered from a sacramental point of view. In fact, for those with

18

eyes to see or ears to hear, a great deal of the Bible, in both Testaments, may be understood in a sacramental fashion.

The Christian gospel is deeply rooted in the piety, wisdom, and worship of the Hebrew people. Jesus Christ does not come to us out of a vacuum, as though his identity as God's Messiah should somehow require him to bypass any association with a particular culture or people or history. The gospel of an incarnate Lord presumes that the "Son of God" would be expected to come to us as one who is embedded in a specific community and tradition. This study will attempt to show some of the many ways that the gospel of Christ can be understood more deeply through examining the ways that it attempts to interpret his identity, ministry, and mission by making use of insights, images, and rites cherished by Israel and recorded in the Old Testament. Even the two sacraments that embody the gospel in its unique witness are not exceptions. While the Old Testament mentions neither baptism nor the Eucharist, it can nevertheless contribute to our discernment of God's grace in the sacraments as we encounter rites and images that shaped Israel's faith and its hope.

The Sacrament
of Baptism

CHAPTER 1

River Jordan:
The Gospel in Water

Luther's "Flood Prayer"

Martin Luther composed for his baptismal liturgy a prayer called the *Sindflutgebet*, or "flood prayer." The prayer evokes Old Testament texts as well as texts from the New Testament. It recalls the universal flood, recorded in Genesis, from which Noah and his family were carried to safety in the ark. The prayer rehearses the exodus story of Israel's escape from Egypt through the waters of the Red Sea. It calls to mind Jesus' own baptism in the Jordan River, described in the three Synoptic Gospels and, somewhat differently, in the Gospel of John. Luther's prayer has served as a model for most of the newer baptismal prayers in the service books of several denominations. (See, for example, the Presbyterian *Book of Common Worship*; *Book of Worship: United Church of Christ*; *The* [Episcopal] *Book of Common Prayer*; *Celebrate God's Presence: A Book of Services for the United Church of Canada*; *Common Worship: Services and Prayers for the Church of England*; *Evangelical Lutheran Worship*; *The United Methodist Book of Worship*.)

Almighty and eternal God, according to Your strict judgment You condemned the unbelieving world through the flood, yet according to Your great mercy You preserved believing Noah and his family, eight souls in all. You drowned hard-hearted Pharaoh and all his host in the Red Sea, yet led Your people Israel through

23

the water on dry ground, foreshadowing this washing of Your Holy Baptism.

Through the Baptism in the Jordan of Your beloved Son, our Lord Jesus Christ, You sanctified and instituted all waters to be a blessed flood and a lavish washing away of sin.

We pray that You would behold this child according to Your boundless mercy and bless him with true faith by the Holy Spirit, that through this saving flood all sin in him, which has been inherited from Adam and which he himself has committed since, would be drowned and die.

Grant that he be kept safe and secure in the holy ark of the Christian Church, being separated from the multitude of unbelievers and serving Your name at all times with a fervent spirit and a joyful hope, so that, with all believers in Your promise, he would be declared worthy of eternal life; through Jesus Christ, our Lord. **AMEN**.

> (http://ematthaei.blogspot.com/2006/08/luthers-flood
> -prayer_11.html, accessed October 11, 2010)

Thanksgiving over the Water
(*Book of Common Worship* [1993])

We give you thanks, Eternal God, for you nourish and sustain all living things by the gift of water. In the beginning of time, your Spirit moved over the watery chaos, calling forth order and life.

In the time of Noah, you destroyed evil by the waters of the flood, giving righteousness a new beginning. You led Israel out of slavery, through the waters of the sea, into the freedom of the promised land. In the waters of Jordan Jesus was baptized by John and anointed with your Spirit. By the baptism of his own death and resurrection, Christ set us free from sin and death, and opened the way to eternal life.

We thank you, O God, for the water of baptism. In it we are buried with Christ in his death. From it we are raised to share in his resurrection, through it we are reborn by the power of the Holy Spirit. Send your Spirit to move over this water that it may be a fountain of deliverance and rebirth. Wash away the sin of all who are cleansed by it. Raise them to new life, and graft them to the body of Christ. Pour out your Holy Spirit upon them, that they may have power to do your will, and continue forever in the risen life of Christ.

24

To you, Father, Son, and Holy Spirit, one God, be all praise, honor, and glory, now and forever. Amen.

The Church of England's *Common Worship* evokes Noah's flood and the drowning of the Egyptian soldiers at the Red Sea as it vividly petitions God, "Drown sin in the waters of judgement" (*Common Worship*, 365).

Several of the denominational books expand the biblical allusions, referring, for example, to the water in which human beings are suspended before birth. *The United Methodist Book of Worship* includes the line, "In the fullness of time you sent Jesus, nurtured in the water of a womb" (*UMBW*, 90). The baptismal font as womb as well as tomb is an ancient and vivid image. The United Church of Canada's *Book of Services* has a similar reference, and adds the petition, "Pour out, O God, your Holy Spirit upon this water, that this font may become your womb of new birth, our fount of blessing and source of grace" (*Celebrate God's Presence*, 344).

The United Church of Christ *Book of Worship* includes other water references from Scripture: "Jesus was baptized by John in the water of the Jordan, became living water to a woman at the Samaritan well, washed the feet of the disciples, and sent them forth to baptize all the nations by water and the Holy Spirit" (*Book of Worship*, 141).

The post–Vatican II Roman Catholic blessing of the water in the baptismal rite for adults follows the same form as Luther's flood prayer, and adds another image from Scripture: "Your Son willed that water and blood should flow from his side as he hung upon the cross" (*The Rites of the Catholic Church*, vol. 1, 201).

Common Misconceptions of Baptism

In December 2004, the BBC reported that David Beckham, the British soccer star, and his wife Victoria "hosted a star-studded christening for sons Romeo and Brooklyn." Victoria Beckham planned the ceremony, which took place in a chapel built especially for the occasion. According to the BBC, the chapel had two Buddhist shrines at its entrance. After Brooklyn was born, David Beckham had remarked, "I definitely want Brooklyn to be christened,

25

but I don't know into what religion yet" (http://news.bbc.co.uk/1/ hi/uk/4120477.stm).

If the Beckham "christening" event seems a bit incoherent, that is nevertheless hardly unique, except perhaps in its flamboyance. The church has not typically done a good job of interpreting the sacrament of baptism, either to its own members or to the general public. Those who seek baptism for themselves or their children, or who observe a baptism in church, tend to fill in the blanks for themselves, interpreting the meaning of the sacrament on their own, with help from the general culture. Baptism as culturally interpreted may be understood to be, variously,

a charming ceremony by which a family publicly celebrates the birth of a child;

a rite parents submit to, either to appease the grandparents or perhaps to ensure the child against some peril in this life or the life to come, if there should be one;

in cases of an older child, a sort of Christian bar or bat mitzvah, a coming-of-age rite of passage timed to occur when a child reaches the cusp of puberty;

any of several other possibilities learned either from folk customs or from treatment of baptisms (or "christenings") in popular culture

In most cases, those who come to the church seeking baptism for themselves or their children at least outwardly conform to the expected churchly forms, whatever their personal understanding of the rite. Only a very few build their own chapels and design their own ceremonies!

The challenge to the contemporary church is clear. We have to be deliberate and intentional in unwrapping the layered meaning of the sacraments, both for newcomers to the church and for continuing members. While baptism has multiple meanings, it is not open to any and every possible meaning. The example offered by the Beckhams no doubt stems from good intentions and from the barest acquaintance with the church's baptismal practice. However, neither good intentions nor lack of information justifies a rite that is only distantly related to the church's understanding and use of the sacraments with which God has entrusted it. Living as we do in a cultural moment marked by widespread biblical illiteracy, it is apparent that the church can no longer depend upon society in general to teach the basics of the faith (if it ever could), nor may it even place too much reliance on occasional exposure to the church's worship or its offerings of instruction for children. What would seem to be required would be an intentionality that grows out of the awareness that the church finds itself in a new cultural position in which we need to learn to think like a minority rather than like a majority (whatever the numbers involved).

A good point to begin reflection on the sacrament of baptism is the Gospel stories of Jesus' own baptism at the hands of John the Baptizer. For at least the first three centuries of the church's life, it was this story that provided the primary model for the rite of baptism, as well as for understanding it and teaching about it. The background for that story begins with John, an Elijah-like character drawing crowds to hear his preaching and witness his baptizing.

An Opening Out of an Old Story

The story of Jesus Christ is one that is drenched in Old Testament precedents, images, and language. It is not a brand-new story as much as it is an opening out of an old story—one that begins with God's choosing of Abraham and his progeny, and God's choosing of David and his royal succession. John the Baptizer is an Elijah-like prophetic figure who points like an arrow to Jesus, identified as God's "son," borrowing an Old Testament image. Jewish people would recognize and resonate with language about repentance, confession of sin, a heavenly voice, and the anointing of the spirit. The baptismal waters, according to the testimony of Mark and Luke, are a washing of repentance and the forgiveness of sins, powerful themes carried forward and developed in Christian proclamation and practice.

John the Baptizer

Matthew 3:1–12; Mark 1:1–8; Luke 3:1–6; John 1:6–8, 19–28

(We will begin with Mark, since that Gospel served as one source for both Matthew and Luke.)

Mark 1:1–8

Baptism plays a prominent role at or near the beginning of all four Gospels. Gordon Lathrop has suggested that all four follow the same shape:

> baptism,
> narratives,
> meal and passion,
> resurrection and sending . . .
> Such a list is, in exactly this order,
> recognizable to us as the emerging shape
> of the Christian Sunday meeting.
> (Lathrop, "Worship in the Twenty-first Century," 283)

The question might be whether the Gospels shaped the liturgical order or liturgical practice shaped the Gospels. It is quite possible that the answer is both. In any case, it is obvious that baptism is not a marginal matter for the Gospel writers. Baptism stands at the beginning of the Christian life, and at the beginning of the gospel story.

The Gospel of Mark opens with a quote that is a blend of the Old Testament books of Malachi and Isaiah (even though the introduction says, "As it is written in the prophet Isaiah").

Malachi-Isaiah as quoted in Mark	*Original Malachi*
"See, I am sending my messenger ahead of you, who will prepare your way; the voice of one crying out in the wilderness . . ." (Mark 1:2–3)	"See, I am sending my messenger to prepare the way before me, and the Lord whom you seek will suddenly come to his temple." (Mal. 3:1)

28 The "wilderness" reference is indeed from the prophet Isaiah. "A voice cries out: 'In the wilderness prepare the way of the LORD'" (Isa. 40:3). Mark immediately identified the "messenger"

mentioned in Malachi 3 as John the Baptist. "John the baptizer appeared in the wilderness, proclaiming a baptism of repentance for the forgiveness of sins" (Mark 1:4).

The fact that John's ministry took place "in the wilderness" is not merely circumstantial, either. For Israel, a primary formative experience had been the forty years of wandering in the wilderness, somewhere between Egypt and the promised land. John may have been by nature more at home in wilderness places at the margins of society, but at the same time the wilderness venue suited his message perfectly. John intended his hearers to understand that their generation stood poised at the beginning of a new sort of exodus-like transformation, a shaking off and leaving behind of the sins that had exiled them from God, a lifting of the eyes toward a renewal of the covenant of promise. Baptism served as a personal revisiting of Israel's experience at the Red Sea, a crossing over to safety, or even their crossing of the Jordan under Joshua's leadership, when they finally laid claim to the land of promise.

Wilderness, by definition, is a wild place, an untamed, in-between place, as it had been for Israel en route to the land of promise and as it was for those who had come out to hear John and witness what he was doing. It is a watershed sort of place, where people are both leaving something behind and moving toward something new. Most of us have experienced wilderness moments. We have spent time in a place where the landmarks are missing and the threats are real, though not so apparent as to be easily avoided, and we have found ourselves standing bewildered at some sort of intersection. Not only individuals but groups find themselves in those in-between moments, and that includes the church, for which the twenty-first-century social and cultural environment has been changing rapidly.

Centuries after the times of prophets seemed to have died out in Israel, John preached with a prophetic voice. Why wasn't preaching enough? Why did he accompany his message of repentance with a summons to baptism?

Hebrew prophets were known to accompany their prophetic messages with symbolic action. The prophet Ezekiel reported that God had told him to construct a model of Jerusalem under siege:

29

Then lie on your left side, and place the punishment of the house of Israel upon it; you shall bear their punishment for the number of days that you lie there. . . . When you have completed these, you shall lie down a second time, but on your right side. . . . See, I am putting cords on you so that you cannot turn from one side to the other until you have completed the days of your siege. (Ezek. 4:4–8)

The sign acts continued as Ezekiel dramatized prophecies of the siege of Jerusalem.

Similarly, the prophet Isaiah heard God tell him to walk naked through the streets of Jerusalem: "Then the LORD said, 'Just as my servant Isaiah has walked naked and barefoot for three years as a sign and a portent against Egypt and Ethiopia, so shall the king of Assyria lead away the Egyptians as captives and the Ethiopians as exiles, both the young and the old, naked and barefoot, with buttocks uncovered, to the shame of Egypt" (Isa. 20:3–4). In the same prophetic tradition of word plus sign, John came baptizing, a ritual washing that dramatized his message that the nation was in need of radical cleansing. Words matter, and using them skillfully can have a powerful impact. However, human beings process experience by means of all their senses, not just the sense of hearing. Juxtaposing a rite to a spoken message adds power and dimension to both. The drenching waters of the Jordan, whether experienced or observed, reinforced John's words, intensified and personalized his preaching.

The Greek word translated "baptism" in Mark 1:4 is *baptisma*, a word found only in Christian sources. The more generic Greek word is *baptismos*, a noun meaning dipping or washing. The verb form is *baptizō*, and may be translated as dip, immerse, wash, plunge, sink, drench, overwhelm (Arndt and Gingrich, *A Greek-English Lexicon*, 131). The fact that a new word had to be coined for Christian usage indicates the need from very early on for a word to represent the rite itself, rather than the more generic word that suggests a method of washing. The *Didache*, a second-century document probably written no more than sixty years after Mark, provides instruction about baptism: "Baptize in the name of the Father, and of the Son and of the Holy Spirit, in living [running] water. But if thou have not living [running] water, baptize in cold water; and if thou canst not in cold, then warm. But if thou have neither, pour on the head water thrice in the name of Father and Son and Holy Spirit" (*Didache*, VII). The linguistic connection to a specific mode of washing had evolved into *baptisma*, a word with a broader liturgical-theological reference.

John's baptism was both similar to and different from ritual washings familiar to observant Jews. The various ritual washings in the book of Leviticus are meant to purify a person of one or another form of ritual uncleanness, whether the priests before making sacrifices, or those who had acquired impurities arising from bodily functions or exposure to the dead or uncleanness related to disease. The washings in the Qumran community were also intended to provide cleansing for ritual uncleanness. However, John apparently understood his baptism not primarily as a means of obtaining purity from ritual defilement but, rather, in ethical terms, as had been earlier enjoined by the prophet Isaiah:

> "Wash yourselves; make yourselves clean; remove the evil of your
> doings from before my eyes; cease to do evil, learn to do good;
> seek justice, rescue the oppressed, defend the orphan, plead for
> the widow . . . though your sins are like scarlet, they shall be like
> snow." (Isa. 1:16–18a)

This text helps to define John's baptizing ministry, which was "a baptism of repentance for the forgiveness of sins" (Mark 1:4), rather than an act of cleansing from ritual uncleanness. The ethically oriented theme of forgiveness of sins begins with John's ministry, but it will carry over into Christian baptism as well.

The ablutions for which the book of Leviticus calls (particularly chaps. 6, 11, and 13–17), and the washings characteristic of the Qumran community differ from John's baptism in that they could be repeated, as often as daily in Qumran, while many times over a lifetime for those who observed the laws of Leviticus. By contrast, John's baptism seems to have been a once-in-a-lifetime affair, a singular move toward a decisive embrace of life in a new dimension. The mainstream of the church has certainly always understood Christian baptism to be unrepeatable. The fact that baptism is given once only, rather than many times, testifies to the reliability of God's promise. God's mercy will not run out! God's promise to be our God and to pour God's mercy and helping strength upon us is a reliable one, not one so feeble that we should have to go back to God again and again to secure another pledge.

Scholars are doubtful that John's baptism derived from proselyte baptism, required of Gentiles who were becoming Jews, a rite that may not have existed or may not have been widely practiced at the time of John's ministry. However, when evidence of proselyte baptism began to be documented, what it had in common with the washings of Leviticus and the frequent baptisms in Qumran is that it was self-administered, with one exception. When Gentile converts to Judaism had small children, baptism was administered to the children, since they were incapable of fulfilling the ritual washing on their own (Spinks, *Early and Medieval Rituals and Theologies of Baptism*, 4).

By contrast, those who responded to John's preaching did not baptize themselves but "were baptized by him [John] in the river Jordan" (Mark 1:5). T. F. Torrance has suggested that in John's baptism (and later, in Christian baptism), "all were treated as though they were children, in that someone baptized them" (Spinks, *Early and Medieval*). What difference might one discern between a self-administered rite and one that is administered by one person for another? It may be that baptism administered by one for another more clearly represents the bestowal of a gift. One is not cleansing oneself, as in an ordinary bath, but is receiving something. John understood, or perceived intuitively, that the act of one baptizing another serves as a representation of the sort of gift that God alone can give—such as, in this case, forgiveness of sins. A sense of indebtedness might be particularly vivid, since the experience of being baptized by someone else demonstrates that the person being baptized is dependent on the action of another, just like a helpless child in the bath.

The people from the Judean countryside and from Jerusalem who sought John out in the wilderness were baptized in the river Jordan, "confessing their sins" (Mark 1:5). Confession of sin, whether corporate or personal, was not a new phenomenon in Israel. Corporate confessions may be found in Nehemiah 9:16–37, for example, and in Daniel 9:3–19. In an example of personal confession, the psalmist prayed to God, "Then I acknowledged my sin to you, and I did not hide my iniquity; I said, 'I will confess my transgressions to the LORD,' and you forgave the guilt of my sin" (Ps. 32:5).

32   Mark hints at a link between John the Baptizer and the prophet Elijah, who in Jewish lore would precede the revelation of the

Messiah, when he describes John as "clothed with camel's hair, with a leather belt around his waist" (Mark 1:6; cf. 2 Kgs. 1:8). John proceeded to fulfill the role of predecessor when he announced that one "who is more powerful than I is coming after me" (Mark 1:7). "I have baptized you with water," John says, "but he will baptize you with the Holy Spirit" (Mark 1:8). Here we discover a crucial distinction between John's baptism and what will later be called Christian baptism. Both are administered by one for another; both relate to repentance, confession, and forgiveness; but Christian baptism has to do with the Holy Spirit.

Matthew 3:1–12

Matthew borrows heavily from Mark's account of John the Baptizer but adds material of his own. In Matthew's account, John came preaching this message: "Repent, for the kingdom of heaven has come near" (Matt. 3:2). John's reference to the kingdom recalls the words of King Nebuchadnezzar, contrasting God's kingdom with his own earthly kingdom: "His [God's] kingdom is an everlasting kingdom, and his sovereignty is from generation to generation" (Dan. 4:3b).

John's preaching of the kingdom of heaven coming near introduces an explicit eschatological dimension to his preaching, which is reinforced with an expansion of the message with material not found in Mark. Seeing Pharisees and Sadducees coming for baptism, Matthew tells the reader that John called out, "You brood of vipers! Who warned you to flee from the wrath to come? Bear fruit worthy of repentance" (Matt. 3:7–8). Matthew chooses to highlight God's judgment as a characteristic of the kingdom that was even then drawing near. John's message is reminiscent of a passage in the book of Ezekiel that also joins an act of purification with water to ethical and eschatological expectations: "I will sprinkle clean water upon you, and you shall be clean from all your uncleannesses. . . . And you shall be my people, and I will be your God. I will save you from all your uncleannesses" (Ezek. 36:25, 28, 29a).

John's vision, as Matthew sees it, points to an imminent judgment, and when he tells the crowds about the one who is coming after him, John declares, "He [the one who is coming] will baptize you with the Holy Spirit *and fire*" (Matt. 3:11, emphasis added). Although Matthew did not introduce John with a scriptural allusion

33

to "my messenger" drawn from Malachi (cf. Mark 1:2), his reference to a baptism of fire shows his reliance on the same passage from which Mark had drawn the messenger image. The prophet Malachi had handed on this word from God:

> See, I am sending my messenger to prepare the way before me. . . . The messenger of the covenant in whom you delight. . . . But who can endure the day of his coming, and who can stand when he appears? For he is like a refiner's *fire* . . . and he will purify the descendants of Levi and refine them like gold and silver, until they present offerings to the LORD in righteousness. (Mal. 3:1–3, emphasis added)

John uses the subsequent image of a winnowing fork and threshing floor to illustrate the division to be made between the righteous and the unrighteous (the wheat and the chaff) and intensifies the theme of judgment, since "the chaff he will burn with unquenchable fire" (Matt. 3:12). The language of fiery judgment seems even more stark since, while John told of the people "confessing their sins" (Matt. 3:6) and described baptism as an act of repentance (Matt. 3:11), nowhere in Matthew's narrative does John have anything to say about forgiveness of sins. Matthew associates the forgiveness of sins with Jesus.

Baptism can, of course, represent forgiveness, judgment, or both. On the one hand, water is essential to life and can symbolically manifest the generous outpouring of God's grace. On the other hand, in large amounts water can also put life at risk. Hurricane survivors bear testimony to the terrible destructive power of water. Flash flooding would have been familiar to people in arid places in the Middle East.

In Matthew's description, as in Mark's, John is the active baptizer, and those being baptized are relatively helpless as he either plunges them beneath the water or drenches them with a great quantity of it. A person being baptized must surely sense, however dimly, a threat to life. Chasing the people down after Pharaoh changed his mind about letting the Hebrews go free, the Egyptian soldiers drowned when the waters of the sea closed over them, certainly leaving behind a communal memory of divine judgment. The flood in Noah's time certainly represented judgment made manifest in water. Matthew characterizes John's baptism as a representation of God's judgment.

34

Judgment is not an antiquated notion that needs to be put on the shelf. Surely judging one another is a risky business, but in God's case, judgment is a form of grace. It represents God's bias toward justice. Judgment is a healing stroke, not intended to annihilate, but to redeem. It is something both to dread and to welcome: "Let the field exult, and everything in it. Then shall all the trees of the forest sing for joy before the LORD; for he is coming, for he is coming to judge the earth. He will judge the world with righteousness, and the peoples with his truth" (Ps. 96:12, 13). When one thinks of judgment in human terms, we are acutely aware that judgments are frequently biased, distorted by the vested interests of those making the judgments. However, God's judgment is free from these limitations and biases. God's judgment is trustworthy and reliably just.

The experiences of judgment we are most likely to remember are of having been judged ourselves, perhaps unfairly, and we tend to picture the kinds of judgment that can be imagined on a small screen. On a larger screen, however, God's judgment can be seen as a promise that God will have the last word when the need is for a strength that is big enough to counter the enormous centers of power in the world that manipulate, crush, mesmerize, or otherwise exploit the many who are small and whose power is narrowly circumscribed. Certainly the time of John's baptizing ministry was a time in which the people of Israel had to be aware of the enormity of the power of the Roman occupying authority, and perhaps also the power of the indigenous authorities who seemed unwilling to risk any of it in protecting their own people. In those circumstances, judgment would come as good news! "A shoot shall come out from the stump of Jesse, and a branch shall grow out of his roots. . . . But with righteousness he shall judge the poor, and decide with equity for the meek of the earth" (Isa. 11:1, 4).

Luke 3:1–18

Luke's account of John's ministry, like Mark's, describes John's baptizing as explicitly linked both to repentance and to the forgiveness of sins (Luke 3:3).

While Luke, unlike Matthew, does not refer to the kingdom directly, his quote from Isaiah 40 is more complete than either Mark's or Matthew's: "The voice of one crying out in the wilderness; 'Prepare the way of the Lord, make his paths straight. Every valley shall be filled, and every mountain and hill shall be made low, and

35

the crooked shall be made straight, and the rough ways smooth; and all flesh shall see the salvation of God'" (Luke 3:4–6).

In the Old Testament, Isaiah's words are, "Then the glory of the LORD shall be revealed, and all people shall see it together" (Isa. 40:5). Clearly, in either version, this is an eschatological promise. It points to a day of eschatological denouement, marked by the kinds of upheaval necessary to refashion the fixed and stubborn landscapes that give shape to human societies: valleys filled, mountains and hills leveled, rough ways smoothed out. The Lukan text invites us to ponder the theme of transformation, which requires a strength beyond our own to reshape the topography of our lives. John's baptism served as that first step into the powerful waters in which God is working personal and communal change.

Luke's paraphrase from Isaiah, "and all flesh shall see the salvation of God," offers an opportunity to ponder how baptism anticipates the ultimate ending/beginning, the new creation for which the whole world longs, characterized by justice and reconciliation. Although believers catch a glimpse of that new creation by faith, it shall ultimately become visible to all. Luke intends to point to Jesus, the coming one, as the embodiment of the kingdom/reign of God (*basileia*) in the world. Where Jesus is, the kingdom/reign of God is, and wherever the *basileia* makes an appearance, here and there, now and then, Jesus is in it; and in the ultimate consummation, Jesus will be in it.

Luke and Matthew have drawn material from a source they shared, portraying John in judgment mode, excoriating the "brood of vipers" (Luke 3:7). Luke follows the strong words of judgment with material that is unique to his Gospel. As Luke tells it, the crowds took John's preaching of judgment very seriously. They asked, "What then should we do?" (v. 10). John replied, according to Luke, with specific ethical directions applicable to anyone, but also including some directed especially to bewildered tax collectors and some to soldiers (Luke 3:11–14). To the crowds John said, "Whoever has two coats must share with anyone who has none"; to the tax collectors, "Collect no more than the amount prescribed for you"; to soldiers, "Do not extort money from anyone by threats or false accusation, and be satisfied with your wages." John's reply points to a way of being in the world that was countercultural then and is countercultural now, an alternative way of understanding what is truly valuable. Baptism is like that. When we take it seriously, it turns us around and points us toward the world as givers and caretakers rather than as exploiters.

Like Matthew, Luke says that the coming one "will baptize you with the Holy Spirit and fire" (v. 16). Luke (or perhaps the source common to both Matthew and Luke) must have had in mind that passage from Malachi 3. "For he [God] is like a refiner's fire."

Fiery judgment is both a challenge and opportunity for the preacher. Judgment is distasteful to those who have been overdosed on judgment as well as to those who are incapable of imagining anything so bad that it might rightly call for divine judgment. Nevertheless, judgment is more than just bad news. "For he is like a refiner's fire" underlies Luke's mention of "fire" in verse 16, representing the baptism to be brought by "one who is . . . coming." Even before Christ, in John's baptism, one may discern in a single ritual act how judgment and grace are intertwined. The fire will *refine*; that is, remove impurities and restore integrity. Baptism as not just one thing but at least two things helps us to understand grace as a kind of judgment, and judgment as a kind of grace.

For Luke, baptism with fire has another meaning as well. Luke, after all, is also author of the Acts of the Apostles, in which he tells the story of the first Pentecost. In that account, Luke describes the experience of the apostles. After a sound "like the rush of a violent wind" had filled the entire house, "divided tongues, as of fire, appeared among them, and a tongue rested on each of them" (Acts 2:2–3).

Luke has a special interest in the Holy Spirit and perceives the "tongues, as of fire" to be a manifestation of the Spirit: "All of them were filled with the Holy Spirit" (Acts 2:4). As Luke tells the story of the early church in the book of Acts, he will also be rehearsing stories of baptism and the gift of the Spirit and various ways in which the two are related. As portrayed by all three Synoptic Gospels, John's baptizing ministry is one that he himself understood to be laying the groundwork for one who was yet to come, who would bring another baptism, this time in the Holy Spirit. When Luke (and Matthew) add "and fire," we may discern both a refining fire, characteristic of the anticipated kingdom/reign of God and also, particularly in Luke, the power of the Spirit that would be made manifest in the ministry of Jesus and of his commissioned apostles.

37

John 1:6–8, 19–28

In the Gospel of John, the author tends to make his theological points with greater directness than the writers of the Synoptic Gospels. The Gospel writer wants everyone, including any continuing disciples of John the Baptizer, to understand that John was not the light, and was not the Messiah, and was not Elijah or any other prophet. The Baptizer said as much himself, according to the Fourth Gospel. The priests and Levites sent from Jerusalem asked, "Who are you?" (John 1:19).

The Baptizer answered quite plainly, "I am not the Messiah" (v. 20).

"Are you Elijah?". . . "I am not."

"Are you the prophet?". . . "No" (v. 21).

When the interlocutors from the city pressed John with this question of his identity, he replied with the by-now familiar quotation from the prophet. "I am the voice of one crying in the wilderness" (John 1:23; cf. Isa. 40:3). In other words, the reader is given to understand that the Baptizer's role is important, but it is a subordinate one. He plays a role in the gospel story, but the gospel is not about him. His role can be understood only in relation to the One to whom he points.

When persons who had been delegated by the Pharisees asked John directly why, if he was neither the Messiah, nor Elijah, nor a prophet, he was baptizing, he responded, "I baptize with water. Among you stands one whom you do not know, the one who is coming after me" (John 1:26–27). The reference is to Jesus, the Messiah, who stands in the crowd anonymously. For us, and all those who have gone before us or will come after us, Jesus will always be one whom we know and yet do not know. More always remains to be revealed, and, in the Baptizer's case, more will soon be revealed when the anonymous one steps up to be baptized. John knows that he [the Baptizer] is "not worthy to untie the thong of his [Jesus'] sandal" (v. 27). In reflecting on our own baptisms, we are able to discern Jesus, the one known and yet unknown, yet certainly known well enough to evoke our own reverence. John's role as witness to the light is an important part of the story, though destined to fade into the background as the light itself grows stronger.

The Baptism of Jesus

Matthew 3:13–17; Mark 1:9–11; Luke 3:21–22;
John 1:29–34

Mark 1:9–11

If you were to organize a Christmas pageant for your congregation using only the Gospel of Mark, it would have to be called off for want of material. Mark's Gospel never mentions Bethlehem, and names Nazareth for the first time in the opening chapter, which had already begun with the ministry of John the Baptizer. "In those days Jesus came from Nazareth of Galilee and was baptized by John in the Jordan" (Mark 1:9).

Mark offers no hint as to why Jesus had come to the site of John's baptizing ministry, nor why he had received a baptism "of repentance for the forgiveness of sins" (v. 4). The Letter to the Hebrews has expressed the traditional and orthodox understanding that Jesus was "without sin" (Heb. 4:15). It may be that Jesus intended to show his respect for John and to affirm his ministry, set outside the ordinary bounds of structured society in the wilderness, where Israel's experience of old had demonstrated the virtue of looking for the hand of God at work. By submitting to John's baptism in the Jordan, Jesus ventured to place himself alongside the sinners, rather than holding himself apart from them. Gordon Lathrop has written that

> Baptism gathers an assembly into Christ and so into identification with the situation of all humanity, not into distinction and differentiation. Paradoxically, Baptism is the washing that makes us unclean, with all the unclean and profane ones of the world. In Christ, Baptism makes us part of humanity, witnesses to the grace of the triune God for us all. (Lathrop, *Holy People,* 182)

Later in his ministry, Jesus became known for associating with sinners and outcasts, running the risk of ruining his reputation and losing his credibility by sharing a table with persons who, under the law, were unclean. Here we find a curious tension. The very rite of washing "for the forgiveness of sins" ought to leave us pure. But what sort of purity will it be? Apparently baptism does not lead to the kind of purity intended to be a distancing barrier that protects the baptized from the impurity of the world's inhabitants. It

39

manifests a different sort of purity, in which the sense of superiority, the smug sense of being "holier than thou," the sense of separation from the defiled masses, is washed away. If the conventional sort of purity is what someone is looking for, it will not be found in Jesus' baptism.

Jesus' later followers exhibited uneasiness about Jesus' having been baptized as though he needed to repent. But Jesus apparently was not worried about being mistaken for a sinner. He will, after all, die as a sinner. Torah says, "Anyone hung on a tree is under God's curse" (Deut. 21:22). A line leads directly from Jesus' baptism with sinners, to his crossing of taboos in order to associate with sinners, to his death in the manner of those who are cursed. Jesus himself, according to Mark, related his baptism to his ignominious death. On the road to Jerusalem, he asked James and John, who wanted to sit at Jesus' right hand and at his left in glory, "Are you able . . . to be baptized with the baptism [*baptisma*] that I am baptized with?" (Mark 10:38). At the beginning, middle, and ending of his earthly ministry, Jesus deliberately took his place among those who desperately needed repentance. If he had not, we would not know him.

Certainly it is good news that Jesus has chosen not to keep a distance from us, who are also sinners; but has drawn near to us— not in indifference to the various moral and ethical distortions that disfigure our lives and deform the communities of which we are a part, but, rather, because by his unequivocal offer to befriend us he offers us strength and help to repair our lives and relationships, for our sake and for the sake of the world. The implications of this for the church and for our personal ministries would seem to be that we also dare to turn our faces toward "sinners," those whom society grants us permission to ignore or despise, rather than away from them. If we seek the virtue of purity, it is purity by a different definition—one that risks drawing closer to those whose lives are broken in notorious ways, in order to discover our common humanity and lend our energies to healing what is broken.

Mark's terse report of Jesus' baptism offers few details, but his choice of language draws the reader's attention. "And just as he was coming up out of the water, he saw the heavens torn apart" (v. 10). Mark was recalling words of the prophet who had called out to God, "O that you would tear open the heavens and come down. . . . But you were angry, and we sinned; because you hid yourself we transgressed" (Isa. 64:1a, 5b).

Mark is sending a message about the identity of Jesus, although a subtle one. Certainly anyone who knew the Old Testament would be likely to catch it. The God who had seemed not to have spoken since the days of the prophets, who appeared to have hidden rather than take up the cause of an oppressed people, had answered Isaiah's heartfelt prayer, had "come down" in an act of self-revelation, drawing near to those who had "transgressed" (even though the transgressors were inclined to place the blame on God for having hidden from them!).

The "torn apart" image continued to be an operative theme as Mark composed his Gospel, since he later would use a form of the same Greek verb *schizō* when describing how, just as Jesus died, "the curtain of the temple was torn in two" (Mark 15:38). The curtain of the temple divided "the holy place from the most holy," in which the ark of the covenant had originally resided, the curtain having served the function of shielding the people from the presence of God (Exod. 26:33). In both the baptism narrative and in the description of the tearing of the temple curtain, Mark was signaling the readers that the hidden God had "torn apart" the barriers and drawn near.

As Mark tells it, "*he* [Jesus] *saw* the heavens torn apart." The use of the third-person singular suggests that this vision was not a public one. "And," Mark continues, "the Spirit descending like a dove on him." Is it Mark's intention to lay the accent on "descending," or on "a dove"? It would seem most likely that he is describing a graceful descent. Nowhere in the Old Testament is the Spirit identified with the image of a dove. Perhaps Mark had in mind the dove from the Noah story (Gen. 8:11–12). The dove's signal that the flood was over preceded God's establishment of a covenant with Noah and his descendants and with every living thing (Gen. 9:8–9). Mark's simile, comparing the descending Spirit to a dove, served as a hint that, in Jesus, God was tending to covenantal business.

One might wonder at the contrast that becomes evident between the apparently gentle, dovelike descent of the Spirit and the ferocity of the Spirit who "drove him [Jesus] out into the wilderness" (vv. 12–13). The Spirit is quiet and gentle, but also fierce. The same Spirit that is active in our baptisms opens our eyes, encourages and consoles us, but may also push us into uncomfortable places. There is no conflict here. Just as a parent can be both gentle and as strongly determined as may be necessary to protect a child

41

and require her or him to face up to responsibilities, the Spirit may comfort us or push us hard, according to God's knowledge of our need.

Certainly the reference to the Holy Spirit intends the reader to see that Jesus is indeed that one whom John had declared would come to baptize with the Holy Spirit (v. 8). The identification of baptism with the Holy Spirit marks a shift in the understanding of baptism that will play a key role in the development of subsequent Christian baptismal theology. Again, Mark may have in mind the words of the prophet: "A shoot shall come out from the stump of Jesse, and a branch shall grow out of his roots. The spirit of the Lord shall rest on him" (Isa. 11:1–2), and "Here is my servant, whom I uphold, my chosen, in whom my soul delights; I have put my spirit upon him; he will bring forth justice to the nations" (Isa. 42:1).

In the case of both of these Isaiah passages, originating in two different periods and from two different hands, the exegete working in the Old Testament alone might deduce that the promise was that the spirit would be given either to a monarchial successor to King David or to Israel ("my servant") as a whole. However, Mark, knowing the whole story of Jesus before ever beginning to write his Gospel, sees a link between the prophecies and Jesus that is a legitimate one, even though it is not likely that "Isaiah" would have been able to foresee the fulfillment of the prophecies with the same specificity with which Christians learned to see it. Mark's use of the Isaiah texts identified Jesus as the one who, immersed in and anointed with God's Spirit, would signal the coming of the eschatological reign of God, which will be characterized by justice filling the whole earth.

In Israel, both kings and prophets were anointed (see 1 Kgs. 19:16), as were priests (Exod. 28:41). Anointing might be understood as a figurative as well as a literal anointing with oil. The prophet uses the word metaphorically while referring to an anointing with the spirit. In the voice of an unnamed prophet, Isaiah wrote, "The spirit of the Lord GOD is upon me, because the LORD has anointed me; he has sent me to bring good news to the oppressed, to bind up the brokenhearted, to proclaim liberty to the captives, and release to the prisoners, to proclaim the year of the LORD's favor" (Isa. 61:1–2a).

Both "Messiah" and "Christ" mean, in their Hebrew and Greek origins, "anointed one." The early church understood the account

42

of the Spirit's descent on Jesus at his baptism to be his anointing, and a rite of anointing with oil would come to play a role in their baptismal liturgies.

"And a voice came from heaven" (v. 11). The Old Testament provides examples of a voice from heaven that is unmistakably God's own voice (e.g., Deut. 5:22–27). Mark does not tell us whether the people present heard the voice or only Jesus heard it, but since it seems to be that only Jesus "saw the heavens torn apart," it may be that only he heard the voice saying, "You are my Son, the Beloved; with you I am well pleased" (v. 11).

The word "Son" was not newly coined, but has a history in the Old Testament, as do all the New Testament titles applied to Jesus. One example of the use of the word "Son" is from the book of Psalms, in which God is speaking to the king: "I will tell of the decree of the LORD: He said to me, 'You are my son; today I have begotten you'" (Ps. 2:7). Mark has borrowed the image of "Son" as one way of pointing to the identity of Jesus. While not precisely defined, it sends an unmistakable signal that Jesus has a special appointment and vocation both like and unlike the appointment and vocation of King David and his successors. Jesus' relationship to God can be understood, at least partially, as similar to the relationship between a parent and an adult offspring who has inherited both a status and an obligation.

While the designation "Son" has a history, Mark (and the other Gospel writers as well) continue to define it, not in precise theological terms, but as they unfold the words, acts, ministry, death, and resurrection of Jesus throughout their narratives. The Gospel of Mark uses the phrase "Son of God" at the beginning of his story and at its climax.

The beginning of the good news of Jesus Christ, the Son of God. (1:1)	Now when the centurion . . . saw that . . . [Jesus] breathed his last, he said, "Truly this man was God's Son!" (15:39)

Between these two verses Mark shows us Jesus first from one angle, then from another, tutoring us as to how we might understand the title "Son of God." So, although the designation of "son" is not new to those who know the Old Testament, it is being made new as we see it realized in Jesus' life, death, and resurrection.

43

The Gospel story of Jesus' baptism played a significant role in the formation of early baptismal liturgies. Although the apostle Paul had already used the powerful image of baptism as sharing in Christ's death and resurrection in his Letter to the Romans (Rom. 6:3–5), the death/resurrection image seems to have had no liturgical influence in the first three centuries of Christianity. The accent fell on baptism as a womb (birth) rather than as a tomb. Even before the Councils of Nicaea (325 CE) and Chalcedon (451 CE) formally defined the doctrine of the Trinity, baptisms in the early church relied on the Trinitarian structure of the Gospel narratives of Jesus' baptism. It is easy to see in the Gospel of Mark that the chief roles are played not by John the Baptizer, but by the *Spirit*, the *Father*, whose voice was heard from heaven, and the *Son*, "the Beloved." One of the very early liturgical actions added to the act of baptizing itself was a ritual anointing with oil, particularly in Syria and other Eastern churches, as a representation of Jesus' anointing with the Holy Spirit as told in the Gospel narratives.

The United Methodist Book of Worship, like many of the other contemporary service books of the several denominations, provides for the laying on of hands while addressing the baptized with these words:

The Holy Spirit works within you,
that being born through water and the Spirit,
you may be a faithful disciple of Jesus Christ.

Then may follow signation with a sign of the cross on the forehead, and "N., child of God, you are sealed by the Holy Spirit in baptism and marked as Christ's own forever" (*UMBW*, 91). The United Methodist service offers a suggestion that might be followed in churches of other traditions as well. The rubric reads that "other persons, including baptized members of the candidate's family, may join the pastor in this action" (i.e., the laying on of hands).

Presuming that the person baptized is a small child, members of the family might come to the font, or the child might be carried to them, that they might also lay their hands on the child's head, or trace the sign of the cross on her or his forehead. In the case of an adult, members to join in the laying on of hands might come to the person at the font, or the pastor might escort a newly baptized person to them.

44

These various words and gestures, all of which relate to the Holy Spirit, serve to draw attention to the expectation that the Holy Spirit is at work in the rite of baptism to anoint us for service, just as the Holy Spirit anointed Jesus in preparation for the public launching of his mission.

Matthew 3:13–17

While the Gospel of Mark showed John the Baptizer as displaying deference toward the one who was to come, saying, "I am not worthy to stoop down and untie the thong of his sandals" (Mark 1:7), Matthew amplifies the theme. Jesus had come to be baptized by John, "but John would have prevented him, saying, 'I need to be baptized by you, and do you come to me?'" (3:14)

It may have been that the ministry of John the Baptizer still exerted influence and perhaps even attracted followers as late as the time in which Matthew was writing his Gospel, toward the end of the first century or early in the second. The intention of all the Gospel writers was to make it clear that, as great as John had been, standing as he did in the prophetic tradition exemplified by the prophet Elijah, John himself had understood that the main story was not about him, but about Jesus.

Jesus' response to John's demurral was enigmatic. "Let it be so now; for it is proper for us in this way to fulfill all righteousness" (v. 15). What can this mean? None of the Gospel writers suggest that the Old Testament had foreseen the Messiah's baptism, or that the Messiah would be ministered to by someone like John, so the reference cannot be to a fulfillment of an explicit prophecy. Matthew, who alone includes the verbal exchange between Jesus and John, may also have intended to address directly those who might be worried by the apparent contradiction of the sinless one being baptized in a rite that represented repentance. Perhaps the best interpretation we can offer of Jesus' statement is simply that being baptized by John made sense to Jesus, and he believed that it made sense in God's mysterious providence, yet to be revealed. Jesus would allow himself to be identified with sinners and to share their circumstances as closely as he could. It is that solidarity with sinners that would "fulfill all righteousness," although such a fulfillment could not possibly have been comprehensible until the whole of Jesus' story had been lived out. The sense of it will be revealed in the unfolding of the story, in particular in the cross and resurrection.

45

Another way of understanding Jesus' having consented to baptism "to fulfill all righteousness" might be that Matthew has portrayed Jesus as replaying in his own person the experience of Israel. Matthew drew parallels between Moses and Jesus. For example, Herod's slaughter of the holy innocents (Matt. 2:16) recalls Pharaoh's order that the Egyptian midwives kill the newborn sons of the Hebrew women (Exod. 1:16). The Lord's command that Joseph flee to Egypt with the holy family to protect Jesus from Herod's wrath serves as a vivid reminder that the children of Israel, following their brother Joseph, had fled to Egypt for refuge in their own time of trial (Gen. 47:1–6). And, just as Israel's journey to the promised land had begun with their crossing through the miraculously parted waters of the Red Sea (Exod. 14:21–22), Matthew tells how Jesus' journey led out of Egypt and ultimately through the baptismal waters of the Jordan River in a pilgrimage that would lead to his death and resurrection. Matthew wants the reader to note the parallels. He tells us that the flight into Egypt "was to fulfill what had been spoken by the Lord through the prophet,

"Out of Egypt I have called my son." (Matt. 2:15)	"When Israel was a child, I loved him, and out of Egypt I have called my son." (Hos. 11:1)	And a voice from heaven said, "This is my Son, the Beloved, with whom I am well pleased." (Matt. 3:17)

In response to John's reluctance to baptize him (who was not a sinner), Jesus said, "Let it be so now; for it is proper for us in this way to fulfill all righteousness" (Matt. 3:13). The fulfilling of righteousness might well be Jesus' assuming in his person the vocation of Israel. When the Baptizer heard Jesus' response, Matthew tells us that "then he consented" (v. 15). John may still have been puzzled, but he was willing to move ahead on faith.

Of course, Jesus' enigmatic words remind us that God is at work in the world in ways that are not always or easily discernible, and those ways may lead into unexpected places. For the Messiah, God's Son, to seek out the waters intended to wash sinners is among those unexpected places. It is certainly possible that God is working in unexpected ways and unexpected places today, and, for us, "fulfilling all righteousness" may include being alert to discerning God's action with obedient hearts, even where we are not accustomed to looking for it.

46

Matthew does not repeat Mark's reference to the heavens "torn apart," saying only that "suddenly the heavens were opened" (v. 16). Whereas Mark reports that the heavenly voice had said, "*You are* my son," Matthew records it as "*This is* my Son," as though others heard the voice as well as Jesus. The sense in which Israel as a whole was God's "son" shed light on the way that Matthew understood Jesus as "son."

"Son" language invites exploration of the relationship between two sons of God: Israel as a whole, chosen for special service to the end of blessing "all the families of the earth" (Gen. 12:3), and Jesus, the Beloved, who has been anointed by the Spirit for the same purpose. Around him is gathered the church, which shares in a sense the filial responsibility of serving the same universal mission by virtue of having been called, chosen, and equipped by the Spirit for such a task.

Luke 3:15–22

A peculiarity of Luke's account is that in verses 18–20 the baptism story has been interrupted with the statement that Herod had added to "all the evil things" he had done "by shutting up John in prison" (Luke 3:19–20). Somehow Luke was not troubled by the digression from the main line of the story to mention an event that must have occurred later, after Jesus' baptism. Perhaps for Luke, underlining the fact that John's preaching had gotten him in trouble with the authorities was more important than a consistent chronology. Luke sends the readers a signal that Jesus' first public appearance must be understood in the context of a larger conflict with the powers that be—a conflict in which his ministry was embedded in beginning, middle, and ending.

While in Mark and Matthew the descent of the Spirit occurs as Jesus was coming out of the water, Luke reports that, after Jesus had been baptized, he "was praying" (v. 21). Prayer is a major interest of Luke's, mentioned more often in his Gospel than in any of the others. While Jesus was praying, "the heaven was opened, and the Holy Spirit descended on him in bodily form like a dove" (v. 22). It may be that by omitting the phrase "he [Jesus] saw" the Spirit descending, Luke is saying he understood the descent of the Spirit to have been a public event, visible to all present. Adding the words "in bodily form" may also indicate that those gathered there could actually witness some manifestation of the Spirit and perhaps hear

47

an audible voice, although, in Luke as in Mark, the voice from heaven is not "This is my Son," but "You are my Son" (v. 22), leaving room for a measure of ambiguity about the public or private nature of the experience.

With Luke's special interest in prayer, it is not surprising that he links the opening of the heavens and the descent of the Spirit with Jesus in prayer after his baptism. While the Spirit does not depend on our prayer, the testimony of the saints would point to prayer as at times creating the perception of a thin space that reduces the distance between heaven and earth, between mortals and God, in such a way as to render us more than ordinarily available to the movement of the Spirit.

John 1:29–34

The Fourth Gospel is distinct from the Synoptics in that, like the book of Genesis, its first words are "In the beginning." The "Word" was in the beginning, and "the Word was God." That "Word," God's self-expression, "became flesh and lived among us, and we have seen his glory, the glory as of a father's only son" (John 1:14). With typical directness, John identifies Jesus as the incarnate Word. While all four Gospels treat the story of Jesus' baptism as a defining moment in which his identity was established, John is unique in preceding the baptismal narrative with testimony to the incarnation. He wants his Gospel to be read with the incarnation in mind.

The Gospel of John does not describe Jesus' baptism directly, referring to it only indirectly as John the Baptizer testified to what he had seen and experienced at Jesus' baptism. The evangelist tells us that it was the day after Jesus' baptism when John the Baptizer saw Jesus coming toward him and called out to everyone, identifying Jesus as "the Lamb of God who takes away the sin of the world" (v. 29).

This text, sung or said, can be found in the service books and/or hymnals of many churches as the *Agnus Dei* (Lamb of God).

> Lamb of God, you take away the sin of the world;
> > have mercy upon us.
> Lamb of God, you take away the sin of the world;
> > have mercy upon us.
> Lamb of God, you take away the sin of the world;
> > grant us peace.
> (*Evangelical Lutheran Worship*, 112 and other pages)

John specifically identified Jesus, the Lamb of God, as the one whose coming he had prophesied, one "who ranks ahead of me because he was before me" (v. 30), both echoing the Synoptics' theme that John understood himself to be subordinate to Jesus and at the same time reinforcing the theology of the Gospel of John that identifies Jesus as the Word who "was in the beginning with God" (v. 2).

In case there should be any doubt about the Baptizer's relative rank, identity, or vocation, John testifies that the reason he had come baptizing with water was specifically so that Jesus "might be revealed to Israel" (v. 31). Jesus' baptism was intended, in God's providence, to be a revealing moment, in which God would identify Jesus as the long-awaited One. It was a clarifying moment, an epiphany, for the crowds who had come out into the wilderness, thus establishing them as witnesses on behalf of all of Israel.

John the Baptizer declares that he had seen the Spirit "descending from heaven like a dove," and that it remained on Jesus (v. 32). The Spirit's visible descent was not ambiguous, not a private experience for Jesus alone, but a public event, to which the Baptizer bears witness.

In verse 33, John repeats the refrain from verse 31, "I myself did not know him." In other words, John's recognition that Jesus was the expected Messiah was not a conclusion he had reached on his own by natural means of gathering information or making a calculated personal judgment. It was the One who had commissioned the Baptizer, presumably God, who had identified Jesus to the Baptizer, saying, "He on whom you see the Spirit descend and remain is the one who baptizes with the Holy Spirit" (v. 33).

It is true, of course, that for every believer faith is a mystery of which the origins are not easily explained. Our natural gifts of perception are not sufficient that we should be able to "know him" on our own. Sometimes we can name an event, a person, a circumstance, or even a sustaining environment to which we might trace the beginnings of our faith, but others exposed to the same influences have not all responded in faith. Jesus' parable of the Sower testifies to the phenomenon of different responses among those exposed to the same stimulus (Matt. 13; Mark 4; Luke 8). In our contemporary environment, which is both secular and at the same time afflicted by various forms of oppressive religious absolutism, it can seem surprising that anyone has faith at all! Where there is faith,

49

the Spirit is at work, showing us what is not accessible to ordinary human perception. Faith is a gift, sometimes springing up against all the odds. The testimonies of Anne Lamott and Sara Miles, each of whom were children of atheists but became adult converts to the Christian faith, point to the unpredictable movement of the Spirit (Lamott, *Traveling Mercies*; Miles, *Take This Bread*). That faith looks to Jesus as the incarnate Word, a profound truth with which the Spirit bears witness to our spirits.

The community for whom John has written his Gospel would have been familiar with the rite of baptism, and with the teaching that the Spirit was given in baptism. The Baptizer's testimony links the community's experience of baptism with Jesus himself, who is the chief actor in the baptismal rite. He, after all, by God's own testimony through the Baptizer, "is the one who baptizes with the Holy Spirit" (v. 33).

Tending to be wary of ambiguity, the Gospel of John takes measures to guarantee that the reader will be sure to get the point by quoting the Baptizer saying, "And I myself have seen and have testified that this is the Son of God" (v. 34). Jesus is not a prophet in the ordinary sense, but "Son" of God. The Gospel writer has already offered his own definition of "Son" in his extended reflection on Jesus as God's self-expression, the Word of God made flesh.

John's disciples had not entirely disappeared even at the time of the writing of the Gospel of John. The interest of the Gospel writer was to make it as clear as possible that John did not understand himself to be a rival of Jesus'. The Baptizer's role was to prepare the way for Jesus and to bear witness to him, after which John's prophetic work would be done.

Baptism and the Forgiveness of Sins

Acts 2:38; Acts 22:16; 1 Corinthians 6:9–11;
Colossians 2:13–14

John the Baptizer came preaching a baptism "for the forgiveness of sins" (Mark 1:4; Luke 3:3; and similarly, John 1:29). Christians, having adopted John's ritual and reframed it as an act specifically related to Christ and the Holy Spirit, also understood it in relation to forgiveness of sins. For example, on the day of Pentecost, Luke records that Peter preached a sermon to the crowd who had

50

gathered in response to a public manifestation of the Spirit in relation to the apostles (Acts 2:4–6): "Repent, and be baptized every
one of you in the name of Jesus Christ so that your sins may be forgiven; and you will receive the gift of the Holy Spirit" (Acts 2:38).
The linking of forgiveness of sins and the Spirit characterizes baptism in its specifically Christian form, in contrast to John's baptism.

Luke also describes an address that Paul made to a rowdy audience when he had been rescued by Roman soldiers after being
identified and mobbed in the temple. Paul recited his story, including his personal credentials, his history as a persecutor of Christians, and his conversion on the road to Damascus. He recalled that
in Damascus a man named Ananias had visited him and spoken
words to him that led to Paul's regaining the sight he had lost in his
encounter with Jesus on the road. Ananias had said to him, "Get up,
be baptized, and have your sins washed away, calling on his name"
(Acts 22:16). At least by the time of Tertullian (160–225 CE), it had
become common in the church to believe that baptism effected the
forgiveness only of past sins. Tertullian argued against the practice
of infant baptism, clearly already an established practice, not on the
grounds that it was not valid, but because, when a child had a whole
life to live after baptism, the risks of committing postbaptismal sins
were so great that such an early baptism put the baptized person at
risk of condemnation. (For similar reasons, he opposed the baptism
of young, single adults.) This concern caused it to become commonplace for converts to postpone baptism as long as they could,
until they reached their deathbeds, if possible. This was the choice
of the Emperor Constantine (272–337 CE), who had embraced
Christianity with fervor, but did not seek baptism until he neared
the end of his life.

Augustine (354–430 CE) exerted a significant influence on
baptismal practice when he interpreted the doctrine of original
sin as inherited guilt that required baptism to wipe the slate clean.
Because infant mortality was high, postponing baptism appeared to
run the risk of imperiling an unbaptized child's salvation. This led to
the practice of baptizing as soon after birth as possible and eventually to a widespread practice of baptism by midwives, thus separating the sacrament from the context of the worshiping community.
The theological problem posed was that it had become evident to   51
pastoral observation and ordinary experience that baptized persons
still committed sins. If baptism was an act of forgiving only original

sin, what hope was there for those who lived long lives after their baptisms? The church found a solution in the fashioning of a whole new sacrament, the sacrament of penance (since Vatican II, the sacrament of reconciliation), which provided a protocol for auricular confession to a priest, who was empowered to forgive postbaptismal sins. This new sacrament posed a problem to the Reformers of the sixteenth century, who observed that the priest's power to forgive could easily be misused in ways that were manipulative and self-serving rather than pastoral.

The fact of such abuses challenged both Martin Luther and John Calvin, as well as others of the Protestant Reformers, to rethink issues related to baptism, particularly to baptism as an act intended for remission of sins. They took the position that baptism for the forgiveness of sins had a future reference as well as a past reference. One interpreter of Calvin's baptismal theology interprets it as the conviction that "in Christ all sins have been washed away, are being washed away, and will be washed away" (Old, *Shaping*, 248). "Of the essence of the Reformed understanding of baptism is the belief that it is a prophetic sign. It is a sign under which the whole of life is to be lived. Our baptism is always with us, constantly unfolding through the whole of life" (Old, *Shaping*, 179).

The baptismal invocation in Calvin's *Genevan Psalter* of 1542 includes a petition for a child being baptized, that he or she be sanctified by the Spirit and "that always he [*sic*] receive from you the remission of his [*sic*] sins" (Old, *Shaping*, 240).

André Benoit, in his study of baptism in the second century, argues that, while remission of sins was a constant in baptismal doctrine in that period, it had to do with the pardon of actual sins, not original sin. In the primitive church, the issue of postbaptismal sins posed no problem, because if baptism needed to be preceded by *metanoia* (repentance), *metanoia* did not end with baptism. Rather, it was necessary to repent ceaselessly while awaiting the future eon. Since repentance was a permanent fixture of the Christian life, sins after baptism raised no particular difficulty, since the Christian assumed a penitent state the whole life long (Benoit, *Le Baptême*, 223–24).

52   The sacrament of baptism initiates the incorporation of a person of any age into a community whose role is to form its members over a lifetime into a people who are capable of hearing a prophetic

word and, in response, confessing their own sins and their complicity in the sins common to all. The priestly role of the community is one that can be learned, and it involves both a proper penitence before the holy God for one's own sins and a commitment to acknowledge before God the sins of the church, the world, and every race, tribe, nation, and affinity group—a communal intercession for others, including those who cannot, do not, will not, or don't know that they ought to repent for themselves. Such formation begins with baptism, and is enabled by its promise of forgiveness.

The Letter to the Colossians specifically referred to baptism, relating it to forgiveness.

> [W]hen you were buried with him in baptism, you were also raised with him through faith in the power of God, who raised him from the dead. And when you were dead in trespasses and the uncircumcision of your flesh, God made you alive together with him, when he forgave us all our trespasses, erasing the record that stood against us with its legal demands. He set this aside, nailing it to the cross. (Col. 2:12–14)

This statement served to support the contention that the Christians of Colossae had been liberated from the oppressive power of "rulers and authorities" (2:15) and "the elemental spirits of the universe" (2:20), presumably referring to invisible powers as well as civil officers and religious officials and false spiritualities, with their prescriptions and regulations. Christians are not to be intimidated: "Why do you live as if you still belonged to the world? Why do you submit?" (2:20).

The homily continues as the writer of the letter expresses a passionate conviction that believers must set their minds on Christ, who is "seated at the right hand of God" (3:1), and put to death sinful behaviors (3:5–9), clothing themselves with virtues, such as "compassion, kindness, humility, meekness, and patience" as well as forgiveness and love (3:12–25).

Paul, or someone from his circle, sees baptism as a kind of dying and being made alive again. Our record has been cleared, and the new life calls for a continuing discipline of repudiating every sort of behavior that does not conform to the good news and dedicating ourselves to a new way of life.

In Colossians, the apostle's view would seem to be congruent with Benoit's summary of second-century views. Chapter 3 sets

53

before the recipients of the letter a charge that they adopt continuing disciplines intended to eliminate sinful behaviors, implying that such behaviors had not automatically dissolved after baptism, but required continuing attention if they were to be avoided; and also that Christians practice virtues fitting to those who have been buried with Christ in baptism and raised with him, as though ways of living appropriate to the gospel could be learned over time.

The contemporary service books of many denominations include rites of confession and pardon, not to forgive postbaptismal sins by means of sacramental acts, but to recall our baptism, which sustains us our whole life long. No Christian outgrows the need for the repentance that is embedded in the church's perception of baptism. The recollection that we are baptized serves to remind us of the promise that God will never abandon us to our sins, but embraces us and the whole church in an outpouring of mercy that never ends. In liturgical use, the person who pronounces the declaration of forgiveness might stand at the baptismal font to indicate that confession and pardon are rooted in our baptism.

Calvin's liturgical approach was to follow the minister's bold announcement of God's mercy with the reading of the Ten Commandments, understood as guidance for living the Christian life—guidance God has generously provided for people already forgiven.

The Presbyterian *Book of Common Worship* suggests following the pardon with either the reading of the commandments, or the summary of the law, or this:

Hear the teaching of Christ:
A new commandment I give to you,
that you love one another as I have loved you.
(*BCW*, 57)

CHAPTER 2

Marking the Transition from Death to Life

The Kansas City International Airport has created foot basins especially for Muslims, whose faith requires both the ritual cleansing of hands above the wrists and the washing of feet up to the ankles before prayers. Ceremonies for purification are familiar in more than one religious community, so it is perhaps not surprising to find rituals related to washing in both the Old and the New Testaments.

Baptism was very early on identified as a kind of washing. After Saul's conversion on the road to Damascus, Ananias exhorted him, "Get up, be baptized, and have your sins washed away, calling on [God's] name" (Acts 22:16). In a message to husbands, exhorting them to love their wives, the apostle Paul uses Christ and the church as an example: "Christ loved the church and gave himself up for her, in order to make her holy by cleansing her with the washing of water by the word . . . yes, so that she may be holy and without blemish" (Eph. 5:25–27). Paul made use of a washing image when he wrote to the Corinthians, "But you were washed, you were sanctified, you were justified in the name of the Lord Jesus Christ and in the Spirit of our God" (1 Cor. 6:11).

The references to washing in these texts may be literal, as in the Acts 22 passage, or perhaps metaphorical, as in the Ephesians passage, or both literal and metaphorical, as is likely in 1 Corinthians. In any case, the references to washing have been informed by a long tradition of washing images in the Old Testament. Read by

55

themselves, Old Testament texts about washing rituals may seem to have nothing to do with the Christian sacrament, but read with baptism in mind, they reveal that, indeed, they do have a contribution to make as we ponder the sacrament's layered meanings, first from one angle, then another.

Both the Old Testament washing rituals and the sacrament of baptism are complex, but both have something to do with death and contagion. Whether having to do with literal, biological death or with death as a metaphor for separation from an infection that corrupts the soul, the washing rites and the sacrament can mutually interpret each other. God's hand extended graciously to us may be discerned in both Old and New Testaments, which alike testify to a God who is at one and the same time both tender in dealings with human beings and a *mysterium tremendum*. Before this mystery, mortals must draw near with humility as well as confidence. The God who created the Levitical priesthood and called Israel to be a priestly people also entrusts the church to be a corporate priesthood, ordained by the sacrament of baptism to be a people whose ministry, testimony, and prayer are meant to contribute to the blessing of all the families of the earth.

Ritual Uncleanness and Death / Ritual Purification and Life

The image of baptismal washing has been influenced by washing rituals in the Old Testament, including some that point to a transition from death to life. While baptism is a New Testament sacrament, a specific action joining us to Jesus Christ in his death and resurrection, the ceremonial washing is not a new phenomenon. To understand it better, it is necessary to look at it in a context broader than the New Testament itself, and particularly to pay attention to the ways that the Old Testament links Israel's experience with water to life-giving things the various writers and editors understood God to be doing.

Shaped by Enlightenment sensibilities, "modern" people typically presume that ritual is inferior to intellectual beliefs, and that the purpose of ritual is to serve as an interpretive representation of some idea or conviction. If a ritual and its "meaning" are understood

56

to be separate and distinct things, then the ritual is construed as a device intended to lead to thought. Contemporary ritual studies, influenced by anthropology as well as psychology, take quite a different view of ritual. Rituals are not merely channels through which an intellectual belief or doctrine may be communicated, but they enable a personal engagement that involves more than the mind—indeed, the whole self. John's baptizing ministry in the wilderness made use of words and action that became a means for an encounter with the holy and righteous God. His washing ritual at the Jordan, like all ritual, clearly was not a device to promote a system of ideas. Rather, it was about meeting the God of Israel. "A ritual approach . . . acknowledges that human nature is embodied and therefore that full knowledge of God requires the engagement of all the senses. We do not come to faith only through our ears" (Moore-Keish, *Do This,* 154).

Although Christian baptism clearly traces its origin to the baptizing activity of John, his baptism is likely to have been rooted in the various Old Testament injunctions related to washing, recorded particularly in the book of Leviticus. Washing was required for both persons and their clothing when there was disease in a house (e.g,, Lev. 14:47), or when persons had recovered from a disease (e.g., Lev. 14:7–9). Washing of the candidates was required in a ceremony for the ordination of priests (e.g., Lev. 8:6), and it was also necessary to wash a garment or bronze vessel that had come into contact with a sin offering (e.g,, Lev. 6:28). The legs and entrails of an animal to be offered in sacrifice were to be washed (e.g., Lev. 1:9). Contact with an unclean animal required the washing of the person and of clothing (e.g., Lev. 17:15).

The various ritual washings emerged not to represent some autonomous "meaning" that participants were required to translate off of the symbolic actions, nor as magic, but rather as means by which mortal beings might expect to be led into the cleansing embrace of the God of Israel. In other words, they were intended to function sacramentally.

"Bodily impurity stands for the forces of death" (Milgrom, *Leviticus,* 129). Those afflicted with leprosy found themselves cut off from the community as though they had died. What the Bible calls "leprosy" is not what contemporary medicine would call Hansen's disease, but might more accurately be called "scale diseases,"

57

according to Jacob Milgrom, because they have a scaly appearance. These diseases resemble the deterioration of a dead body, which is what caused them to be declared ritually unclean.

The Gospel of Luke tells the story of Jesus' healing ten lepers as he was on the road somewhere between Samaria and Galilee. The lepers had called out to him, "'Jesus, Master, have mercy on us!' When he saw them, he said to them, 'Go and show yourselves to the priests.' And as they went, they were made clean" (Luke 13:14). Jesus' injunction that the lepers go to the priests was rooted in rules in the book of Leviticus. It was the priest who had the authority to declare that a person with a disease was ritually unclean and required to be separated from the community.

Leviticus 13:2–14:9

> When a person has on the skin of his body a swelling or an eruption or a spot, and it turns into a leprous disease on the skin of his body, he shall be brought to Aaron the priest or to one of his sons the priests. The priest shall examine the disease on the skin of his body; . . . after the priest has examined him he shall pronounce him ceremonially unclean. . . . The person who has the leprous disease shall wear torn clothes and let the hair of his head be disheveled; and he shall cover his upper lip and cry out, "Unclean, unclean." He shall remain unclean as long as he has the disease; he is unclean. He shall live alone; his dwelling shall be outside the camp. (Lev. 13:2–3, 45–46)

The law also provided rules for the ritual of cleansing for the leper whom the priest has examined and found to be free from disease (Lev. 14:2–9). First, the leper "shall be brought to the priest; the priest shall go out of the camp, and the priest shall make an examination. *If the disease is healed in the leprous person*" (Lev. 14:2b–3, emphasis added), certain things must be done. The ritual that follows involves two birds, one of which is slaughtered over a vessel of water. The priest sprinkles water, into which the blood of the slaughtered bird has drained, seven times over the person with the disease:

> Then he [the priest] shall pronounce him clean, and he shall let the living bird go into the open field. The one who is to be cleansed shall wash his clothes, and shave off all his hair, and bathe himself in water, and he shall be clean. After that he shall

come into the camp, but shall live outside his tent seven days. On the seventh day he shall shave all his hair: of head, beard, eyebrows; he shall shave all his hair. Then he shall wash his clothes, and bathe his body in water, and he shall be clean. (Lev. 14:7b–9)

The Leviticus text does not provide a ritual intended to *heal* the person with a leprous disease. Rather, if the priest has determined upon examination that the person is free of disease, the priest then provides the ceremony necessary to remove the ritual uncleanness.

> Thus the entire purification process is nothing but a symbolic ritual, a *rite of passage*, marking the transition from death to life. As the celebrants move from the realm of impurity outside the camp, and are first restored to their community, then to their home, and finally to their sanctuary, they have passed from impurity to holiness, from death to life. In so moving, they are reinstated with their families and are reconciled with their God. (Milgrom, *Leviticus*, 134)

When the ten lepers in the Lukan story begged Jesus for mercy, his only recorded response was to say, "Go and show yourselves to the priests" (Luke 17:14a). No mention is made of any word or gesture intended to effect a cure. But "as they went, they were made clean" (v. 14b). Presumably, when they presented themselves to the priests, the priests would certify that they were indeed cured and provide the cleansing ritual as prescribed, which would enable reconciliation with the community.

Neither Luke's story nor the ceremony for ritual cleansing in the book of Leviticus is about the sacrament of baptism. Nevertheless, two observations are relevant. The first is that a word from Jesus was sufficient for the healing of the ten. Likewise, in the sacrament of baptism, it is Jesus himself who is the primary actor, whose work is a work of healing. He lays claim to the baptized, uniting them with himself and the community of the faithful. It is not simply the authority of the person administering baptism or some special power in the water itself that effects what has been promised in the sacrament. It is Jesus who baptizes, joining his reliable promise to the words and actions of those who administer the rite.

The second observation is that the ritual cleansings described in the book of Leviticus serve, in retrospect, as a foreshadowing of the sacrament of baptism. They are different from the sacrament,

59

of course, because they can be repeated and because they have prescriptive and limited purposes. Nevertheless, they point to ways that God's power may be made manifest in a tangible sign—in this case, washing in water—for our benefit. The ceremony for ritual cleansing points to a way of understanding baptism that, similarly, using the Pauline images, has to do with passing from death to life; brings inside those who have been "outside the camp"; removes any stigma that clings to us and separates us from God and God's servant people; and sets us in the mainstream of the community of the faithful.

Martin Luther, when afflicted by depression and anxiety, reminded himself that he was baptized. Baptism takes death seriously, along with all the things that shadow life and threaten it, but above all, it testifies that in Christ's resurrection, God has definitively overcome every power of death and in our baptism has joined us to Christ and united us with a people. Baptism marks God's triumph, which has been, is being, and will be made manifest in our lives, singly and together.

The Revised Common Lectionary lifts up the note of celebration and thanksgiving as it calls for reading the Luke passage on Thanksgiving (Year A) and on Proper 23 (Year C), pairing it with Psalm 111.

> Praise the LORD!
> I will give thanks to the LORD with my whole heart,
>   in the company of the upright, in the congregation.
> (Ps. 111:1)

Death and Resurrection

The apostle Paul has provided a key image for baptism that serves as a lens through which to read some of the Old Testament references to washing rituals.

Romans 6:1–23

60

Do you not know that all of us who have been baptized into Christ Jesus were baptized into his death? Therefore we have been buried with him by baptism into death, so that, just as Christ was raised from the dead by the glory of the Father, so we too might walk in newness of life. For if we have been united with him in a death like his, we will certainly be united with him in a resurrection like his. (Rom. 6:3–5)

After Jesus' death and resurrection and in light of them, Paul reframes Christian baptism, which is a practice already in place (see Acts 9:18), as a participation in the Lord's dying and rising. Paul does not offer any systematic theology of baptism. When he mentions it, he uses it to make a point in the course of discussing some other issue. He takes for granted that those whom he is addressing already know about baptism and value it. Paul feels no need to explain in detail how baptism is performed or in precisely what circumstances, even as he opens it up to reveal a new dimension. He depends on his audience to see the connections he is making and grasp his point.

The Romans 6 passage, chronologically one of the early references to baptism in the New Testament writings, is of course clearly related to Jesus Christ and also exhibits a characteristic eschatological dimension ("we will certainly be united with him in a resurrection like his"). Paul uses the vivid image of participation in Christ's death and resurrection in the course of developing an argument about sin and grace and the role of the religious law. It is quite likely that an issue had arisen around these themes, one that could have been stated in terms of Paul's rhetorical question, "Should we continue to sin in order that grace may abound?" (Rom. 6:1).

Even the most beautiful and the healthiest of religious doctrines are susceptible to distortion and misuse, including the doctrine of grace. If it is true that God's grace reaches out to counter sin, then surely someone will be tempted to make an argument that since God's response to sin is grace, those who put their faith in God's grace might cross forbidden boundaries and behave as willfully as though there were no rules, all to demonstrate that grace abounds. Antinomianism has made more than one convert over the centuries, and it can still seduce those who are willing to be seduced.

Paul repudiated those who would revel in grace by scorning the rules embodied in the law. His argument goes something like this: Because of our sin, which has been embedded in human life both individual and communal ever since the first human beings, none of us is innocent, and all are rightfully condemned (Rom. 5:12, 18).

61

We are not capable of pulling ourselves free from this tangled pattern of sin, even by exerting a resolute determination to escape it. The only liberation from the cycle of sin is death, which is its radical, though bitter, remedy. It is at this point that the apostle evokes Christian baptism. In baptism, having been united with Christ in his death, we have already died (Rom. 6:3).

As Paul's reasoning goes, we died by having been baptized "into his death," but that is not the end of it, as anyone knows who is acquainted with the story of Christ's cross and his resurrection. United with him in his death, we shall also be united with him in his resurrection, although this union is described in the future tense— "we will certainly be united with him in a resurrection like his." In other words, our lives have been sacramentally joined to Christ's. "We know that our old self was crucified with him so that the body of sin might be destroyed, and we might no longer be enslaved to sin. For whoever has died is freed from sin" (6:6–7). The baptized have died to sin, but they are "alive to God in Christ Jesus" (6:11). A new possibility has been opened where there had been only one, and that a sad one. The new possibility is not one that we have created for ourselves out of our own determination and resolve, but the pure gift of God. "For sin will have no dominion over you, since you are not under law but under grace" (6:14).

The apostle continued, then, to develop his point, which is that walking "in newness of life" (6:4) does not involve abusing God's grace or taking it for granted. Instead, we find ourselves in a circumstance of having been liberated from a demeaning servitude to ugly and destructive ways of living because we belong no longer to them as our mentors and masters, but to God, whose will for us is not to crush us, but to set us free to live as those who have been created to bear the divine image. "But now that you have been freed from sin and enslaved to God, the advantage you get is sanctification. The end is eternal life" (6:22–23). "Eternal life" is not simply a life, following biological death, that never ends. It is also to participate to the extent possible for temporal human beings in tasting by anticipation the delight and enjoyment of the *basileia*, the reign of God, here and now, even in the midst of the contradictions and ambiguities of this life, expectantly awaiting the final consummation, the healing of the whole creation.

62

In Galatians, written even earlier than the Letter to the Romans, Paul had already used a similar image in the course of developing an argument about justification and faith, although without mentioning baptism. "I have been crucified with Christ; and it is no longer I who live, but it is Christ who lives in me" (Gal. 2:19b–20a). Although scholars debate the authorship of the Letter to the Colossians, it also links baptism with death and resurrection in Christ. "When you were buried with him in baptism, you were also raised with him through faith in the power of God, who raised him from the dead" (Col. 2:12). Unlike Romans, the Colossians text testifies to a transformation that the author believes has already occurred, rather than one that is yet to be fulfilled eschatologically.

Raymond Brown believes that the link between baptism and Christ's death may be discovered in Jesus' own words, recalled in the Gospel of Mark. In response to a request from James and John, who wanted to sit on either side of Jesus in his glory, Jesus had replied, "Are you able to drink the cup that I drink, or be baptized with the baptism [*baptisma*] that I am baptized with?" (Mark 10:38). The "baptism" is clearly his death. Jesus' question confronts them with something the two disciples may not have adequately considered: to belong to Jesus costs something. "Whoever does not take up the cross and follow me is not worthy of me. Those who find their life will lose it, and those who lose their life for my sake will find it" (Matt. 10:38–39).

For Paul, and for the author of Colossians if that is not Paul, "death" needs to be understood metaphorically rather than literally, just as taking up the cross refers to something other than a literal physical action. If Christians "lose their life"—die, in some sense, with Christ in their baptisms—what is being left behind? What is left behind—inundated, drowned—is a culture that nurtures in us a practical atheism. There is not an absence of belief, indeed, for belief of all sorts may very well proliferate; but, for all practical purposes, the God of Israel and of Jesus Christ is typically pushed to the margins of our attention. Other masters govern us, even while we may imagine ourselves to be in charge of our own lives. This atheism-for-all-practical-purposes takes different forms in different societies and eras; in our own, it is incarnated in a culture of unrelenting distractions.

Karl Marx taught that religion is the opiate of the people (paraphrased, from Marx, *Critique of Hegel's Philosophy*). He believed that religion served the powers that be, those who had a vested interest in distracting the general population from paying attention

63

to ways that they were being exploited. Religion, he said, caused people to look for justice in the next world, while passively going with the flow in this one.

Some religion, in some places and some times, does indeed seem to function as a drug, but even in a society like ours, in which religious faith is relegated to a kind of religion department that has authority only in the private and personal spheres of life, there are abundant influences that have the same intended effect. I don't mean to imply that there is some kind of sinister cabal at work plotting conspiracies against God. It is subtler than that. Neil Postman has written a book called *Amusing Ourselves to Death.* Certainly entertainment may serve as an opiatelike distraction, particularly when it is available and indeed pressed upon us 24/7, but the vitriol of public discourse also serves very well, turning us all into vicious partisans so absorbed in our righteous quarrels that we fail to notice who is profiting by our distractedness.

Short-term thinking that refuses to see long-range consequences is built into our economic system and our political systems. One can learn how to use words and images in all sorts of settings to the effect of manipulating people to vote against and make economic decisions against their own interests and the interests of society; the teaching of such skills is even incorporated into university curricula. Those who associate the word "sin" only with sexual offenses or with criminal acts may not recognize that this distracted-to-death way of life is, in fact, one way of describing the power of sin to separate us from our God and from God's purpose for us, both personally and corporately. It is, in fact, a culture of spiritual death, most often described in the Bible in terms of sins against the poor and sins against justice—sins so well disguised as to seem beneficial to us and to righteousness in general that we fail even to notice them.

Spiritual death, described in these or other terms, is one in which we turn away from God, either in indifference or in pursuit of other gods who are malleable enough to be more suitable for enlisting in the service of our desires and our great causes. Spiritual death is what Paul has in mind when he writes about sin, which is an omnipresent distraction that obscures our vision and distorts our hearing and exploits our insecurities to set us running off in wrong directions. Alexander Schmemann, the Orthodox theologian, writes that "death is above all a *spiritual reality*, of which one

64

can partake while being alive, from which one can be free while lying in the grave. Death here is [one's] *separation from life*, and this means from God Who is the only Giver of life, Who Himself *is* Life" (Schmemann, *Of Water and the Spirit*, 62–63).

The "spiritual death," what I have called "practical atheism," according to Schmemann,

> fills the entire life with "dying" and, being separation from God, makes [our] life solitude and suffering, fear and illusion, enslavement to sin and enmity, meaninglessness, lust and emptiness. (Schmemann, *Of Water*, 63).

Schmemann argues that, until we recapture some sense of "death" as something destructive that we live with and are immersed in, even while alive, "we will not be able to understand the significance of Christ's Death for us and for the world. For it is this spiritual death that Christ came to destroy and to abolish" (Schmemann, *Of Water*, 63). He adds that Christ's death "is nothing but love, nothing but the desire to destroy the solitude, the separation from life, the darkness and despair of death" (Schmemann, *Of Water*, 64).

Our part, in Schmemann's vision, is to accept Christ's faith, Christ's love, and Christ's desire as our own. In no other way can we know him. "It is indeed impossible to know Christ without desiring a radical liberation from 'this world,' which Christ revealed as being enslaved to sin and death" (Schmemann, *Of Water*, 65).

The sacrament of baptism is Christ's act, in the church, to claim us as his own, united with him in his death, which is to say, individually and collectively shedding that life (death) we all share that is so deeply rooted in the deceptions and self-deceptions pointing us away from the self-giving love that is made manifest in Jesus' death and resurrection, in which we find our best selves and our truest calling. At every celebration of baptism, the Spirit is poured out for the benefit of the whole congregation, in order that all might be strengthened to live into our shared baptismal vocation, which is a calling to assist one another in shaking off everything that obscures life, while embracing the gift of the risen life in Christ, which is both present reality and promise for the future.

That promise is symbolically represented by the fact that at least by the early third century, Easter, the celebration of the resurrection of the Lord, had become a day for baptism. In *De Baptismo*,

65

Tertullian commented that "the Passover [i.e., Easter] provides the day of most solemnity for baptism, for then was accomplished our Lord's passion, and into it we are baptized. . . . After that, Pentecost is a most auspicious period for arranging baptisms, for during it our Lord's resurrection was several times made known among the disciples, and the grace of the Holy Spirit first given" (*De Baptismo*, 19, in Johnson, *Rites*, 64). Many congregations today group baptisms at Easter, especially, or at Pentecost, or on the Sunday after Epiphany celebrated as Baptism of the Lord.

The Contamination of Death

Numbers 19:14–22

This text provides specific directions for washing oneself and one's clothing when anyone goes into a tent where someone has died, or when someone touches someone killed by a sword or who has died naturally or comes in direct contact with a human bone or a grave. The result of such contact is that persons become ritually unclean and are cut off from the assembly until they purify themselves.

As in the cases of the scale diseases (generically, "leprosy"), when someone died within a tent (enclosed structure), the impurity caused by the death was believed to rise upward to fill the whole environment and contaminate it. Anyone who then entered the tent or other enclosed environment would become ritually unclean, with the risk of polluting the sanctuary where the community worshiped. The cleansing ritual was intended to counter the forces of death.

The purification ritual involves a person who is ritually clean taking "ashes of the burnt purification offering" (v. 17), adding water, and dipping hyssop into it. Then the ritually clean person is to sprinkle water on the tent, its furnishings, the people who were in it, and whoever may have touched "the bone, the slain, the corpse, or the grave" (v. 18). "The clean person shall sprinkle the unclean ones on the third day and on the seventh day, thus purifying them on the seventh day. Then they shall wash their clothes and bathe themselves in water, and at evening they shall be clean" (v. 19).

Note the similarity of this ritual to actions described in the Letter to the Hebrews alluding to baptism: "And since we have a great priest over the house of God, let us approach with a true heart in full assurance of faith, with our hearts sprinkled clean from an evil conscience and our bodies washed with pure water" (Heb. 10:21–22). In this case, "an evil conscience" represented a sort of spiritual death. It is a fact that the evils we have done, the memory of which tends to torment our consciences, have the power to contaminate people other than those directly affected by our actions. Today we are likely to explain such a phenomenon in psychological terms, but there may be more emotional weight conveyed by the ancient language that testifies to the power of death, in its many manifestations, to contaminate the whole community.

When a group of adolescents attacks and beats an immigrant, a homeless person, or someone perceived to be gay, it will be found that habits of speech common in the community will have seemed to the perpetrators to possess the kind of authority that grants permission for such an act. Though one neighbor talking to another or small talk in the kitchen or the car seems insignificant and harmless, the fear and antagonism embedded in both words and tone contaminate children and adults alike until everyone in the shared space has been affected.

Competition can be healthy and play a useful role in personal development, but when carried to bitter extremes, as is not uncommon in the proliferation of "reality" television shows and many video games, it can contribute to a me-against-them or a tribalistic we-against-them mentality that treats "the other" only as an enemy and a threat to one's own success. The evolution of political speech in the twenty-first century, energized in some cases by the relative anonymity of the Internet, has made space for the vicious and the polarizing, which undercuts possibilities for honest dialogue and debate, and can poison communities and fair processes.

It is not possible even to keep up with the daily news without discovering for oneself how all are pulled down by the actions of some, and most of the acts that feed "an evil conscience" are undiscovered and unreported. Unscrupulous persons enrich themselves by exploiting weaknesses in the rules governing public programs like Medicare. Financial gurus exploit trusting investors who end up impoverished. The power to exploit others may be dressed in the guise of freedom and liberty, as though the right to get rich supersedes obligations owed one another. It is as though we have all agreed to minimize our own vices while damning those of others. The culture of demonizing, exploiting, and keeping silent about exploitation when we see it, either to protect ourselves or in hopes

67

that others will grant us the same favor, is a culture of death, a viral culture that spreads spiritual poison. We are all both perpetrators and victims, sharing a profound need for hearts "sprinkled clean."

Ezekiel 36:22–32

The image of purifying by sprinkling with water can be found as well in the book of Ezekiel. God had accused Israel of having failed to keep God's law, for which the Babylonian exile had served as punishment. "Mortal, when the house of Israel lived on their own soil, they defiled it with their ways and their deeds" (Ezek. 36:16). In words of judgment, God accused Israel of having profaned God's holy name among the nations. God made a pledge: "I will sanctify my great name . . . and the nations shall know that I am the LORD" (v. 23). God will gather the Diaspora of Israel, and bring them into their own land. "I will sprinkle clean water upon you, and you shall be clean from all your uncleannesses, and from all your idols I will cleanse you. A new heart I will give you and a new spirit I will put within you . . . and you shall be my people, and I will be your God. I will save you from all your uncleannesses" (vv. 25–29; cf. Num. 19:19).

The promised forgiveness is based entirely on God's free decision: "It is not for your sake, O house of Israel, that I am about to act, but for the sake of my holy name" (Ezek. 36:22). In other words, the forgiving action moves from God toward those who are the beneficiaries of the gift, without their having to earn it. Sprinkling of clean water serves, in this case, as a rite of purification from uncleanness caused by moral and ethical failures.

Similarly, Ezekiel had carried to Jerusalem, the symbolic heart of Israel, a word from the Lord. Jerusalem's origin, God declared, was of alien parentage, and "you were abhorred on the day you were born" (Ezek. 16:5). But God took pity on Jerusalem. "I pledged myself to you and entered into a covenant with you, says the Lord GOD, and you became mine. Then I bathed you with water and washed off the blood from you, and anointed you with oil" (16:8–9). Here is an example of God's tenderness toward the people, represented in the act of washing and anointing.

It would not be hard to see in the Ezekiel 36 text, particularly, a ritual act that provided a model for framing one perspective on the Christian sacrament of baptism: cleansing water, anointing, a "new spirit within you," a renewal of the covenant. "'[S]pirit' in the Old Testament is never simply an 'insight, understanding,' but a power which gives [one] strength to do new things (1 Sam. 10:6). The new thing here is the obedience which is now possible with regard to Yahweh's commands and the new way of life . . . and in this way . . . allows Yahweh to participate directly in [a human being]'s new obedience" (Zimmerli, *Ezekiel,* 249).

Ezekiel 36:28 testifies to God's promised renewal of the covenant, "You shall be my people, and I will be your God," in the same words as God's earlier promise in Ezekiel 11:20b, "Then they shall be my people, and I will be their God." While the image in Ezekiel is related to the Numbers "sprinkling" passage, it differs from it especially in that it is directed toward the whole household of Israel, which corporately shared moral responsibility for failure to keep God's law, rather than to just those few who had become ritually unclean by direct contact with an unclean person, place, or object. In this case too, one can perceive a similarity to baptism. While baptisms occur one by one, the sacrament is one that is shared by the whole community of Jesus Christ.

The Life-Giving Work of God

We may discern in the passages from Leviticus, Numbers, and Ezekiel a concern for the healing of estrangements that separate people from one another, from their best selves, and from the God who has made covenant with them—a God who heals the contaminating sins that affect the entire community. The story of Naaman, possibly the most dramatic healing story in the Old Testament, deals explicitly with the theme of *physical* healing—notably effected through washing.

Naaman was not only a Gentile but an enemy. As a military officer, he had fought against Israel—and won! (See 1 Kgs. 22:29–36.) The story of his healing testifies to a God whose concern for human beings is not narrow or parochial, but reaches beyond typical boundaries. In this way, his story helps to open a perspective on baptism.

2 Kings 5:1–15a

Naaman, commander of the army of the king of Aram . . . suffered from leprosy. . . . Elisha sent a messenger to him, saying, "Go, wash in the Jordan seven times, and your flesh shall be restored and you shall be clean." . . . So he went down and

> immersed himself seven times in the Jordan, according to the word of the man of God; his flesh was restored like the flesh of a young boy, and he was clean. (2 Kgs. 5:1, 10, 14)

Naaman commanded the forces of the king of Aram (Syria), which was Israel's perennial enemy. Curiously, part of Naaman's enormous military success was due to the fact that "by him *the LORD* had given victory to Aram" (v. 1). Thus the narrator establishes the fact that the affairs of the nations are in the hands of the only God who is sovereign over all the peoples of the earth. However, it is only through his "leprosy" that Naaman comes to see and understand his debt to Israel's God. In Naaman's household in Damascus lived a young girl taken captive during one of Naaman's raids into northern Israel. Out of sympathy for her master's suffering, she told Naaman's wife about a prophet in Samaria who could assuredly cure Naaman's disease. Desperate for relief, Naaman told his king what the girl had said, and the king sent Naaman to the king of Israel along with a letter and a lot of money and expensive gifts.

"When the king of Israel read the letter, he tore his clothes and said, 'Am I God, to give death or life, that this man sends word to me to cure a man of his leprosy?'" (2 Kgs. 5:7). As Scripture sets the scene in Israel's royal court, it is comical. One might imagine the king of Israel reading the letter, red faced, bug eyed, his hair standing on end! What was the Syrian king up to? Was this incredible request setting up a pretense to rationalize an unprovoked attack?

The prophet Elisha heard about the king's distress and sent a message asking the king to send Naaman to him, "that he may learn that there is a prophet in Israel" (2 Kgs. 5:8). When Naaman and his entourage arrived at the prophet's door, Elisha didn't even come out, but sent a message to Naaman that he should wash seven times in the Jordan River. Naaman was angry. Surely the prophet could have made an appearance and come up with a ceremony worthy of the name! And what's so great about the Jordan River? "Are not Abana and Pharpar, the rivers of Damascus, better than all the waters of Israel? Could I not wash in them, and be clean?" (2 Kgs. 5:12). And so, he sulked and fumed.

Nevertheless, Naaman followed the counsel of his servants, did what the prophet had directed him to do, and emerged from the water healed. In verse 15, Naaman makes a testimony of faith: "Now I know that there is no God in all the earth except in Israel."

In his sermon at the synagogue in Nazareth, Jesus made the point that God's concern is not for the people of Israel alone. He said, "There were also many lepers in Israel in the time of the prophet Elisha, and none of them was cleansed except Naaman the Syrian" (Luke 4:27). Needless to say, the congregation was not pleased to hear this message, in which they heard that God's mercy extended further than they were ready or conditioned to accept!

Naaman's sevenfold washing in the Jordan was not Christian baptism. It has some affinities with the various cleansing rituals in the book of Leviticus but is far from identical to them. Nevertheless, Naaman's water-bath in the river and his subsequent healing offer some relevant perspectives on the sacrament of baptism.

Naaman's objection that the rivers of Damascus should not be considered inferior to the rivers of Israel had a point. It was not the water, after all, that healed Naaman. God had done it, of course, even though the healing had become manifest in the waters of the Jordan, which happened to be nearer at hand than the rivers of Damascus. In the sacrament of baptism, we look for no intrinsic power in the water, but look through the baptizing action to discern the power and work of God. No special water is necessary—not even water brought back to Kansas all the way from the Jordan River. The Directory for Worship of the Presbyterian Church (U.S.A.) makes the point explicitly: "The water used for Baptism should be common to the location" (Directory, W-3.3605). In every place, clean and pure water serves God's purpose, whether sacramentally or in ordinary uses.

The sacrament may not be understood as a cure for a physical disease, but nevertheless it manifests a kind of healing. As a sign of God's forgiveness, baptism heals the wounds left by a bad conscience or by the anxiety and uncertainty that accompany the dawning awareness of one's own fallibility and capacity for doing harm to others. It embodies God's work of healing hopelessness and aimlessness as it incorporates adults and children, from the most sophisticated to the simplest, into the community of the Spirit, gathered around Jesus Christ in expectation of the ultimate healing of the whole creation. It exhibits the gospel's power to heal the alienation of those who have been strangers to God and distant from the things of God.

In the early Christian church, baptism served to incorporate both Jews and Gentiles into the community of Christ, thus healing

71

the separateness that had led each community to be suspicious of and even disdainful of the other. Baptism joins each of us to Jesus Christ, not to a denomination or confessional family only. It is always a mistake to say, "I was baptized Methodist," or "I was baptized Catholic." Good ecumenical practice is to receive members from another denomination without rebaptism, recognizing the legitimacy of Trinitarian baptism in the other body.

Neither confessional differences nor even excommunications, however painful, can overcome the fact that we who have been joined to Christ are at the same time joined to one another. Baptism is a means by which God's healing force is at work in subtle ways to undermine confessional exclusiveness and to erode the kind of spiritual elitism based on gender or race or status. "As many of you as were baptized into Christ have clothed yourselves with Christ. There is no longer Jew or Greek, there is no longer slave or free, there is no longer male and female; for all of you are one in Christ Jesus" (Gal. 3:27–28).

The pathologies of sin continue to manifest themselves even in and among the baptized, so that excluding people by categories (rich and poor, gay and straight, "liberal" and "conservative") persists, to our embarrassment and as a scandal to the world, but God will have the last Word, and that Word is proleptically made visible here and now in the sacrament that testifies to God's healing of estrangements. The God who might have turned away from Gentile Naaman instead turned toward him, as seen in Naaman's experience of having been cleansed in the Jordan. God continues to heal, and to exhibit the intention of healing, in the sacrament of baptism.

God's healing, as set before our eyes in baptism, is intended for each of us, but also for the community of nations and for the whole creation. Our intercessions and the church's work in the world are intimately related. The church longs to see the fulfillment of that universal healing—the healing of injustices, of violence, of hurts passed from one to another. Baptism evokes the eschatological promise of a healed creation, toward which the sacrament is meant to lead us and on behalf of which we are privileged to participate.

The Revised Common Lectionary pairs the Naaman story with Psalm 30, no doubt because the psalm expresses joy of the sort that Naaman experienced as he discovered himself to have been healed by the God of Israel. Psalm 30 celebrates a healing from illness:

"O Lord my God, I cried to you for help, and you have healed me" (v. 2). Our baptism marks an occasion for thanksgiving to the God whose work it is to heal our spiritual brokenness and our many estrangements from God and one another. Can you imagine Naaman joining the dance as we sing our gratitude to God?

> You have turned my mourning into dancing;
> you have taken off my sackcloth and clothed me with joy,
> so that my soul may praise you and not be silent.
> O Lord my God, I will give thanks to you forever.
>   (Ps. 30:11–12)

John 5:1–9

Washing in water as a means of healing is a theme that recurs in the New Testament. Tourists visiting Jerusalem can still see the well-attested site of the pool of Bethesda. The Gospel of John tells us that Jesus had gone up to Jerusalem for a festival, which is not identified. Jesus visited the pool, where there were many "invalids—blind, lame, and paralyzed" (v. 3). He encountered a man who had been disabled for thirty-eight years, and asked him whether he wanted to be made well. The man replied that he had no one to help him into the water, and he moved so slowly that "someone else steps down ahead of me."

Presumably, the propitious moment of entry into the pool must have been when the water was "stirred up," a stirring associated with the action of the Spirit. Some ancient authorities add a verse 4 that reads, "for an angel of the Lord went down at certain seasons into the pool, and stirred up the water; whoever stepped in first after the stirring of the water was made well from whatever disease that person had" (*New Oxford Bible*, NT 155). The man to whom Jesus was speaking either must have been pushed aside or his entry into the pool was so delayed that he could only lie there year after year, in futile hope that one day the timing might work out in his favor. But Jesus told him to pick up his mat and walk. "At once the man was made well, and he took up his mat and began to walk" (v. 9).

Although the story takes place at the pool of Bethesda, it does not include any actual scene in the water. Even though the scene is reminiscent of Naaman's healing in the Jordan, on this occasion no one gets wet. But, of course, none of the Israelites crossing the Red

73

Sea or the Jordan ever got wet, either! Nevertheless, the washing background of the narrative at the pool invites an interpretation in terms relevant to baptism.

In response to the religious authorities' objections to his having healed someone on the Sabbath, Jesus said, "My Father is still working, and I also am working" (5:17). Jesus is the link that joins traditional Jewish washing rites and messianic cleansing, life-giving work, which is physically embodied in the sacrament of baptism. The linkage becomes explicit in the story of the wedding at Cana.

John 2:1–11

Marianne Meye Thompson believes that the story of the wedding at Cana (John 2:1–11) early in the Gospel of John is key to understanding John's interpretation of Jesus' mission. In the Cana story, Jesus turned water into wine. The water in question came from "six stone water jars for the Jewish rites of purification, each holding twenty or thirty gallons" (v. 6), an enormous amount of water! Jesus had already been identified as "Son of God" (1:34), as well as "Messiah" (1:41), "King of Israel" (1:49), and "Son of Man" (1:51). Thompson says that

> Jesus is portrayed as Israel's *Messiah*, and the miracle at Cana [signals] messianic *fullness*, in keeping with the words of the prologue, "from his fullness have we all received." But the account in which this point is scored has to do with the "Jewish rites of purification." Messianic fullness thus entails messianic cleansing. Early on, the Gospel forges an integral link between the Messiah, the "King of Israel," and the Jewish rites of purification. . . . Just as the temple symbolized the purity of Israel and of Israel's God, so too Jesus embodies, manifests, and transmits true purity. (Thompson, "Reflections," 266 and 267)

Unless I Wash You

New Testament references to the act of washing include some that point directly to baptism in water, but they sometimes have a broader meaning, referring to the cross of Christ, which represents a sort of universal baptism, a cleansing of all the sins of humankind, of which we discover a glimpse in the story of Jesus washing his disciples' feet.

John 13:1–11

John's version of the Last Supper focuses on Jesus' washing the feet of his disciples more than it does on the meal. The pericope begins by referring to the fact that "Jesus knew that *his hour* had come to depart from this world" (13:1, emphasis added). In the Fourth Gospel, John uses "hour" to refer to Jesus' death, the climactic moment toward which his whole ministry was moving (e.g., John 2:4 and 7:30). Rising from the table, Jesus "took off his outer robe, and tied a towel around himself" (13:4). The Greek verb translated in the NRSV as "took off" (*tithēmi,* more helpfully, "laid aside") is the same one used in John 10 to describe the Good Shepherd's "laying down" his life for the sheep (10:11, 15, 17). Like the Synoptic Gospels, John interprets the Last Supper in terms of Jesus' death, even though he does not record the words or actions associated with the meal.

Then Jesus "poured water into a basin and began to wash the disciples' feet" (v. 5). To wash feet was a menial act, reserved for servants. Peter was appalled. He said, "You will never wash my feet" (v. 8a). Jesus' reply was stunning. "Unless I wash you, you have no share with me" (v. 8b). Peter did an about-face: "Lord, not my feet only but also my hands and my head!" (v. 9).

Jesus was asking his disciples simply to receive the act of hospitality he was offering them and also, indirectly, asking them to accept the act of washing "as a sign of his love for them and of his own humiliating death in their behalf" (Gench, *Encounters,* 97). "Being bathed by Jesus means being symbolically taken into the event of the cross" (Sloyan, *John,* 169). Just as Jesus, in his baptism, deliberately joined himself to sinners—in other words, to those made unclean by what they have done as well as by what they have left undone—in baptism the movement is reversed, so that the baptized become joined to Christ, who can never be separated from his cross. According to the church's memory, Peter, whom Jesus washed in response to his plea, eventually encountered his own cross (see John 21:18–19), and everyone who is joined to Christ in baptism is exposed to the likelihood of bearing a cross at some time or another. Even if only a few are martyrs, many there are for whom the service of the Servant will require sharing some measure of his self-offering, whether intentionally or involuntarily, perhaps occasionally, perhaps consistently over a lifetime, and all will experience the tension and sometimes open conflict of belonging to the

75

crucified One in societies in which "success" in its several definitions is glorified. Nevertheless, to be taken into the event of the
cross is an occasion for joy. A hymn in the African American tradition expresses that joy while not forgetting for a moment the cost of
it, so vividly expressed in the cross.

> Down at the cross where my Savior died,
> Down where for cleansing from sin I cried,
> There to my heart was the blood applied;
> Singin' Glory to His name, His name!
> Glory to His name, Precious name.
> I'm singin' Glory to His name, Precious name,
> There to my heart was the blood applied;
> Singin' Glory to His name, His name.
> (Elisha A. Hoffman, 1839–1929)

As the Servant, Jesus cleanses his disciples for participation in
the climactic moment of his ministry. It is he who makes pure by his
word and his grace, and that purity is manifest in our baptism. "The
righteous one, my servant, shall make many righteous, and he shall
bear their iniquities. . . . He poured out himself to death, and was
numbered with the transgressors; yet he bore the sin of many, and
made intercession for the transgressors" (Isa. 53:11–12).

Jesus' death on the cross was an act of voluntarily embracing
human rage, meant for God but directed toward the apparently
helpless target at hand, without passing it on. Usually, our free-
floating anger strikes out in retaliation, sometimes coldly, sometimes in fierce heat; and when retaliation is not possible because of
an inequity of power, the anger seeks an object that is not likely to
strike back. By embracing the rage that proceeds from the realization by mortals that we are not in charge of the universe, and that
the way the universe is set up does not always work in our self-
defined interests, Christ has transformed the energy of that rage
into love, as he opens his arms outward toward us from the cross. In
that sense, the cross of Christ marks God's will to heal us and reconcile us and re-create us and our passionate energies, and it calls us to
share in the work of redirecting rage toward injustice, while refusing to return evil for evil. In other words, on the cross the Christ
who returns good for evil manifests a kind of universal baptism, a
saving gift that does not need to be earned, but to be received. It

76

is that universal baptism that is represented and serves as an active force in every particular act of baptizing. It is that universal baptism that is suggested in Jesus' sermon in Nazareth, in which he lifts up Naaman as the example of an "outsider" whom God healed and embraced in boundless mercy.

Interpreters differ over whether the footwashing scene was meant to make a statement about baptism, but whatever the intention of John the evangelist, or of Jesus himself, the text is certainly resonant with a baptismal theme, particularly in the words of Jesus, "Unless I wash you, you have no share with me." Peter himself immediately grasped that Jesus was not talking about washing as a simple matter of removing the dust of the road, but rather about a metaphorical sort of washing that had to do with the whole self, body and soul.

It is typical of human nature to find it difficult to accept a gift or to accept a generous act of hospitality that clearly costs something to the one who provides it or the one who accepts it. Even in matters of faith, at least in Western, Enlightenment-influenced society, we imagine that religious devotion is chiefly a matter of doing something. Even the sacraments may seem to us to be chiefly pious things that we do, when in large part, they are actions through which God is working for our benefit. Certainly, both baptism and Eucharist call for a human response ("you also ought to wash one another's feet"), and, indeed, Jesus assuming the servant role exhibits for us the meaning of our own priesthood, as part of the church as well as personally. But the sacraments are first of all about something given, and the primary focus of attention should be on the Giver. "Unless I wash you . . ."

Christ, the Servant, serves us, and in that intimate service his love for us is made manifest. Herman G. Stuempfle's hymn "Lord, Help Us Walk Your Servant Way" exhorts us to humble service, as we might expect, but it also points to Christ the Servant and to the character of his servanthood.

> You came to earth, O Christ, as Lord,
> But pow'r you laid aside.
> You lived your years in servanthood,
> In lowliness you died.
> (Stuempfle, © 1997,
> GIA Publications, Inc.)

77

Soul-Shaking Encounters

In the Revelation to John, he hears these words: "Blessed are those who wash their robes, so that they will have the right to the tree of life and may enter the city by the gates" (Rev. 22:14). It is typical in the African American church for worshipers to put on their finest clothes for church. While the Bible certainly does not provide a liturgical dress code, the expectation of meeting the holy God may at least inspire us to prepare ourselves. Whether it is combing one's hair, washing one's face, putting on a clean shirt, or engaging in a disciplined act of self-examination, it is prudent to put ourselves in order before risking an encounter with God.

Exodus 19:10–14

> The LORD said to Moses: "Go to the people and consecrate them today and tomorrow. Have them wash their clothes and prepare for the third day, because on the third day the LORD will come down upon Mount Sinai in the sight of all the people. . . ." He consecrated the people, and they washed their clothes. (Exod. 19:10–11, 14b)

These verses are part of a larger narrative (Exod. 19:1–20:21) that leads up to and includes God's giving of the Ten Commandments. The third month after the exodus from Egypt, the people had reached Mount Sinai (Horeb). God had declared to the people of Israel that "you shall be for me a priestly kingdom and a holy nation" (Exod. 19:6). In response, the people vowed to do everything that God had commanded. Moses reported to the people that God had promised "to come to you in a dense cloud, in order that the people may hear when I speak with you and so trust you ever after" (Exod. 19:9). When Moses had delivered the message, the Lord spoke again, ordering that the people be consecrated and that they wash their clothes in preparation for God's appointment to appear to the people directly.

Brevard Childs comments that the act of washing their clothes is one that "traditionally precedes a great and solemn happening" (Childs, *Exodus*, 368), and he cites a passage from Genesis. When God had commanded Jacob to pack up and go to Bethel and make an altar there, Jacob had set about to obey, first announcing to his household and the rest of his entourage that they should "put

78

away the foreign gods that are among you, and purify yourselves, and change your clothes; then come, let us go up to Bethel" (Gen. 35:2–3a).

The dramatic contrast between the status of mortal human beings and the holy God is one that calls for the people to exhibit a proper awe, humility, and respect. The larger narrative in Exodus accents the reasons for awe, humility, and respect as God meets the people. "Any who touch the mountain shall be put to death" (Exod. 19:12). They will experience thunder and lightning, a thick cloud on the mountain, "and a blast of the trumpet so loud that all the people who were in the camp trembled" (Exod. 19:16). When God drew near, "the whole mountain shook violently" (Exod. 19:18). What can the people do to prepare themselves for a terrifying brush with the holy? They can show their respect by doing what the Lord has commanded: "Have them wash their clothes and prepare" (Exod. 19:10).

John the Baptizer expected some sort of encounter between God and God's people Israel, one that would bring judgment, "the Holy Spirit and fire" (Matt. 3:11). The heavens would be "torn open" (Mark 1:10), "every mountain and hill . . . made low, and the crooked . . . made straight" (Luke 3:5). Facing such a prospect, John called the people to repent and be baptized—to undergo a thorough scrubbing, body and soul—a not-too-distant parallel to God's direction to the people through Moses that they "wash their clothes" in preparation for a soul-shaking encounter with the holy.

The washing of clothes and baptism both served as the people's enacted prayer that they might be clothed with a proper humility as they prepared to present themselves with dignity before the sovereign Lord. Such humility may seem quite quaint and antique in the twenty-first century, when even our relationship with God has been democratized to the extent that it is difficult to conceive of God as in any way remotely dangerous. The rubric for our time is "casual," and the rubric holds even when we have to do with holy things. After all, God is our friend, eager to see that everything works out for us as we expect it to. Grace has trumped judgment, so it seems, and we can relax before the Holy One.

God is gracious, certainly, and God's astonishing generosity is manifest in Jesus Christ. Nevertheless, that grace is never to be taken for granted, nor are we to imagine that there are no risks at stake when human beings, so limited and so fallible, find ourselves dealing with God; "O come, let us worship and bow down, let us kneel before the LORD, our Maker!" (Ps. 95:6). When the church's worship takes God seriously, however joyful it may be, it will at the same time cause us to bow down and to kneel, whether literally or metaphorically, in humility before the magnificence of God. The purifying God whom we meet in the sacrament is a holy God, not to be trifled with. Every act of baptism reminds us that the life of faith can be dangerous.

Annie Dillard has written,

> It is madness to wear ladies' straw hats and velvet hats to church; we should all be wearing crash helmets. Ushers should issue life preservers and signal flares; they should lash us to our pews. (Dillard, *Teaching a Stone*, 40)

Perhaps she was thinking of Uzzah, whom God struck dead when he reached out his hand to touch the ark of the covenant (2 Sam. 6:6–7), or of Aaron's sons Nadab and Abihu, priests whom God consumed with fire at the altar (Lev. 10). Their stories might well serve as cautionary tales, warnings even to the well intended that there is risk in handling holy things. While fire and brimstone may be out of fashion in so-called mainline churches, the opposite risk is to imagine that God may be domesticated, tamed, represented as always friendly and just plain nice, not inclined to embarrass ministers or congregations with anything resembling bolts of heavenly lightning in the middle of the sermon or the anthem. Yet God is a God of justice, and most of us are camped out with the unjust at least part of the time and prefer that divine judgment be expressed tastefully (and quietly) and aimed in a direction that doesn't include us. Those whose vocation is precisely to handle holy things know by experience how easy it is to begin to think of ourselves as privileged, perhaps even as channels without whom God might be helpless either to speak or act in the congregation.

Priesthood—Intimacy with the Things of God

The Levitical priests, whose work it was to approach God and to handle holy things, also needed to prepare themselves, as the people had needed to prepare themselves to meet God at Sinai. In the last chapter of the book of Exodus, God gave Moses instructions for setting up "the tabernacle of the tent of meeting" (Exod. 40:2). The tabernacle was a temporary structure that could be transported from place to place as the people traveled. It would serve as a portable predecessor to the Jerusalem temple, representing the presence of God among the people of Israel. God directed Moses to place in the tabernacle the ark of the covenant. A pillar of cloud stood over the tabernacle in the daytime, and fire was in the cloud at night, the cloud and the fire representing the glory of God. Unless the cloud was removed, no one, not even Moses, dared enter the tabernacle. When God took the cloud away, it would signal a time for the people to pack up and resume their pilgrim journey. Water for washing played a role in the rites of the tabernacle.

Exodus 40

> You shall set the altar of burnt offering before the entrance of the tabernacle of the tent of meeting, and place the basin between the tent of meeting and the altar, and put water in it. . . . Then you shall bring Aaron and his sons to the entrance of the tent of meeting, and shall wash them with water. . . . He [Moses] set the basin between the tent of meeting and the altar, and put water in it for washing, with which Moses and Aaron and his sons washed their hands and their feet. When they went into the tent of meeting, and when they approached the altar, they washed; as the LORD had commanded Moses. (Exod. 40:6–7, 12, 30–32)

God gave Moses instructions for preparing the liturgical materials necessary for the tabernacle, including a table, lamps, altars, and a basin of water. At the appropriate moment, Moses must bring his brother Aaron and Aaron's sons to the entrance, and wash them with water as part of their ceremony of ordination to a priesthood that would extend to their descendants throughout the generations. The basin of water would serve Aaron and his sons for washing their hands and feet each time they were preparing to begin their priestly duties.

Those ordained to be priests were, of course, ordinary human beings. They were not immune from the spiritual disorders common to all mortals. Yet their calling was one that required a particular intimacy with the things of God—holy things. The washing rituals, both in the ordination rite and whenever they were called to duty at the altar, represented God's requirement that those who

81

approached God on behalf of the people be clean in heart, mind, and soul. The actual physical washing served as a reminder of this requirement and an acceptance of it, an enacted prayer, acknowledging one's need of cleansing and asking for God to make up for the insufficiencies of the priest.

Priesthood Shared by All

While Israel possessed the Levitical priesthood, it is true also that Israel believed that God had made Israel as a whole to serve in the world as a corporate priesthood, a priestly people. Early in the wilderness journey, following the exodus from Egypt, while Israel was encamped at the foot of Mount Sinai (Mount Horeb), God gave the people a message through Moses:

> Now therefore, if you obey my voice and keep my covenant, you shall be my treasured possession out of all the peoples. Indeed, the whole earth is mine, but you shall be for me a priestly kingdom and a holy nation. These are the words that you shall speak to the Israelites. (Exod. 19:5, 6)

Echoing Exodus, the baptismal service of the Presbyterian Church in Canada identifies the sacrament as a participation in Christ's priesthood, saying that "God washes us clean by forgiving our sin; commissions us to be a royal priesthood with Christ in his ministry to the world; empowers us to live in newness of life as people of the Word; and invites us to be renewed at the Lord's Table until we feast with him in glory" (*BCW, Canada*, 149).

Baptism is a kind of ordination, in which Christians are commissioned to share with Israel the priestly responsibility that comes with "election," which includes bearing witness to God's mighty acts, whether by word or deed or simply by the manifestation of a presence in the world of a community bearing God's name. Joel Kaminsky points out that "the total purpose of Abraham's and thus Israel's election are never fully articulated in the Hebrew Bible" (Kaminsky, *Yet I Loved Jacob*, 85). God's election, or choosing, of Israel is grounded in the mystery of divine love, and not done merely for an instrumental purpose. At the same time, "any privilege this entails carries with it a higher level of responsibility" (Kaminsky, *Yet I Loved Jacob*, 140–41).

One of the principles of the Protestant Reformation, often invoked, affirms "the priesthood of all believers." It is quite common to mistake this affirmation with the idea that each believer is her or his own priest, not in need of any other, or the idea that there need be no distinction of roles in the church. However, it might better be understood to say that each of us is called to serve as a priest to the other and that all the baptized together share a vocation to be a corporate priesthood for the world.

The nature of Israel's special role as a priestly people can be traced to the promise that God made to Abram, and repeated to his sons: "I will make of you a great nation, and I will bless you, and make your name great, so that you will be a blessing. I will bless those who bless you, and the one who curses you I will curse; *and in you all the families of the earth shall be blessed*" (emphasis added). God remembers the promise in Genesis 18:18 and repeats it first to Isaac (26:4) and then to Jacob (28:14).

The priestly role is one of blessing, for which God had called Israel on behalf of "all the families of the earth." How shall this blessing be communicated to the peoples of the world? Perhaps, at its simplest, the very existence of Israel in the world serves to point to God and God's claims upon every human being. It may be that this service as God's marker in the world has been the ultimate source of the world's hostility toward the Jews, a displaced rage that is actually meant for God, as we see also in the cross. In that cruel device, designed to shed the victim's very lifeblood, one recalls that Old Testament sacrificial and liturgical language about anointing with blood or sprinkling that is paradoxically about making the ordinary holy as well as restoring and reconciling those who have been cut off.

In the New Testament, the opening verses of Revelation include a doxology, "To him who loves us and freed us from our sins by his blood, and made us to be a kingdom, priests serving his God and Father" (Rev. 1:5b–6; see also Rev. 5:10). The First Letter of Peter also understands Israel's corporate priestly vocation to have been extended to include those "who have been chosen and destined by God the Father and sanctified by the Spirit to be obedient to Jesus Christ and to be sprinkled with his blood" (1 Pet. 1:2). While sprinkling with blood recalls liturgical practice in Leviticus, it also serves as a vivid reminder that the Christians in Asia Minor for whom the letter of Peter was written were experiencing persecution, which

83

must have served as an ominous warning that it was not inconceivable that they might be called to shed their own blood. "But you are a chosen race, a royal priesthood, a holy nation, God's own people, in order that you may proclaim the mighty acts of him who called you out of darkness into his marvelous light" (1 Pet. 2:9).

The church that testifies to the light then shares with Aaron and the Levitical priesthood the charge to bless in the name of the God who "makes his face to shine upon you."

> The LORD spoke to Moses, saying: Speak to Aaron and his sons, saying, Thus you shall bless the Israelites: You shall say to them, The LORD bless you and keep you; the LORD make his face to shine upon you, and be gracious to you; the LORD lift up his countenance upon you, and give you peace. (Num. 6:22–26)

Every member of this corporate priesthood, which is to say, all the baptized, have been "sanctified by the Spirit" and "sprinkled with [Christ's] blood." The sprinkling of blood, often seven times, upon persons or objects, was a rite of cleansing, recorded most frequently in the book of Leviticus. Blood, of course, represents the very essence and power of life. The sprinkling of an animal's blood served as a sin offering (e.g., Lev. 4:3, 6; 5:9) or as a ritual for cleansing a person of a leprous disease in order that he or she may return to the life of the community (Lev. 14:6–7, 14), or for the purpose of cleansing the sins of the whole people (Lev. 16:19). When 1 Peter described the church as those "sprinkled with his [Christ's] blood," he was writing metaphorically rather than literally, but clearly he was recalling rites familiar to those who knew the Old Testament Scriptures and who were perhaps aware of the rituals of the temple as a way of saying that, for the baptized, Christ serves as the one and only sin offering, whom God has provided. He is the one who cleanses, heals, and reconciles, who makes a place among the priestly people even for Gentiles, who had been outsiders.

God spoke to Moses, saying, "Now this is what you shall do to them to consecrate them, so that they may serve me as priests" (Exod. 29:1), and "You shall then ordain Aaron and his sons" (Exod. 29:9). The text includes the rubric that blood from a ram should be taken from the altar, with anointing oil added to it, and the mixture sprinkled "on Aaron and his vestments and on his sons and his sons' vestments with him; then he and his vestments shall be holy, as well as his sons and his sons' vestments" (Exod. 29:21).

The First Letter of John testifies that "if we walk in the light as he himself is in the light, we have fellowship with one another, and the blood of Jesus his Son cleanses us from all sin" (1 John 1:7). "Blood" language can be uncomfortable for many people, but ancient Jewish liturgical practice nevertheless illuminates some aspects of baptism—like the sprinkled blood that was part of the ceremony for ordaining the first priests.

The role of priests is not to lord it over others or enjoy special status or privilege but, rather, to bear a special responsibility to be intercessors. Whether each for the other or as a people, we are intercessors and advocates whose corporate ministry as the church is meant to share with Israel in such a way that it will have as an effect the blessing of "all the families of the earth" (Gen. 12:3). Intercession and advocacy are two sides of the same coin, advocacy also being part of the job description of the priestly community and its members. John the Baptizer must have known these words from the prophet Isaiah: "Wash yourselves; make yourselves clean; remove the evil of your doings from before my eyes; cease to do evil, learn to do good; seek justice, rescue the oppressed, defend the orphan, plead for the widow" (Isa. 1:16–17).

Advocacy and intercession are priestly work in two movements. We are meant to do what we pray, and to pray what we do. Bearing corporate witness in the world has historically included establishing hospitals, lobbying governments, distributing food, building houses, circulating petitions, cultivating a sense of responsibility for those who have been treated as a nuisance or a threat, refusing to return evil for evil, offering refuge, as well as speech about holy things and the Holy One. Baptism ordains us to take our part in these and other ways of bearing witness, as well as to share liturgically in God's outreach to a broken world.

Intercessions were part of the liturgy in the early church. "First of all, then, I urge that supplications, prayers, intercessions, and thanksgivings be made for everyone" (1 Tim. 2:1). The church would do well to rediscover its corporate priestly role and to embed that role in its worship as well as its work. Such a rediscovery could help bring the actual work and mission of the local congregation and larger ecclesiastical bodies into sharper focus. Continually reflecting on the church's calling to serve as a corporate priesthood, looking toward a universal blessing, will also strengthen a parish's liturgical life, particularly its prayers of intercession. Good Friday, when the church remembers that Christ died for the sins of the whole world, has historically been an occasion particularly devoted to prayers of intercession (e.g., the Solemn Intercessions for Good Friday in *BCW*, 283). "On this day the church prays for the entire creation for which Christ died" (Stookey, *Calendar*, 100). Of course, some part of every Lord's Day service is devoted to prayers for those outside the congregation. To heighten awareness of the church's priestly role, the prayers of the people (variously called) might be led by persons whose parish responsibilities are directed specifically outward, beyond the boundaries of the congregation. A person responsible for the congregation's diaconal ministry (deacons) might lead the intercessions, or a person chairing a committee leading a particular mission project, such as building a Habitat for Humanity house or gathering food for the food bank or filling backpacks for schoolchildren or raising funds for a feeding station in Malawi, or simply someone known to the congregation for reaching out to those who need a hand.

The priestly role of the whole church catholic depends entirely, however, on the fact that it is joined to the priesthood of Jesus Christ. "Therefore he had to become like his brothers and sisters in every respect, so that he might be a merciful and faithful high priest in the service of God, to make a sacrifice of atonement for the sins of the people" (Heb. 2:17).

The Letter to the Hebrews reflected on Jesus as high priest, contrasting his eternal priesthood with the human priesthood of Aaron and his descendants: "Unlike the other high priests, he has no need to offer sacrifices day after day, first for his own sins, and then for those of the people; this he did once for all when he offered himself" (Heb. 7:27).

The writer of the letter includes a reference linked to Torah's purification and ordination rituals and to the sacrament of baptism: "And since we have a great priest over the house of God, let us approach with a true heart in full assurance of faith, with our hearts sprinkled clean from an evil conscience and our bodies washed with pure water" (Heb. 10:21–22; cf. Ezek. 36:25).

Our baptism joins us to our "great high priest" and to his ministry of intercession and advocacy. "Like living stones, let yourselves be built into a spiritual house, to be a holy priesthood, to offer spiritual sacrifices acceptable to God through Jesus Christ" (1 Pet. 2:5).

The work of the Levitical priesthood was to offer sacrifices, including the literal slaughtering of animals. The church as "holy priesthood" has nothing to do with the sacrifice of animals, but rather with sacrifices of thanksgiving (Ps. 50:14); our bodies (Rom. 12:1), which is to say, our whole selves, including the work of our hands and the sharing of goods; and praise (Heb. 13:15–16). Certainly such sacrifices include testimony (1 Pet. 2:9), intercession (1 Tim. 2:1), and the pursuit of justice and kindness (Mal. 6:8).

We are baptized only once. However, just as Aaron and his sons washed their hands and feet before serving at the altar, to demonstrate the proper disposition of those entrusted with interceding for the people, some Christians like to remind themselves of their baptism (which is a sharing in the corporate priesthood of the whole church) by touching the water in the open baptismal font as they pass it while entering or leaving the place of worship. Beginning in the Middle Ages, it became necessary to cover baptismal fonts, often with locked covers, to protect against those who would steal some of the "holy" water for superstitious uses. Since that is not a big problem in the twenty-first century, the need for covering the font (or leaving it open but empty) would seem to be obsolete. Many churches are removing the covers and leaving their fonts filled so that worshipers passing by may at least see and take note of the water (or touch it) and be reminded of their baptismal calling—the washing that served as their priestly ordination.

Some churches practice *asperges*, the sprinkling of water on the people and/or the place where they assemble for worship. This act calls us to take hold of our baptismal identity. In some churches not otherwise accustomed to *asperges*, water is sometimes scattered over the congregation during services for the reaffirmation of the baptismal covenant, perhaps using a leafy branch that has been dampened in water.

CHAPTER 3

Baptism: Life, Spirit, and Covenant

Viewed from space, the most consistent color of the earth is blue, because most of its surface is covered with water. Water is essential to all life—animal, vegetable, and microscopic. Without it, the planet would dry up and life would disappear. Yet too much water in the wrong places poses a threat. Depending upon circumstances, a direct line can be drawn from water to life or from water to death. Because of this dual linkage, water can in certain situations serve as a bridge—a transitional state—from life to death or from death to life.

Most of the time water plays a less dramatic role in our lives. We use it to wash everything from the lunch dishes to our cars. We wash our hands, our feet, our faces, our whole bodies, and feel cleansed and refreshed. A bath or shower not only washes away the grime of the day, but it serves our psychological well-being too, providing a sense that we have shed the traces left by our labors and are ready to start over. When we are parched with thirst, a drink of cool water renews us.

In many parts of the world, bodies of water facilitate transportation. Rivers, lakes, coastal waters, and canals carry boats and ships from one place to another with their animate and inanimate cargos.

The Bible has a number of stories in which water plays a key role. The waters of creation and the water that supports a fetus in the womb: life. The flood waters of Noah's time and the waters that

89

seemed to close off the means of Israel's escape from Pharaoh's pursuing soldiers: death. Or, differently viewed, the waters that lifted Noah and his entourage to safety, the waters that opened to provide the Israelites a means of escape from reenslavement or destruction, and the water of the Jordan, through which Israel crossed from the wilderness into the land of promise: life. Stories of abundant water, source of life and growth and nourishment in a dry land, reach back all the way to Eden and all the way forward to the *eschaton*. The New Testament compares baptism to Noah's new beginning, with its covenantal promise, and tells stories about Jewish rites transformed by the presence of Jesus and his significant conversation with a Samaritan woman on a hot day at an ancient well.

One biblical image of God is that of a fountain. Another is "living water." Jesus uses the image of living water to speak of the Spirit—Holy Spirit, "the Lord and Giver of life," to borrow the language of the Nicene Creed.

It is not surprising that the sacrament of baptism has drawn so deeply on the Bible's water stories, descriptions of rituals with water, and water-related images to embody the testimony that in baptism we encounter the God who reaches out to lift us from the dangerous flood and pull us to safety.

The God whom we encounter in baptism is the same God who covenanted with Abraham and Noah and their descendants and who has renewed that covenant in Jesus Christ, extending it to us who were far off, sealing the covenantal promise with the sacrament. This covenant-making God keeps the promise, giving us a taste of the waters of the river of life, the living water of the Spirit.

Deep, Unordered Water

After several days of heavy rain, the local television channels begin to run flash-flood warnings for particular localities at the bottom of the screen. The evening news is likely to show pictures of stalled cars, inundated homes, and even boats paddling down a city street. Seldom does a summer go by without our being reminded that water is dangerous, particularly for coastal regions in hurricane season. Footage of raging surf and rogue waves chills the heart. Pounding waves and sudden floods are particularly frightening when the power goes out and the stars are hidden behind the clouds. The total darkness can be terrifying.

Genesis 1:1–3

In the beginning when God created the heavens and the earth, the earth was a formless void and darkness covered the face of the deep, while a wind from God swept over the face of the waters. Then God said, "Let there be light"; and there was light. (Gen. 1:1–3)

The reader is barely able to conceive the scene. The text evokes a certain terror of the wind, the storm, the raging water, the darkness, the absence of any place of refuge. The word translated "wind" is *ruach*, which can also mean "spirit," as in the RSV translation, "and the Spirit of God was moving over the face of the waters" (Gen. 1:2). Gerhard von Rad believes that a better translation is "storm of God" (von Rad, *Genesis*, 47). He suggests that humankind "has always suspected that behind all creation lies the abyss of form-lessness; that the chaos, therefore, signifies simply the threat to everything created" (49). The chaos, the storm, the formlessness are not conditions permanently altered, forever left behind, but rather possibilities that still exist except for God's continued work of creating and sustaining what has been created. The "deep," then, is a reminder of the threatening power of chaos, and of the danger that it might overcome us and every familiar landscape and, indeed, have the last word over our common life.

The baptismal rite, a combination of actions and words, may appropriately serve as a reminder that chaos, whether in the world generally or in one's personal life, is not in our power to eliminate or control. Rivers still overflow their banks, and drownings still occur. Nevertheless, it is in God's power to subdue chaotic forces and subject them to some kind of order. The sacrament of baptism indeed bears testimony to the God who is able with a word to cre-ate life where there had been and still could be a terrible absence of life; who is able with a word to create a habitable space for those who otherwise have no place to stand. All the contemporary service books include in their several versions of the thanksgiving over the water a reference to the watery chaos preceding the creation. One example is from the *United Methodist Book of Worship*: "Eternal

Father: When nothing existed but chaos, you swept across the dark waters and brought forth light" (*UMBW*, 90).

Sylvia Dunstan's hymn "Crashing Waters at Creation" evokes the creation story's sense of the awesome power of water and the power of the Spirit to wrest daylight out of perpetual night. The "Spirit's breath" is the breath of life.

> Crashing waters at creation,
>   ordered by the Spirit's breath,
> first to witness day's beginning
>   from the brightness of night's death.
>   (Dunstan, © 1991 GIA Publications,
>   Inc.; used by permission)

One might discern in the primeval waters some suggestion of the watery amniotic fluid that supports a fetus in utero. The watery chaos described in the first verse of Genesis becomes, when God's word is added to it, the starting point of a period of gestation that leads to the brightly illumined world of daylight alternating with nighttime, to sea and land, plants and animals and human beings. Every human being begins life in the water of the womb, and from early times, baptism was often likened to a new birth. Jesus said to Nicodemus, "Very truly, I tell you, no one can enter the kingdom of God without being born of water and Spirit" (John 3:5). Gabriele Winkler, describing early Syriac and Armenian writers, says that "baptism is always conceived of as a birth, and the baptismal water is seen as a womb" (Winkler, "Original Meaning," 76). Theodore of Mopsuestia (350–428 CE) declared that "the one baptized settles in the water as in a kind of womb, like a seed showing no sign of an immortal nature" (Spinks, *Early and Medieval*, 45). Baptism represents a movement from what in retrospect seems like formlessness toward the beginning of a lifelong process of formation "in Christ" (e.g., Rom. 8:1; Gal. 3:26; 4:19).

Noah, the Flood, and the Ark

Genesis 6:5–8:22

The Lord saw that the wickedness of humankind was great in the earth. . . . And the Lord was sorry that he had made humankind on the earth, and it grieved him to his heart. . . . And God said

92

to Noah, "I have determined to make an end of all flesh, for the earth is filled with violence because of them. . . . Make yourself an ark. . . . I am going to bring a flood of waters on the earth. . . . But I will establish my covenant with you. . . ."

All the fountains of the great deep burst forth, and the windows of the heavens were opened. The rain fell on the earth forty days and forty nights. . . . [God] blotted out every living thing that was on the face of the ground. . . . Only Noah was left, and those that were with him in the ark. . . .

And the waters gradually receded from the earth. . . . The waters were dried up. . . . So Noah went out with his sons and his wife and his sons' wives. . . . Then Noah built an altar to the Lord . . . and offered burnt offerings. . . . The Lord said in his heart, "I will never again curse the ground because of humankind." (Gen. 6:5–6, 13, 14, 17, 18; 7:11–12, 23; 8:3, 13, 18, 20, 21)

When you visit a church nursery, you are very likely to find a miniature ark with its cargo of animals, or a storybook about Noah, or a colorful poster depicting elephants and giraffes peeking out of a porthole. Though elements of it are appealing to children, the story as a whole is really chilling. It is a narrative of watery destruction.

The story begins with a sobering diagnosis of the state of humankind. "Now the earth was corrupt in God's sight, and the earth was filled with violence" (Gen. 6:11). Even in the twenty-first century, the daily news seems to support a similar diagnosis. Violence is all around, sometimes physical violence in the form of terrorism or the military responses it inspires, or gang violence or the violence of criminal cartels. Sometimes the violence takes the form of careless and hateful words, of which there is no lack, and sometimes it is embodied in policies designed to manipulate the poor and the vulnerable to the advantage of the strong and the rich.

"And the LORD was sorry that he had made humankind on the earth, and it grieved him to his heart" (Gen. 6:6). This sympathetic observation of God's sorrow and grief runs the risk of reducing God to the dimensions of a very *human* being. However, von Rad observes that "It was apparently easier in Old Testament faith to tolerate the danger of lessening God's greatness and 'absoluteness' by human description than to run the risk of giving up anything of God's lively personalness and his vital participation in everything earthly" (von Rad, *Genesis*, 114). The God of Scripture must not be characterized simply as a divine abstraction or an impersonal

93

principle. A charming example of this humanization of God appears in 7:15–16: "They went into the ark with Noah. . . . And those that entered, male and female of all flesh, went in as God had commanded him; *and the* L*ORD* *shut him in*" (emphasis added). Picture God, if you will, carefully closing the doors of the ark with its precious cargo! Here we see tenderness, not cold-bloodedness.

Rain fell for forty days and forty nights. The "windows of the heavens" were opened and the "fountains of the great deep burst forth," so that the chaos that existed before the earth's creation pressed in upon the world both from above and below (Gen. 7:11; cf. Gen. 1:6–7). The ark floated to safety, carrying Noah, his wife, their three sons, Shem, Ham, and Japheth, and the sons' wives—a total of eight people—and the nonhuman cargo as well.

Luther's "flood prayer" begins by remembering Noah:

> Almighty and eternal God, according to Your strict judgment You condemned the unbelieving world through the flood, yet according to Your great mercy You preserved believing Noah and his family, eight souls in all.
> (http://ematthaei.blogspot.com/2006/08/luthers-flood-prayer_11.html, accessed October 11, 2010)

Luther perceived a link between the Noah story and the sacrament of baptism. God sent the flood to cleanse the created order, corrupted by wickedness, evil, and violence. In the sacrament, God means to rescue human beings, who, though capable of nobility and generosity, nevertheless clearly need the cleansing that is God's gift in Christ, a gift that becomes ours by water and the Spirit. Quite likely Luther perceived that the Noah story has two dimensions— one highlighting the need for cleansing and the other accenting the fact that the waters of the flood lifted the ark and carried it to safety, preserving the seedbed of new life. In the Noah story, water both destroys and saves. It is the occasion of a crisis and the gift of life beyond the crisis. The Noah story, with its foreshadowing of death and resurrection, contributes a perspective on the sacrament.

The Genesis story reports that Noah had sent out from the ark a dove "to see if the waters had subsided from the face of the ground" (8:8). It is very likely the case that the Gospel writers' perception of the Spirit at Jesus' baptism descending "like a dove" was shaped by the Noah story, from which they drew a tangible image for an experience not easily reduced to words. As Noah's dove finally found it safe to leave the ark, it signaled a new beginning, just as the descent of the Spirit at Jesus' baptism, "like a dove," signaled a new beginning.

Noah's first act after leaving the ark was to worship. He built an altar to the Lord and made a burnt offering (Gen. 8:20). In response, God said, "I will never again curse the ground because of humankind . . . nor will I ever again destroy every living creature as I have done" (Gen. 8:21). "So far as that is concerned—says Calvin in his exposition of this passage—[if floods were the way to make things right] God would have to punish man with daily floods" (von Rad, *Genesis*, 119). But God, thankfully, is gracious! The conclusion of the flood story is that God makes a covenant with Noah's family in which God promises that never again shall a flood destroy the earth.

In the flood story, God's covenant is accompanied by a sign: "This is the sign of the covenant that I make between me and you and every living creature that is with you, for all future generations: I have set my bow in the clouds, and it shall be a sign of the covenant between me and the earth" (Gen. 9:12–13). The "bow" is a warrior's bow, a weapon set aside in the heavens as a reminder to God and to humankind of God's covenantal promise to set aside any design to destroy living things a second time. The flood drowns, but it lifts those in the ark to safety, and God adds to this very tangible salvation a covenantal sign. So also does baptism sacramentally drown the old self and lift us up to participate in Christ's resurrection life, with the water bath itself serving as a sign of God's covenant, the divine promise.

The sacrament of baptism has been understood as a covenantal sign, particularly in the Reformed tradition, but also in late-sixteenth- and seventeenth-century Anglican theology (Spinks, *Reformation and Modern*, 151), with evidence of its continuation to this day in the confirmation service of the American Episcopal *Book of Common Prayer*: "Renew in *these* your *servants* the covenant you made with *them* at their Baptism" (*BCP*, 309). As a covenantal sign, baptism confirms and seals God's promise of salvation. In the flood story, God made a covenant with the whole created order. Later, God made a covenant with Abraham and his descendants: "This is my covenant, which you shall keep, between me and you and your offspring after you: Every male among you shall be circumcised" (Gen. 17:10). Those who understand baptism in covenant terms see it as parallel to the rite of circumcision, each serving as a sign or seal of the covenant.

The Presbyterian *Book of Common Worship* frames baptism as a covenantal act. The profession of faith begins with this statement by the minister:

> Through baptism we enter the covenant God has established.
> Within this covenant God gives us new life,
> guards us from evil,
> and nurtures us in love.
>
> (*BCW,* 406)

The rubric then calls for the following question to be put to candidates for baptism or parents or guardians of children being presented for baptism:

> As God embraces you within the covenant, I ask you
> to reject sin,
> to profess your faith in Christ Jesus,
> and to confess the faith of the church,
> the faith in which we baptize.
>
> (*BCW,* 407)

The service provides these words to accompany signing the cross on the forehead of one newly baptized: "N., child of the covenant, you have been sealed by the Holy Spirit in baptism, and marked as Christ's own forever" (*BCW,* 442).

Signing with the cross is one example of a physical action that, taken together with others, communicates the heart of the sacrament nonverbally. The actual practice of the sacrament of baptism is, of course, more than simply getting through printed liturgical texts. Pastors and parish worship planning committees might profit from looking carefully at the details of the physical actions of the sacrament. How might the doing of the rite represent more fully the fact that the sacrament brings us into deep waters where peril and potential salvation intersect? One place to start might be by considering the way that water is seen, heard, and used in the rite. It is not a question of validity, but rather that more water, rather than less, can help to ensure that those present in the congregation can see it and hear the sound of it and sense something of its power.

Are there ways of enacting a rite in such a way that a child or adult being baptized might actually appear to be wet enough that a

96

towel needs to be provided, perhaps one especially prepared both to serve a practical purpose and to be kept as a reminder of one's baptism? Sung pieces can help to unwrap some of the multiple dimensions of the sacrament, particularly, in this case, to include some sense of baptism as a descent into deep spiritual waters, in which something is at risk.

David Hoekema's "You Are Our God; We Are Your People" begins with a stanza that recalls the destructive power of the flood as well as the rainbow sign:

> It rained on the earth forty days, forty nights,
> and all of the world was destroyed.
> The ark Noah built at the calling of God
> saved God's chosen ones from the flood.
> God gave Noah the rainbow sign:
> "Such a flood I will not send again—
> I am your God; you are my people."
> *(David A. Hoekema. © 1985 Faith Alive Christian*
> *Resources; reprinted with permission)*

Christ's Triumph over Death

As the bow in the heavens was the sign of God's covenant with Noah, the Eucharist, rooted in the death and resurrection of the Lord, is the sign of the "new covenant" (e.g., 2 Cor. 3:6). N. T. Wright states, "The 'new covenant' beliefs of the early Christians meant that, in hailing Jesus as 'son of god,' they believed that Israel's god had acted in him to fulfill the covenant promises by dealing at last with the problem of evil" (Wright, *Resurrection*, 727). Evil has to do with the disorder that human beings bring into the world by turning away from God to serve lesser claimants to their loyalty, with the result that these promiscuously chosen centers of loyalty lead to competition that serves to turn people against one another. Evil opens the way for death, in all its dimensions.

If the creator god was also the covenant god, and if the covenant was there to deal with the unwelcome problem that had invaded the created order at its heart and corrupted human beings themselves, it was this intruder, death itself, that had to be defeated. To allow death to have its way—to sign up, as it were, to some kind of compromise agreement whereby death took human bodies but

97

the creator was allowed to keep human souls—was no solution, or not to the problem as it was perceived within most Second Temple Judaism. That is why "resurrection" was never a *redescription* of death, but always its *defeat* (Wright, *Resurrection*, 727–28).

In Jesus' resurrection God's covenant plan was fulfilled: "For since death came through a human being, the resurrection of the dead has also come through a human being; for as all die in Adam, so all will be made alive in Christ" (1 Cor. 15:21–22).

Paul declares, "So if anyone is in Christ, there is a new creation" (2 Cor. 5:17). The resurrection is God's promise that points ahead to the *basileia*, the reign/kingdom of God in which the old creation will be repaired and restored. "See, I am making all things new" (Rev. 21:5).

> God himself will be with them;
> he will wipe every tear from their eyes.
>   Death will be no more;
> mourning and crying and pain will be no more,
>   for the first things have passed away.
> (Rev. 21:3–4)

The *eschaton*, in which God's rule will be made manifest to the whole creation indisputably and unmistakably, lies in the future, from which God is coming to meet us. Yet in Christ's resurrection it has already established a foothold in the present by the power of the Holy Spirit, "by putting his seal on us and giving us his Spirit in our hearts as a first installment" (2 Cor. 1:22).

The "new covenant" is not a replacement of the covenant God made with Noah or Abraham, but rather consistent with it and an extension of it. In baptism, God immerses us in the Spirit that testifies to the faithfulness of God's promise in Christ, and embraces us in the covenant with which God had already embraced Noah, Abraham and Sarah, and their descendants.

In the New Testament, 1 Peter understands the story of Noah to "prefigure" Christian baptism.

1 Peter 3:18b–22

[Christ] was put to death in the flesh, but made alive in the spirit, in which also he went and made a proclamation to the spirits in prison, who in former times did not obey, when God waited patiently in the days of Noah, during the building of the ark, in which a few, that is, eight persons, were saved through water. And baptism, which this prefigured, now saves you—not as a removal of dirt from the body, but as an appeal to God for a good conscience, through the resurrection of Jesus Christ, who has gone into heaven and is at the right hand of God, with angels, authorities, and powers made subject to him. (1 Pet. 3:18b–22)

The 1 Peter text is one that has long puzzled biblical interpreters, as it offers a glimpse of Christ making a proclamation to "the spirits in prison," whose identity is uncertain. A tradition dating to at least the second century treats this passage and 4:6, which is similar, as testifying to the crucified Lord having descended to the dead to preach the gospel to them. The magnificent Church of the Holy Savior in Chora (Istanbul) graphically represents this tradition in a fresco of Christ "harrowing hell." Christ, in the center of the fresco, has trampled down the broken gates of hell. Holding Adam in one hand and Eve in the other, he is pulling them out to safety. The same tradition is likely the root of the line in the Apostles' Creed, "He descended into hell" (or, in the contemporary ecumenical version, "He descended to the dead"). The tradition expresses the theological point that Christ's salvation extends backward in time as well as forward.

Some interpreters believe that the 3:19 text is about Christ's triumph over evil. Whoever the writer may have understood these "spirits" to be, the reader has been told that they were guilty of disobeying God "in the days of Noah." Paul Achtemeier expresses doubt that the "spirits" to whom the text refers represent human beings who have died, since nowhere else in the Bible is "spirits" used in that sense. He thinks it more likely that "Christ in this passage is . . . announcing to the imprisoned evil angels of the time of Noah their final doom" (Achtemeier, *1 Peter,* 245). The reference is to the peculiar passage in Genesis 6:1–4, in which supernatural creatures (rebellious angels?) had inappropriate sexual relations with human women, which forms the background for God's resolve to destroy all living things. If Christ was preaching to these "spirits," it was not, apparently, the gospel of salvation he preached, but rather a pronouncement of condemnation.

The context of the letter is the suffering of the Christians in the period in which the letter was composed (see 3:14). These words

99

may have been intended to encourage them with assurance that Christ has overcome every power that threatens to come between them and their God. Baptism serves as the guarantee that those who now suffer for their faith cannot be snatched out of the hand of God, because "Christ has triumphed over the most powerful forces of the universe" (Achtemeier, *1 Peter,* 246).

We who live in North America or Europe may justifiably complain that in countries that have historically had a Christian majority we now suffer from the general public's ignorance of the faith or indifference to it. Yet we are not likely to suffer persecution, even in this era of the new, bolder atheism. However, in some parts of the world, people of various religious traditions still suffer for their faith, including many Christians. In Iraq, extremists have targeted churches for bombing at Christmastime, and terrorists have kidnapped and murdered Christian clergy. Is it because they have been aggressively evangelizing? No. Exhibiting contempt for the dominant religion of the country? No. Like people of many faiths who have experienced persecution because they are a minority or "different," Christians suffer merely for existing, even though their churches have been in the region since before the rise of modern terrorist agendas and have for centuries coexisted peaceably with Islam. Might these persecuted but peaceful Christians experience some comfort in the assurance that in their baptism "angels, authorities, and powers" have been made subject to Christ, and "the reign of evil is finite and coming to an end in this world" (Davis, *Wondrous Depth,* 143)? May it be so.

Verse 21 uses the Greek word *antitypon* ("antitype"), translated in the NRSV as "prefigured," to characterize how God's salvation of Noah and his family provides a paradigm for understanding baptism. The word "antitype" is rare in the New Testament, but it serves here to draw attention to the continuity of God's redemptive work both in ancient Israel and in the time of the church. As Noah and his family were rescued by the buoyant power of the water that lifted the ark, so persecuted Christians are being rescued by baptism from an evil world into the new world prefigured by the Christian community.

Verse 21 describes baptism as "an appeal to God for a good conscience." The NRSV translates the Greek *eperōtēma* as "appeal," but Achtemeier believes that a better translation would be "pledge," as in "baptism . . . now saves you . . . as a *pledge* of a good conscience to God." The Greek word itself is ambiguous, but the fact that in the early church the baptismal liturgy included a question and a responding confession of faith would seem to make plausible the translation as "pledge." The First Letter to Timothy commends him for having made "the good confession" (1 Tim. 6:12), which may not always have taken the same form, but certainly included some pledge of faith in Jesus, perhaps resembling Peter's confession, "You are the Messiah, the Son of the living God" (Matt. 16:16). It is neither water nor our pledge that has the power to save, however, but rather the resurrection of Christ (v. 21). We would not be able to keep such a pledge by our own strength or resolve; but since Christ has defeated the angelic powers who serve to represent the very source of evil in the world, nothing can come between us and the One to whom we have pledged our faith.

When we think of the sacrament in terms of an action that moves from God toward the baptized, the sacrament looks like God's generous grace and assisting strength made visible in cleansing water. It is possible also to perceive baptism as, in part, representing movement from those being baptized toward God, as enacted prayer offered to God through the intercession of Jesus Christ, who "is at the right hand of God." Baptism is the enacted prayer of the baptized, whether or not they are capable of conceptualizing it and putting it into words, but it is always communal prayer, the prayer of the community for those being baptized and for the community of the baptized as a whole.

However, if understood as enacted prayer, baptism is also an *appeal* to God (following the translation preferred in the NRSV) for that state of innocence for which we long, but which is beyond our power to grasp by our own strength alone. The text from 1 Peter concludes with an exhortation that suggests the form of the prayerful appeal dramatized in the sacrament: "Since therefore Christ suffered in the flesh, arm yourselves also with the same intention . . . *so as to live for the rest of your earthly life no longer by human desires but by the will of God*" (1 Pet. 4:1–2, emphasis added). Were the same words to be framed in the form of a prayer, the appeal to God might look like this: "Most gracious God, help us to live for the rest of our earthly lives no longer by human desires, but by your most holy will." Such a prayer is reminiscent of these lines in Psalm 51, a penitential psalm: "Wash me thoroughly from my iniquity, and cleanse me from my sin" (Ps. 51:2).

Of course, those who actually penned the words that became Scripture often said more than they knew themselves to be saying. For example, Christians read Isaiah's messianic prophecies through the lenses of the gospel, seeing Jesus Christ in the words of the Old Testament prophet. We may also take seriously the teaching authority of the church as it interprets this text and the resulting faith of the church as expressed in the Apostles' Creed, "he descended into hell" (or "he descended to the dead"). Even presuming that the writer of 1 Peter had a clear sense of who were meant by the phrase "spirits in prison," we who read his words with uncertainty about the original intent may nevertheless read them through the eyes of those who believe both that Christ's death and resurrection overcame every sort of death-dealing spiritual power, and also that Christ's offer of freedom to those held captive by any and every manifestation of "hell" may extend backward in time as well as forward, and is not limited even by the boundaries of mortality.

Baptism joins the baptized to Noah and his kin, all carried to the safety of a new beginning solely by the grace of God, who in Christ has subdued every destructive spiritual power and refuses to turn a back on those imprisoned in any sort of hell. Baptism is both a pledge of good faith, enabled not by our own strength only, but by the resurrected Christ who alone has the power to help us and the church as a whole keep faith with our pledge; and at the same time, baptism is the community's enacted prayer, its heartfelt appeal to the most generous of Givers for one more gift—the gift of a pure heart.

God's Faithfulness to the Covenant

Exodus 14

Then Moses stretched out his hand over the sea. The LORD drove the sea back by a strong east wind all night, and turned the sea into dry land; and the waters were divided. The Israelites went into the sea on dry ground, the waters forming a wall for them on their right and on their left. The Egyptians pursued, and went into the sea after them. . . .

So Moses stretched out his hand over the sea, and at dawn the sea returned to its normal depth. As the Egyptians fled before it, the LORD tossed the Egyptians into the sea. The waters returned and covered . . . the entire army of Pharaoh; . . not one of them remained. But the Israelites walked on dry ground through the sea, the waters forming a wall for them on their right and on their left. (Exod. 14:21–23a, 27–29)

The service books of the several denominations follow the model of Luther's "flood prayer," including a citation of Israel's escape from Pharaoh's army by God's intervention at the Red (Reed) Sea.

Since the story of the crossing of the sea has been fashioned from more than one source, it is not surprising that the parting of the waters is portrayed both in miraculous terms and as an event made manifest by natural causes. God had told Moses to "lift up your staff, and stretch out your hand over the sea and divide it, that the Israelites may go into the sea on dry ground" (Exod. 14:16), but the text also tells the reader that "the LORD drove the sea back by a strong east wind all night, and turned the sea into dry land" (Exod. 14:21). The editor(s) of Exodus 14 saw neither problem nor contradiction but, rather, perceived the hand of God at work, whether the safe crossing be ascribed to a miracle or ordinary processes or a combination of the two.

Brevard Childs writes, "It is fully clear that Israel was not saved because of her faith. Rather, Israel failed to believe right up to the moment before her deliverance. The faith of Israel did not provide the grounds of her salvation in any sense" (Childs, *Exodus*, 238). Clearly, in Exodus 14:10–12, when the people saw the Egyptians advancing, they moaned and complained to Moses, saying, "Was it because there were no graves in Egypt that you have taken us away to die in the wilderness?" (v. 11). Moses cautioned them not to be afraid, but to watch for the Lord's deliverance. "The LORD will fight for you," he said, "and you have only to keep still" (vv. 13–14). Likewise, the sacrament of baptism may be given to people who have already acquired faith or at least begun to; but from a very early period the church has also baptized the dependent children of members of the faith community. God may act in, upon, and with those who at the moment have no faith at all, just as God saved the Israelites, despite their lack of faith, and however many infants and children they carried with them to safety.

The New Testament itself affirms the link between the sacrament of baptism and divine intervention on Israel's behalf at the Red Sea. "I do not want you to be unaware, brothers and sisters,

103

that our ancestors were all under the cloud, and all passed through the sea, and all were baptized into Moses in the cloud and in the sea" (1 Cor. 10:1–4). The "cloud" refers to the pillar of cloud (Exod. 14:19) that positioned itself between the Israelites and the Egyptians, lighting up the night. It represents God's presence standing guard over Israel to protect the people from Pharaoh's army, which was preparing either to drive them back to Egypt or kill them, presumably, if they could not be taken back into involuntary service. In the 1 Corinthians passage, the apostle Paul sees Israel's experience in the cloud and the sea as a baptism "into Moses," creating a parallel with baptism "into Christ Jesus" (Rom. 6:3).

The waters of the sea divided as though to form a wall to the right and the left of the people, making it possible for them to pass between "on dry ground" (Exod. 14:29). As in the Noah story, water is a threat, in this case because it posed a barrier that could have trapped the Israelites and left them and their children exposed to the power of Pharaoh's army. At the same time, when God divided the sea, the people fled to safety on a path that led through the waters. Water is perilous, with death as a real possibility; yet in the midst of it the people are led to safety. Where there had been no hope, God provided a way forward. One may discern here a resonance with the Pauline themes of death and resurrection.

The book of Deuteronomy establishes an ethical link between the exodus, including the safe crossing of the sea, and a resulting obligation to keep God's commandments. After a charge to "love the LORD your God" . . . and keep "his charge, his decrees, his ordinances, and his commandments always" (Deut. 11:1), followed by a rehearsal of God's saving deeds, including "how he made the water of the Red Sea flow over [the Egyptians] as they pursued you" (Deut. 11:4), God said in Moses' voice, "Keep, then, this entire commandment that I am commanding you today" (11:8). Later in the same book, God articulates the divine law, including this admonition: "You shall not deprive a resident alien or an orphan of justice; you shall not take a widow's garment in pledge. Remember that you were a slave in Egypt and the LORD your God redeemed you from there; therefore I command you to do this" (Deut. 24:17–18). Patrick Miller observes that "as [the Israelites] were redeemed from their plight by the grace and mercy of God, so now they are called to act in ways that will ensure the well-being of the most vulnerable of the community," including foreigners

(Miller, *Ten Commandments*, 360). God's action on our behalf is not meant to end there, but to invite our own action for God's sake. Baptism is a gift, but as we grow into it, there is formed in us a sense of responsibility for our neighbors and for the life of the world we share with everyone, believer and unbeliever, baptized and unbaptized. As Brian Gerrish has demonstrated in *Grace and Gratitude*, grace evokes gratitude. The baptismal gift is meant to lead us, out of gratitude, to a commitment to will and to do those things that will contribute to the blessing of "all the families of the earth."

The psalmist celebrated the deliverance at the Red Sea as part of the exodus story, which is foundational to Israel's faith.

> He rebuked the Red Sea, and it became dry;
>   he led them through the deep as through a desert.
> So he saved them from the hand of the foe,
>   and delivered them from the hand of the enemy.
>   (Ps. 106:9–10; see also Ps. 136:11–15)

In baptism, God leads us through the water to take our place in the continuing story of God's engagement with the people called to God's service. It is a deliverance from death that, in contrast to the crossing of the Red Sea, does not require the death of our enemies. The thanksgiving over the water in most contemporary services of baptism, recalling God's saving acts at the Red Sea, serves to highlight the sacrament as embodying the revisiting of an event that represented both peril and promise, with expectations that baptism will also lead to a thankful state of mind and build up in us a community ethos of gratitude that will have a significant formative effect on the ethical lives of those who have been claimed by God in the sacrament:

> By water and the Holy Spirit,
> we are made members of the church, the body of Christ,
> and joined to Christ's ministry of love, peace, and justice.
>   (*BCW*, 432)

The exodus, with its story of passing through the waters, is God's central saving event in the Old Testament, while the resurrection of the crucified Lord (his journey through death to life) is the central saving event in the New Testament and a primary motif in the sacrament of baptism. An eighth-century Easter hymn by

John of Damascus sings of the crossing of the sea and of the resurrection in subsequent stanzas:

> Come, ye faithful, raise the strain of triumphant gladness!
> God hath brought his Israel into joy from sadness;
> loosed from Pharaoh's bitter yoke Jacob's sons and daughters;
> led them, with unmoistened foot through the Red Sea waters.
>
> Now the queen of seasons, bright with the day of splendor,
> with the royal feast of feasts, comes its joy to render;
> comes to glad Jerusalem, who with true affection
> welcomes in unwearied strains Jesus' resurrection.
> *(The Hymnal 1982, #199 and #200; public domain)*

Joshua 3

After the death of Moses, God spoke to Joshua: "My servant Moses is dead. Now proceed to cross the Jordan, you and all this people" (Josh. 1:2). Joshua became, in effect, a new Moses, leading the people across the river into the land of promise, just as Moses had led them through the sea. (Similarly, both Elijah and Elisha had also been linked to Moses redivivus in 2 Kgs. 2:8, 13–14, where each also parted the water of the Jordan.) For the crossing under Joshua's leadership, the priests went first, carrying the ark of the covenant. It was spring, a rainy season, and the Jordan was overflowing, so that it would be difficult if not impossible to cross the swollen river by ordinary means. When the feet of the priests carrying the ark touched the water, "the waters flowing from above stood still. . . . Then the people crossed over opposite Jericho" (Josh. 3:16).

Once again, where it seemed as though the story might have reached an ending, God wrote a new chapter. One cannot help but discern in the story of crossing the Jordan an anticipation of the perspective formed by the gospel, that where God is, endings may become beginnings—that death will be overcome by resurrection.

Reminiscent of the Israelites' washing their clothes in preparation for a theophany at Sinai (Exod. 19:10–11), Joshua also directed the people to "sanctify yourselves; for tomorrow the Lord will do wonders among you" (Josh. 3:5). To come into God's presence was perilous, requiring ritual purification by way of preparation.

106

The approaching proximity of the kingdom was the stimulus for the baptizing ministry of John the Baptizer. Working from a sense of what is necessary and appropriate when anticipating an encounter with the holy, John would call for the people of Israel to "repent, for the kingdom of heaven has come near" (Matt. 3:2). For Christians, the sacrament of baptism also witnesses to an eschatological dimension. In the opening chapter of Ephesians, the apostle has written of the mystery of God's will in Christ "as a plan for the fullness of time, to gather up all things in him, things in heaven and things on earth" (Eph. 1:9–10), and then concludes the section by reminding the Ephesians that they had been "marked with the seal of the promised Holy Spirit," which is "the pledge of our inheritance toward redemption as God's own people" (Eph. 1:13–14). "The seal" is associated with baptism, serving as a down payment (cf. 2 Cor. 1:22) on a share in the eschatological redemption of the whole cosmos in fulfillment of God's plan. Baptism is a sanctification, of sorts, by which the church prepares for the ultimate christophany, the Parousia of the Lord.

The eighteenth-century hymn "Guide Me, O Thou Great Jehovah" and an updated version, "Guide Me, Ever Great Redeemer," portray the crossing of the Jordan in a way that points forward in eschatological hope.

> When I tread the verge of Jordan,
> bid my anxious fears subside;
> death of death and hell's destruction,
> land me safe on Canaan's side.
> Songs and praises, songs and praises
> I will raise forevermore,
> I will raise forevermore.
> (*Evangelical Lutheran Worship*,
> #618; public domain)

Eschatological Images

The sacrament of baptism has three "time" references: past, present, and future. Baptism links us to the past, when God made covenants with Noah and every living creature (Gen. 9:11) and then with Abraham and his descendants (Gen. 17:7) and proved faithful to the divine covenant by making a way for Israel through the sea (Exod. 14:29) and by leading the people across the Jordan into the land of promise (Josh. 3:17), and in the fullness of time sent Jesus to

107

John the Baptizer to be baptized in solidarity with those who came repenting for their sins.

In the present, baptism unites us with Jesus Christ and those with whom he has established solidarity, particularly joining us to the priestly people of God and their ministry in the world, by which together we participate in God's covenantal mission intended as blessing for "all the families of the earth."

Baptism also points toward the future. It manifests God's eschatological future in the present moment, strengthening our confidence in the triumph of God's justice and comforting us as we live out the gospel amidst the ambiguities of the world. Both the Old and New Testaments provide images of living water, serving as representations of the life-giving Spirit, and the sacrament of baptism, with its reliance on the Spirit's power, provides a participatory foretaste of the Edenic *basileia*, the reign (or kingdom) of God.

Genesis 2:10–14; Ezekiel 47:1–12; Zechariah 14:8–9; Revelation 22:1–5, 16–17

Baptism's tilt toward the future has roots in Old Testament images of a new world, represented in an abundance of water to support life of all kinds. The second of the two creation stories in Genesis includes a reference, before the creation of humankind, to a stream that "would rise from the earth, and water the whole face of the ground" (Gen. 2:6). A few verses later, we read, "A river flows out of Eden to water the garden" (2:10). Subsequent verses describe the division of that river into four branches, three of which, in the ancient world, would have been recognizable geographical landmarks. One interpreter notes that the image from Genesis testifies that "the inhabited world lives on the surplus of the riches of paradise" (Zimmerli, *Ezekiel*, 510). Subsequent biblical narrators will return to the image of a river flowing out of Eden as the symbol of a future state that will resemble that paradisiacal place of innocence.

The book of Ezekiel provides a vivid example, reminiscent of the Genesis passage. In a vision, Ezekiel saw himself brought to the entrance of the temple, where he saw water flowing "from below the threshold of the temple toward the east" (Ezek. 47:1). At first, the water was shallow, only ankle-deep (v. 3), but then deeper, and finally, "it was a river that I could not cross, for the water had risen;

108

it was deep enough to swim in, a river that could not be crossed" (47:5). When the water reached the Dead Sea ("sea of stagnant waters"), the water would become fresh. "Wherever the river goes, every living creature that swarms will live . . . and everything will live where the river goes" (47:9).

Ezekiel subtly recalled the river that flowed out of Eden, the river of paradise that emerged from the very spot from which the whole creation had blossomed, and suggested that, when the exile ended, the God whose presence was represented by the temple ("this is the place . . . where I will reside") would send from it water that would nurture trees that would not only produce fruit but whose leaves would serve for healing the wounds of the people of Israel returned from their Babylonian captivity.

The New Testament book of Revelation picks up on the Old Testament images of an abundance of life-giving and healing water, flowing from the presence of God. However, in John's vision, the river does not flow from Eden, or just from Jerusalem, or even from the temple itself, but directly "from the throne of God and of the Lamb" (Rev. 22:1). The text picks up the "river of the water of life" images, including their eschatological themes. "Then the angel showed me the river of the water of life, bright as crystal, flowing from the throne of God and of the Lamb" (Rev. 22:1). Like the above passage from Ezekiel, Revelation speaks of "the tree of life," which represents an eschatological vision not just for the healing of the returned exiles, but for universal healing. "And the leaves of the tree are for the healing *of the nations*" (v. 2, emphasis added).

Susan Palo Cherwien's baptismal hymn evokes the tree of life image, identifying it with Jesus Christ and celebrating how word and water join us to him, the life-giving tree.

> Christ, holy Vine,
> Christ, living Tree,
> be praised for this blest mystery:
> that word and water thus revive
> and join us to your Tree of Life.
> (© 1993 Susan Palo Cherwien, admin.
> Augsburg Fortress; used by permission)

The *basileia*, the reign/kingdom of God that is to come, will be the expression of God's healing of the whole world's brokenness, alienation, and disappointment. Cutthroat competition that sets one community against another will be transformed into another sort of energy, in which justice will be embraced as a delight rather than a threat.

That the Bible projects an image of an abundance of water as one characteristic of the *eschaton* might well cause us to reflect on the role of water in ordinary life, and on our stewardship of this resource that is, because of its vital necessity, worthy of being called holy. A layman in Nebraska answered the appeal of mission workers in Malawi who sought help for a village in which there was no easy access to a reliable supply of clean water. With the help of his congregation and a local factory whose work for generations had been to make windmills for midwestern farms, he arranged to have a windmill sent to East Africa.

Church members and others have organized letter-writing campaigns and visits to their representatives in Congress to appeal for strong laws regulating the protection of rivers and streams from pollution by industrial emissions or runoffs from factory farms. Mining by mountaintop removal is a threat to streams that run at the foot of the mountains and to those who depend on them when the soil and rocks removed by the mining process are dumped into them. City water supplies need to be protected from chemical pollution accumulated from recycled wastewater. If clean, clear water is symbolic of paradise, it is because the loss of it is both hell and death.

Since the need for water is immediate and daily and necessary to sustain life, it is not surprising that it should acquire a mystical aura, an association with the holy, the sacred, and the very substance of life understood in an even deeper sense than the merely biological, *eternal* life. Just as the garden of Eden lacked nothing necessary for an abundant life, including a reliable supply of water, so, in the eschatological visions of the prophets and the psalmist, water from God's very presence would bring sustenance and delight to God's people, and cause to flourish the tree of life, the leaves of which will serve a universal purpose, "the healing of the nations," recalling God's covenantal promise to Abraham that the mission of his descendants was to be a blessing "to all the families of the earth." In Revelation, John points to Christ offering to the thirsty "the water of life" as a gift to any and all who thirst for it: "Let anyone who wishes take the water of life as a gift" (Rev. 22:17; cf. Isa. 55:1).

The church's experience of the sacrament of baptism brings together these several streams derived from eschatological images in both testaments and joins them in a rite that wraps them all together in a way that is fundamentally doxological, in praise for God's work in the past, the present, and the age to come.

The Gospel writers identified Jesus himself as God's answer to Israel's eschatological hope, he himself being the sign of God's promised rule and the ultimate healing of the whole creation. At Jesus' baptism, the Spirit descended upon him, and in the hour of Jesus' glorification, the promised *paraklētos* (Advocate, Helper; see John 14:16), the Holy Spirit who in the Old Testament had been associated with charismatic figures or with kings, judges, and prophets, would be poured out extravagantly on sons and daughters, young and old, and even upon slaves (Joel 2:28–29). The image of "living water" represents the Spirit, and the Spirit is a sign of the messianic age. In the Gospel of John, Jesus uses a festive religious occasion to dramatize an announcement of the inauguration of the new age.

John 7:37–39

> On the last day of the festival, the great day, while Jesus was standing there, he cried out, "Let anyone who is thirsty come to me, and let the one who believes in me drink. As the scripture has said, 'Out of the believer's heart shall flow rivers of living water.'" Now he said this about the Spirit, which believers in him were to receive; for as yet there was no Spirit, because Jesus was not yet glorified. (John 7:37–39)

The festival referred to in the text is the festival of Sukkot, which originated as an agricultural festival, but after the exile had been supplemented by the addition to it of the celebration of Israel's survival during the years of wandering in the desert, when they had had to live in temporary shelters (Neh. 8:13–18). One aspect of the Sukkot celebration was the water drawing, related to the occasion when, in the wilderness, Moses struck the rock to provide water for the people (Num. 20:2–13 and Exod. 17:1–7). For the seven days of the celebration, water was collected in a golden pitcher from the pool of Siloam, which was believed to be the place where the Davidic kings had been anointed, recalling the words of the prophet, "With joy you will draw water from the wells of salvation"

111

(Isa. 12:3). The water from Siloam was carried to the water gate of the temple, and a priest poured it into a bowl designed to drain onto an altar. The ceremony was a joyful one, anticipating the coming of the anointed one, the descendant of David, the Messiah. The juxtaposition of the occasion and the words John attributes to Jesus underlines the significance of the moment, a signal to those who know the festival that the messianic moment is at hand in him.

Jesus' words, "Let anyone who is thirsty come to me" (John 7:37), recall God's promise through the prophet:

> But now hear, O Jacob my servant,
> Israel whom I have chosen!
> Thus says the Lord who made you,
>   who formed you in the womb and will help you:
> Do not fear, O Jacob my servant,
>   Jeshurun whom I have chosen.
> For I will pour water on the thirsty land,
>   and streams on the dry ground;
> I will pour my spirit upon your descendants,
>   and my blessing on your offspring.
> (Isa. 44:1–3)

Jesus draws on the biblical prophecies, and his reference to "rivers of living water" (running water) draws upon Old Testament metaphors. "Now he said this about the Spirit" (v. 39). But, John added, the abundant manifestation of the Spirit would occur only after Jesus had been glorified. The Spirit is the milieu that forms the environment in which the baptized are plunged with the intention that we grow and flourish like well-watered plants—a sustaining environment in which we strain upward in hope for the new creation, of which we have already experienced a foretaste.

We know that the whole creation has been groaning in labor pains until now; and not only the creation, but we ourselves, who have the first fruits of the Spirit, groan inwardly while we wait for adoption, the redemption of our bodies (Rom. 8:22–23).

The water of baptism is the water of the Spirit, which satisfies our dryness, quenches our thirst. "We were all made to drink of one Spirit" (1 Cor. 12:13), as the apostle said. The Gospel of John reinforces the connection between water and the Spirit, and the link between the Spirit and the messianic age.

John 4:7–15

Jesus, sitting by Jacob's well at midday, encountered a Samaritan woman and asked her for a drink. She was puzzled at his request, since it challenged the traditional boundaries not only between the genders but between Jews and Samaritans as well. Jesus told her that, if she had known who he was, she would have asked him for a drink, and God would have given her "living water" (John 4:10). "Living water" is the running water one finds in rivers and streams and is presumably fresh rather than stale. To the Samaritan woman, Jesus promised a drink of "living water." In Jeremiah 2:13, God is described, metaphorically, as "fountain of living water."

Brian Gerrish reports that John Calvin's fundamental definition of God was as "the spring or fountain of all good" (Gerrish, *Grace and Gratitude*, 26): "Moreover, although our mind cannot apprehend God without rendering some honor to him, it will not suffice simply to hold that there is One whom all ought to honor and adore, unless we are also persuaded that he is *the fountain of every good*, and that we must seek nothing elsewhere than in him" (Calvin, *Institutes* 1.2.1, p. 41, emphasis added). The psalmist says, "They feast on the abundance of your house, and you give them drink from the river of your delights. For with you is the fountain of life" (Ps. 36:8b, 9). "River of your delights" is literally, in Hebrew, "torrent of your Edens." The psalm rejoices in the temple, which serves as a symbolic garden of Eden in which pilgrims may enjoy intimacy with God.

The alternative service of baptism in the *Book of Common Worship* includes a response that may be sung or said following the actual baptismal act:

> This is the fountain of life,
> water made holy by the suffering of Christ,
> washing all the world.
>
> > (*BCW*, 427)

At the end of another exchange with the Samaritan woman, Jesus said, "Everyone who drinks of this water [from the well] will be thirsty again, but those who drink of the water that I will give them will never be thirsty. The water that I give will become in them a spring of water gushing up to eternal life" (John 4:13–14).

113

Living water, like the Spirit, may be "poured." Through the prophet God had said, "Then afterward I will pour out my spirit on all flesh" (Joel 2:28), a text that Peter quoted in his sermon on the day of Pentecost (Acts 2:17). In the same sermon, Peter referred to the manifestation of the Spirit, saying, "He has poured out this that you both see and hear" (Acts 2:33). Titus is even more explicit. "But when the goodness and loving kindness of God our Savior appeared, he saved us, not because of any works of righteousness that we had done, but according to his mercy, through the water of rebirth and renewal by the Holy Spirit. This Spirit he poured out on us richly through Jesus Christ our Savior" (Titus 3:4–6).

The image of the pouring out of the Spirit may indicate that baptism was accomplished with the pouring of water at least some of the time. This was explicitly mentioned as an option in the early-second-century *Didache* (*Didache*, VII). It is reasonable to make the case that even in the New Testament period baptism may sometimes have been by submersion in water and sometimes by pouring, and that each method served to dramatize different aspects of the one baptism.

The Church of England's *Common Worship* draws upon the pouring image in a blessing that follows the act of baptism:

May God, who has received you by baptism into his Church,
pour upon you the riches of his grace,
that within the company of Christ's pilgrim people
you may daily be renewed by his anointing Spirit,
and come to the inheritance of the saints in glory.
(Common Worship, 357)

CHAPTER 4

Early Baptismal Theological Themes and Developing Rites

The Pre-Nicene Baptismal Rites

Historical studies have long since established that there was no such thing as a single "New Testam̲ ̲urch" to which later generations might return for an absolutely authoritative model. From the beginning, several Christian communities existed, each one framing the gospel story somewhat differently, with the accents falling in different places, depending on time and location. The fact that we have four Gospels and not just one is testimony to that diversity.

"For the most part the New Testament did not inform worship in the early days, but the other way around. The New Testament was shaped by worshiping communities among whose members were authors whose works were eventually canonized. Early churches worshiped not because stories are in the New Testament, but the stories and symbols are there, at least in part, as fruits of social, ritual experiences of early worshipers" (Connell, "On Chrism," 233).

With the passing of time, churches geographically and culturally different from one another began to experience more and more contact with each other. One result was an increased sharing of ways of expressing the faith and embodying it in common practices. Historians researching practices of a variety of churches in the second, third, and fourth centuries discover both differences in practice and a growing congruence, as the churches matured and

115

influenced one another. As we ponder the sacramental life of the churches today, we may benefit by reflecting on the ways developing practice in the early centuries made use of biblical images and narratives, continuing to shape and reshape their understanding of the gospel.

The New Testament itself does not describe baptismal rites in detail, apparently presuming that they were well enough known not to require description. A number of sources in the period before the Council of Nicaea (first quarter of the fourth century) provide at least offhand references to actual baptismal practices (see Spinks, *Early and Medieval*, chap. 2, 1437). What we learn from these sources is that there was no one clear pattern for the way baptisms were done. Diversity may be the most useful word with which to describe them, although diversity does not mean that the early rites shared no typical characteristics. In pre-Nicene rites both of the East and of the West, it was typical to find these elements at least:

anointing with oil (before or after)
baptism in water
ritual torches (in some places) as a sign of illumination
Trinitarian language

Anointing

The practice of anointing with oil has roots in secular history as well as biblical history, because the use of oil in bathing was common practice in the ancient Mediterranean world:

> One of the first ritual supplements to baptism was anointing. Although attempts have been made to find an original pattern and linear development, the diversity found in the ancient texts seems to reflect a diversity found in common secular bathing etiquette. There we find evidence of anointing before or after, or before and after bathing, and also of oil being poured into the baths themselves. All these are reflected in the diversity we find in the early centuries in the emerging baptismal rituals. (Spinks, *Early and Medieval*, 157)

116

The other root of anointing is biblical, because the kings, prophets, and priests we read about in the Old Testament had been anointed and because the word "Messiah" (Greek, *Christos*) means "anointed one." In the first chapter of the Gospel of John, Andrew found his brother, Simon Peter, and said to him, 'We have found the Messiah' (which is translated Anointed)" (John 1:41).

The Old Testament records the act of anointing, that is, pouring oil over the head of the new king. A wedding psalm addressed to the king includes a reference to anointing, which was the central act of the coronation rite: "Therefore God, your God, has anointed you with the oil of gladness beyond your companions" (Ps. 45:7). In Scripture, anointing can be associated with the giving of "the spirit of the Lord," as in the biblical description of the prophet Samuel's anointing of David.

1 Samuel 16:1–13

> The LORD said to Samuel, "How long will you grieve over Saul? I have rejected him from being king over Israel. Fill your horn with oil and set out; I will send you to Jesse the Bethlehemite, for I have provided for myself a king among his sons. . . . I will show you what you shall do; and you shall anoint for me the one whom I name to you." . . . The LORD said, "Rise and anoint [David]; for this is the one." Then Samuel took the horn of oil, and anointed him in the presence of his brothers; and the spirit of the LORD came mightily upon David from that day forward. (1 Sam. 16:1, 3, 12–13; cf., e.g., 1 Sam. 9:16; 15:1; 1 Kgs. 1:34; 2 Kgs. 9:3, the anointing of Saul, Solomon, and Jehu)

A prophet might also be anointed. Elijah, perhaps an early multitasker, is charged to anoint a prophet and two kings as well: Hazael as king over Aram, Jehu as king over Israel, and Elisha as his own successor (1 Kgs. 19:15–16).

The high priest was also anointed (Num. 35:25), beginning with Aaron, the very first one. "You shall anoint Aaron and his sons, and consecrate them, in order that they may serve me as priests" (Exod. 30:30; cf. 28:41 and 29:7). When Moses anointed his brother Aaron, "he poured some of the anointing oil on Aaron's head and anointed him, to consecrate him" (Lev. 8:12). Then some of the anointing oil was mixed with blood from the sacrificial lamb and sprinkled "on Aaron and his vestments, and also on his sons and their vestments. Thus he consecrated Aaron and his vestments, and also his sons and their vestments" (Lev. 8:30).

117

When Samuel anointed David, the anointing was accompanied by "the spirit of the LORD" falling upon David (1 Sam. 16:13).

Isaiah 61:1 and Luke 4:18

The spirit of the Lord GOD is upon me,
because the Lord has anointed me;
he has sent me to bring good news to the oppressed,
to bind up the brokenhearted,
to proclaim liberty to the captives,
and release to the prisoners.

(Isa. 61:1)

Isaiah referred to one whom he did not identify, one to whom the spirit of the Lord had been given, one who had been anointed for a special mission. Christians have read this text, retrospectively, as one that describes Jesus, supported in such a reading because Jesus had quoted it in his sermon in the synagogue at Nazareth (Luke 4:18). When Jesus makes use of this text, and adds, "Today this scripture has been fulfilled in your hearing" (4:21), "anointing" no doubt should be understood in a metaphoric and spiritual sense rather than recalling an occasion in which there was an actual pouring of oil. The Gospel writers, describing Jesus' baptism, do not use the word "anointing," but imply it, again in a metaphorical sense, when they refer to the Holy Spirit descending upon him. As the anointed one, classical theology has understood Jesus to be prophet, priest, and king (the so-called *munus triplex*). When New Testament writers describe Jesus as "anointed," the implication is that God has designated him as king, a title ascribed to him ironically as he approached his passion.

The book of Acts records a prayer of Peter and John that refers to "your holy servant Jesus, whom you anointed" (Acts 4:27), and, relating the image of anointing to the Spirit, also records Peter as having spoken to Cornelius and his assembled guests about "how God anointed Jesus of Nazareth with the Holy Spirit and with power" (Acts 10:38). Other texts link the Spirit and power; for example, "But you will receive power when the Holy Spirit has come upon you" (Acts 1:8a) and Paul's statement to the Corinthians that he did not come to them with any claim based on his own strength or sophistication, but "with a demonstration of the Spirit and of power" (1 Cor. 2:4). The apostle prayed for the Ephesians

118

that God "may grant that you be strengthened in your inner being with power through his Spirit" (Eph. 3:16). According to the writer of the First Letter to the Thessalonians, the gospel had come to them "in power and in the Holy Spirit" (1 Thess. 1:5).

2 Corinthians 1:21–22 and 1 John 2:18–29

We know that a literal anointing with oil was part of many of the pre-Nicene baptismal rites, sometimes before the washing in water, sometimes after, and sometimes both. New Testament references to anointing of persons after Jesus' resurrection may refer to actual anointing with oil or to a metaphorical anointing as a way of speaking of the gift of the Holy Spirit. "But it is God who establishes us with you in Christ and has anointed us, by putting his seal on us and giving us his Spirit in our hearts as a first installment" (2 Cor. 1:21–22).

Similarly, 1 John includes a text that affirms that the Holy Spirit, at work in the faithful community, makes it possible to identify false testimony: "I write these things to you concerning those who would deceive you. As for you, the anointing [*chrisma*] that you received from him abides in you, and so you do not need anyone to teach you. But as his anointing [*chrisma*] teaches you about all things, and is true and is not a lie, and just as it has taught you, abide in him" (1 John 2:26–27). First John may refer to a literal act of anointing or to a spiritual gift of discernment, with or without an actual ritual act with oil. However, the use of the Greek noun *chrisma*, which means oil, a word found only in 1 John, suggests a literal imposition of a specific substance.

The pre-Nicene baptismal rites linked the act of baptizing and the gift of the Spirit, but the gift of the Spirit was identified with the entire rite, not with any specific moment in it. The anointing itself was derived from the Gospel accounts of the descent (anointing) of the Spirit at Jesus' baptism and served to identify every baptism as an occasion in which the Spirit was given. The act of anointing was typical, but it was not understood as though the Spirit were given explicitly in the act of anointing. It is not surprising, however, that eventually, at least in some parts of the church, anointing with oil, rather than the whole baptismal rite, became identified as the specific occasion for the giving of the Spirit.

Much later, the Roman Church, identifying the laying on of hands and the anointing as the acts by which the Spirit was

119

communicated to the newly baptized, separated those actions from the baptismal washing into a separate rite—indeed, a distinctly separate sacrament—called confirmation. This separation took place not for specifically theological reasons, but by reason of historical circumstance. Originally, the bishop (the pastor whose responsibility was to lead the church in a particular community) presided at baptisms. When the bishop's role had been expanded to that of pastor of churches spread over a regional area (diocese), he might not be able to visit each congregation frequently enough to be present at every baptism. When, out of fear for the child's spiritual safety, children were baptized a few days after birth, the local pastors presided in the absence of the bishop, whose visitation a few weeks, months, or years later would include completing the baptismal rite with the laying on of hands. No such separation occurred in the Eastern churches, where there has never developed a rite or sacrament of confirmation. For them, anointing has always been embedded in the baptismal rite itself.

Contemporary service books of most denominations include, as part of the baptismal rite, signing of the cross on the forehead of the person baptized, with at least optional use of oil. The rubric in the Presbyterian *Book of Common Worship* reads, "The minister may mark the sign of the cross on the forehead of each of the newly baptized. . . . Oil prepared for this purpose may be used" (*BCW*, 413). The rite is not understood as "confirmation," nor does the *BCW* include any rite designated as confirmation, although there are rites for persons making a first profession of faith.

The act of anointing with oil, though not essential, has something to commend it, though it would be prudent to take care that it not be interpreted in a way that would make the baptismal washing appear to be incomplete without it. The typical pre-Nicene practice, in which each element of the rite participates in the meaning of the whole, is no doubt right. The *BCW* has carefully chosen the words used by the minister when anointing is part of the rite, in order to ensure that the act is not presented as though anointing alone is related to the giving of the Spirit:

N., child of the covenant [or "child of God"],
you have been sealed by the Holy Spirit in baptism,
and marked as Christ's own [or "grafted into Christ"] forever.
(*BCW*, p. 442)

The key words are *"have been* sealed" (past participle) by the Holy Spirit." When? *"In baptism."*

Certainly the word "Christ," or "anointed one," shaped the perception that baptism, with its rite of anointing, rooted, as it is, in Old Testament ordinations, served to incorporate the baptized into Christ and the corporate priesthood that the church has been called to share with and through him. What better way to mark the union between the "anointed one" and his disciple than by an act of anointing? What better way to "ordain" each baptized person into the "royal priesthood" (1 Pet. 2:9) exercised by the church than by the same act by which prophets and priests were ordained?

One might also make a case that anointing and the sacrament of baptism have in common a concern for healing. The sacrament is a testament to God's power to heal us of estrangements from God and one another and to heal us of aimlessness and hopelessness. One use for anointing is as an enacted prayer for healing. "Are any among you sick? They should call for the elders of the church and have them pray over them, anointing them with oil in the name of the Lord" (Jas. 5:14). Contemporary service books often include services for wholeness, with explicit petitions for healing, that offer the possibility of laying on of hands and anointing with oil (e.g., *UMBW*, 621–22). The inclusion of anointing in the baptismal rite heightens the relation to baptism as a prayer for and promise of healing, broadly understood.

Baptism in Water

"But we, little fishes, after the example of our ΙΧΘΥΣ Jesus Christ, are born in water, nor have we safety in any other way than by permanently abiding in water." So writes . . . Tertullian, in the introduction to his *De Baptismo* . . . the earliest treatise on baptism ever written . . . (ca. 198–200 C.E.). (Johnson, *Rites of Christian Initiation*, 61)

While baptism was always in water, it is less clear exactly how the water was used. The Greek verb does not settle the question. In non-Christian sources, the Greek *baptizō* can mean "dip, immerse, wash, plunge, sink, drench, or overwhelm" (Arndt and Gingrich, 131). Even in the earliest Gospel, a version of this Greek verb is translated simply as "washing" in reference to "cups, pots, and bronze kettles" (Mark 7:4).

If we take the Pauline image of death and resurrection (as in Rom. 6) as a model, it would lead us to visualize baptism in such a way as to suggest burial and resurrection, and the method most likely to evoke such an image would be to plunge the body beneath the water, and then, after a moment, to raise the person to a standing position in the water. This, of course, is the practice in many churches today, particularly Baptist churches.

However, in the pre-Nicene period, the dominant interpretation of baptism was of washing or of rebirth—womb, rather than tomb—with the death and resurrection image far less common. The washing and rebirth models might, of course, also have involved the complete submersion of the person being baptized, but it is not inevitable that they would. The *Didache*, or Teaching of the Twelve Apostles, a document that may date from as early as the late first century, lists several options for the rite, in order of priority: the use of (1) running water, (2) or cold water, (3) or warm water, (4) or pouring water three times over the head (*Didache*, VII). Even in the first three instances, the only rubric is to baptize in the name of the Father, Son, and Holy Spirit, with no description of what action is meant by "baptize." However, since the fourth option (pouring) is offered as a contrast with the first three, those three obviously involved *more* water.

The New Testament provides several examples in which the Spirit has been described as having been "poured out." Acts 2 quotes the prophecy from Joel 2:28, "In the last days it will be, God declares, that I will *pour out my Spirit* upon all flesh" (Acts 2:17, emphasis added). The Greek is consistent in translating the Hebrew root *shapakh* as "pour." The same Greek verb, *ekcheō*, may be found in a description of the response to Peter's testimony to those in Cornelius's household: "The circumcised believers who had come with Peter were astounded that the gift of the Holy Spirit had been *poured out* even on the Gentiles" (Acts 10:45, emphasis added). In Titus the image of pouring the Spirit is linked to language that suggests baptism: "This Spirit he poured out on us richly through Jesus Christ our Savior" (Titus 3:6).

122 Swedish scholar Lars Hartman reasons that the last clause in 1 Corinthians 12:13, translated in the NRSV "We were all made to

drink of one Spirit," might as easily be translated "We all had the one Spirit poured over us." He suggests that "the image of pouring may indicate how baptism was practiced" (Hartman, "Into the Name . . . ," 67).

"The earliest known [baptismal] font is that preserved in the house church at Dura Europos [Syria], and this was a cistern in which someone could stand and have water poured on them" (Spinks, *Early and Medieval*, 16). In the early centuries, frescoes that picture the baptism of Jesus typically show him standing in the water while John pours water over him. When special buildings began to be built as baptisteries, the pools in them varied in depth, some permitting a complete submersion and others not likely deep enough.

No direct evidence exists for Jewish proselyte baptism until after the beginning of the Christian era, so it is doubtful that it would have served as a model. In fact, it may be just the reverse—that Christian baptism influenced the manner of bathing proselytes to Judaism. The Old Testament models available to John the Baptizer and early Christians, then, would have been the references to various sorts of ablutions in Leviticus, Exodus, and so forth, which are simply "washing," or sometimes the sprinkling of water or mixtures of water and blood or water and oil, as well as bathing. It is not at all certain whether these several precedents would have served to shape John's baptizing in the Jordan River.

Unfortunately, for those who would really like to achieve some certainty about the practice of baptism in the New Testament period and soon after, no one thought to provide a definitive description, probably because they did not have posterity in mind, and descriptions did not seem necessary for contemporaries. It may well be that, as the list of options provided by the *Didache* would indicate, even basic baptismal practice was not everywhere the same. The one consistency would seem to be the use of water, most likely in abundance.

John 3:1–10

> Very truly, I tell you, no one can enter the kingdom of God without being born of water and the Spirit. What is born of the flesh is flesh, and what is born of the Spirit is spirit. Do not be astonished that I said to you, "You must be born from above."

123

The wind blows where it chooses, and you hear the sound of it,
but you do not know where it comes from or where it goes. So it
is with everyone who is born of the Spirit. (John 3:5–8)

When Nicodemus, a Pharisee who held some position of religious authority, had come to Jesus under cover of darkness, Jesus
responded to his spiritual quest by telling him, "Very truly, I tell
you, no one can see the kingdom of God without being born from
above" [anōthen] (John 3:3). The Greek word is ambiguous, and
older translations translate it as born "again," but the translators of
the NRSV prefer "from above," which is more clearly the meaning
of *ano-* elsewhere in the Gospel of John (8:23; 19:11). Nicodemus,
who plays the role of the literalist, was puzzled by the reference to
a new birth. Jesus then added to the puzzle by telling Nicodemus
that entrance to the kingdom of God required "being born of water
and the Spirit" (3:5).

In the first three centuries of the church's life, baptism was
understood predominantly in terms of rebirth, which could appeal
to this text to provide a certain authority, or to Titus 3:5, which
refers to "the water of rebirth."

"Born again" language has played a role in U.S. politics and
culture, particularly when a public figure claims to have been born
again, as though the experience serves as a divine guarantee of honesty and authenticity that entitles the claimant to authority in politics, business, or finance. The birth image, whether "again" or "from
above," might better serve to say that the reborn person is starting
over, like a tiny child, learning the ropes of living all over again,
this time as an apprentice to Jesus Christ. Rather than a badge of
authority, the claim to having been reborn more nearly resembles
a badge of humility.

In this reading from John's Gospel, Jesus juxtaposes "water" and
"Spirit." This is not the only instance in which Scriptures of both Old
and New Testaments link water and Spirit, a link that is especially
prominent in the Gospel of John. The juxtaposition with "Spirit"
certainly raises the profile of "water," which, as an essential for
Christian baptism, was already entirely familiar in the liturgical uses
of the church. Water and Spirit have some characteristics in common, particularly when they have to do with quenching thirst both
physical and spiritual (Ps. 42:1–2; John 4:7–15; Rev. 21:6; 22:17) or
with life, whether agricultural, biological, or the life of the soul.

124

Water is a particularly apt symbol for Spirit, not only in the ways just mentioned. Anyone who has ever had a wet basement or leak in the roof knows that water flows pretty much where it wants to. It is difficult to create permanent obstacles to water with 100 percent success. Water searches out the tiniest, least visible route to penetrate whatever barrier has been erected to shut it out. The similarity to the Holy Spirit should be obvious. The Spirit also seeks out the most unexpected and unlikely routes to penetrate barriers, whether erected consciously or unconsciously, intentionally or not. Spirit and water share a relentlessness. Neither can be easily discouraged! So the church has from the beginning baptized in water, a powerful representation of the Spirit, who is our life, our health, and our peace.

Illumination

The contemporary practice of lighting a paschal candle at baptisms bears an obvious resemblance to some early practices associated with baptism, as early as the pre-Nicene church. The lighting of torches at some point during the rite interpreted baptism as illumination, the bringing of light. Justin Martyr, writing to Emperor Antoninus Pius about 148 CE, describes baptism: "This washing is called illumination since they who learn these things become illuminated intellectually" (Johnson, *Rites of Christian Initiation*, 38).

The Letter to the Hebrews uses the image of enlightenment as a description of the experience of those who have come to faith: "For it is impossible to restore again to repentance those who have once been *enlightened*, and have tasted the heavenly gift, and have shared in the Holy Spirit, and have tasted the goodness of the word of God and the powers of the age to come, and then have fallen away" (Heb. 6:4–6a, emphasis added).

John 9:1–41
The narrative in John 9 focuses on a man who was "blind from birth" (9:1). The Gospel spends a few verses working with the question as to whether this congenital condition was the consequence of some moral fault, either of the man himself (though that is hard to imagine), or of his parents. The traditional view held that suffering was punishment for some sin, acknowledged or unacknowledged.

125

The book of Job served as a direct challenge to the conventional and convenient way people have of assuring ourselves that, if we are careful to keep the rules, we can avoid illness, bankruptcy, or whatever catastrophe and, further, that, when people are hurting, they have probably brought it on themselves. Nevertheless, long after the book of Job, people in Jesus' time and our own still cling to the old explanations, since having no explanation introduces a possible randomness that raises all sorts of questions and anxieties.

To the disciples' question about who might be to blame, Jesus says, in effect, that no one is to blame. Certainly God did not cause the man to be born blind in order to use him as an object lesson. The man is not beyond God's care, and, whatever his circumstances, he can become a vessel of God's grace and manifest God's glory, just as he is, as anyone can. God can work with us, whatever our abilities and disabilities, to manifest divine love and providential purpose (9:3).

The story is one that functions on two levels. First, it is specifically about Jesus' encounter with a particular person. Second, it served to enlighten and encourage disciples in a later era, when their discipleship could cause them to be vilified. "We," Jesus says. Why the first person plural? "We," including those later disciples, members of the evangelist's community, "must work the works of him who sent me while it is day; night is coming when no one can work" (9:4). The images of day and night form the background for the miracle of illumination that is soon to follow. "As long as I am in the world," Jesus says, "I am the light of the world" (9:5).

Jesus "spat on the ground and made mud with the saliva and spread the mud on the man's eyes" (9:6). This resonates with the second creation story in Genesis: "Then the LORD God formed man from the dust of the ground" (Gen. 2:7). The Gospel intends that those who hear the story understand that a new creation is at hand.

Then Jesus said to the man, "Go, wash in the pool of Siloam" (John 9:7). The order recalls Elijah's directions sent out to Naaman the Syrian to go and wash in the Jordan and Jesus' encounter with the paralyzed man at the pool of Bethesda. However, the Gospel writer is sending another message here as well. Siloam "means Sent" (9:7). Certainly, Jesus has sent the blind man to the pool, but, more strikingly, the Gospel of John uses the word "sent" a number of times to refer to Jesus in his calling and mission. For example, "I seek to do not my own will but the will of him who *sent me*" (5:30, emphasis added). Siloam—Sent—it is as though John is posting a sign: providential action at work here!

The healing miracle follows: "Then he went and washed and came back able to see" (9:7b). The sequence of events is striking: Jesus anointed the man's eyes, and commanded the blind man to wash in the pool of Siloam. Then followed the washing, and, behold, a new creation—he was able to see! "We are meant to identify the pool somehow with Jesus and given to understand that the blind man, by washing in water, is plunged into Jesus' own life—that his cure resides not in the waters but in his contact with the Sent One" (Gench, *Encounters*, 66). Just to be sure that no one misses the point, the Gospel sets the event against the background of Jesus' statement, "I am the light of the world" (9:5).

The remainder of John 9 describes a hostile questioning of the healed man by the Pharisees. When asked how he had recovered his sight, the man simply replied, "He put mud on my eyes. Then I washed, and now I see" (9:15). Clearly the religious authorities (Pharisees) were hostile. Yet the man who now sees was not intimidated. When they asked him to tell them what he thought of the man who had healed him, he was not afraid to say, "He is a prophet" (9:17).

John's narrative then moves to the second level of the story. Thus far in the account of the man born blind, Jesus had not been identified as "Messiah." The man had confessed Jesus to be "a prophet." Conflating the two levels, John tells us that the man's parents were not as courageous as their son had been, probably because the authorities "had already agreed that anyone who confessed Jesus to be the Messiah would be put out of the synagogue" (9:22). This likely reflects conditions on the second level of the story, at the time of the writing of the Gospel, when the relation between Jews and Jewish Christians had become unfriendly. When questioned, the parents identified the man as their son and verified that he had been born blind, but otherwise claimed ignorance about how he had recovered his sight: "We do not know. . . . Ask him" (9:21).

The authorities once again called the man to testify, pushing him to denounce Jesus, because they knew that, since his having made the "mud" qualified as having broken the law by working on the Sabbath, "he is a sinner" (9:24). Again, the healed man was not intimidated. He would not argue with them, but only say,

"One thing I do know, that though I was blind, now I see" (9:25). The dialogue between the man and the authorities proceeded with escalating bitterness. The man would not back away from his testimony, and so the authorities finally "drove him out" (9:34). Like the man born blind, Christians contemporary with the Gospel writer "had found their eyes opened by the one who is the light of the world. As a result, they found themselves under intense scrutiny, even suffering expulsion from the synagogue for their confession of faith. . . . Thus his story both informed and fortified their own" (Gench, *Encounters*, 67).

When Jesus heard what had happened, he sought out the man whom he had healed, and asked him, "Do you believe in the Son of Man?" (9:35). The man with new sight asked who that might be, and Jesus responded, "You have seen him, and the one speaking with you is he" (9:37). In response, the man "worshiped him" (9:38). His eyes had been opened to see who it was who stood before him.

The event is summed up in Jesus' statement, "I came into this world for judgment so that those who do not see may see, and those who do see may become blind" (9:39). Light can produce clarity, or it can obscure. During much of the day, the light is gentle and welcome, when one is not looking into it directly, and it illuminates the landscape in every direction. But when the angle of the light is close to the horizon and directly in the line of sight, it can be blinding, making it almost impossible for a driver to see the road ahead. Similarly, when "the light of the world" shone in and through an itinerant rabbi in Judea, the light had a dual effect. While it enabled some to see more clearly, it blinded others. "Jesus is the Light that judges and saves the world. He is also a blinding Light—not to those who admit their blindness, for to these he gives sight—but to these who proclaim that they see and in their boast of vision are blind (see v. 41)" (Sloyan, *John*, 122). Those who admit that they struggle with intellectual or emotional obstacles that prevent them from "seeing" Jesus as the one who illumines what otherwise is in shadows should not so easily be called "blind," in the sense that John uses the word, but, rather, those whose blindness has taken the bitter form of "rejection and opposition" (Meyer, *The Word in This World*, 251).

128   Even in the very early generations of the church, one of the ways Christians understood baptism was as illumination, an eye-opening moment of enlightenment (Heb. 6:4; 10:32; Eph. 1:18) in

which the gospel of Jesus Christ shed a whole new light on what had been familiar terrain. "But you are a chosen race, a royal priesthood, a holy nation, God's own people, in order that you may proclaim the mighty acts of him who called you out of darkness into his marvelous light" (1 Pet. 2:9). (Somewhat similar stories of Jesus healing the blind occur in Mark 10:46–52 and parallels, Matt. 20:29–34 and Luke 18:35–43.) Of course, seeing the light, so to speak, does not imply that those who have been enlightened know everything there is to know about matters sacred or secular, but rather that they know from Whom true wisdom comes. The truth of the gospel, represented in the sacrament of baptism, is not the sort that cannot be overlooked. It is always possible to miss it or to shut one's eyes against it. Holy things are, by necessity, profound enough as to require a measure of openness and sensitivity to mystery. Mystery is not a problem to be solved, but something to ponder—to live with, very probably for a lifetime. The lifelong investment is a worthy one, because in the mystery there is light, and in it is the One who opens the eyes of the blind.

> No sign to us you give
> That eye can plainly see.
> Beyond our bounds of sense you live
> In deepest mystery.
>
> Lord, touch our eyes, still blind,
> With faith, transcending sight,
> And show us truth we cannot find
> Apart from you, the Light.
> (Herman G. Stuempfle, © 1997 GIA
> Publications, Inc.; used by permission)

Frescoes in the Roman catacombs picture the healing of the man born blind as a graphic interpretation of baptism. As the liturgical calendar developed, the John 9 text came to be read during Lent, when catechumens were preparing for baptism, and it is still a Lenten reading in the Revised Common Lectionary. For the man born blind, the gift of sight had been given quickly. For many others, light dawns gradually, and, indeed, more light may break as time goes on.

What is this light that generations of disciples have claimed clears their sight? This text in particular would say that what

129

Christ's light enables us to discern is that the God whose heart has been revealed in him is for us, not against us, no matter what our circumstances. We may not be entirely defined as victims of those conditions over which we have had no control. Whatever our circumstances, we are more than victims, because God is able and willing to work with us and in us and through us in gracious ways for gracious purposes. Heartache there has been, may be, and will be, but heartache is neither the only word nor the last word. This is the mystery beyond the ability to describe or define: there is no obstacle or suffering that can prevent God's work from being revealed in us (9:3).

What may be a fragment of an early baptismal hymn links the themes of new life and illumination:

> Sleeper, awake!
> Rise from the dead,
> and Christ will shine on you.
>   (Eph. 5:14b)

In some churches, a smaller candle, lighted from the larger paschal candle where there is one, may be given to a person being baptized or to parents of children being baptized. The candle can be relighted on baptismal anniversaries. The candle represents illumination given in Christ, and light to be shared. In the United Church of Canada, these words may be used as the candle is presented:

> N., let your light shine before others,
> that they may see your good works,
> and give glory to God.
> **Amen.**
>   (*Celebrate God's Presence*, 352)

Trinitarian Language

Matthew 28:18–20

The so-called Great Commission includes instruction that Jesus gave to his eleven remaining disciples after the resurrection: "Go therefore and make disciples of all nations, baptizing them in the name of the Father and of the Son and of the Holy Spirit" (Matt.

28:19). It used to be conventional scholarly wisdom that these verses that conclude the Gospel of Matthew were not present in the original, but now it is more common to accept them as authentic. "The baptismal formula in the name of three divine agents was presumably in use in the Matthean church at this period, having replaced an earlier custom of baptizing in the name of Jesus" (Brown, *An Introduction*, 203). In any case, verse 19 is indisputably canonical. It is not at all certain when what we have come to call the "baptismal formula" began to be used, but scholars believe that the Gospel of Matthew was written sometime between 80 and 90 CE, although it might have been a decade earlier or later. Hartman notes that the Matthean formula is also found in the *Didache*, which probably originated at about the same time as Matthew's Gospel, and in writings of Justin, Irenaeus, and Tertullian, all of which predate Nicaea.

Although the doctrine of the Trinity was not officially formulated and adopted by councils of the church until the fourth century, the New Testament uses "Father" language to refer to God and "Son" or "Lord" language to refer to Jesus, and it also speaks of the Holy Spirit. Paul wrote, "Now there are varieties of gifts, but the same *Spirit*; and there are varieties of services, but the same *Lord*; and there are varieties of activities, but it is the same *God* who activates all of them in everyone" (1 Cor. 12:4–6, emphases added). Ephesians exhibits a similar linkage of the three: "For through *him* [Christ] both of us have access in one *Spirit* to the *Father*" (Eph. 2:18), and the conclusion of 2 Corinthians reads, "The grace of the Lord Jesus Christ, the love of God, and the communion of the Holy Spirit be with all of you" (2 Cor. 13:13).

The Nicene Creed (see text at end of chapter) is the product of a long process of reflection and debate about how the church ought to understand the relation of Father, Son, and Holy Spirit. The creed was formulated as a result of careful thought about what could be said and what could not be said about the God who is undivided and yet whom the church experiences as, at one and the same time, sovereign over all, incarnate in Christ, and present in and among us in the Spirit. Behind the creed is a history of pondering what the church had been saying all along in the various ways it had used Father, Son, and Spirit language in its worship and proclamation, its missionary work, and its catechesis. The church also drew upon its experience of ways the language had been employed in worship.

We have no way of knowing exactly what words were used in very early baptismal rites. Luke records Peter's sermon on the first Pentecost as concluding with an appeal to his hearers, "Repent, and be baptized every one of you in the name of Jesus Christ" (Acts 2:38). The Greek for "in" is *epi*, contrasting with Romans 6:3, which says we have been baptized "into"—Greek *eis*—Christ Jesus. Baptism may have been "in the name of Jesus Christ" or "into the name of Jesus Christ." Another possibility is that no "formula" was used at all; rather, the one baptizing may have asked, "Do you believe in Jesus Christ?" or some variation of that question, with the act of baptism following a positive response. Or perhaps the presiding minister asked a series of questions: "Do you believe in God the Father? Do you believe in Jesus Christ? Do you believe in the Holy Spirit?" The person presiding may have performed the act of washing three times, once after each positive response to the three questions.

In any case, the description of Jesus' baptism in the Synoptic Gospels served as the chief paradigm for baptism in the pre-Nicene era, and those accounts are all Trinitarian, if we may borrow the term that came into use only in a later era. Each reports a voice from heaven, the Father's voice, identifying Jesus as "my Son, the Beloved" (Mark 1:11; Matt. 3:17; Luke 3:22), and each reports the descent of the Spirit. Christian baptism borrowed a rite from John the Baptizer but adapted it by adding to its reference to God an explicit link to Christ and to the Spirit.

As Christians have become more sensitive to gender issues and to the ways that language can serve to marginalize women, some have grown impatient with traditional Trinitarian language, even in baptism, and have looked for alternatives. The alternatives that have been offered have problems of their own, theological for the most part, but also linguistic. One of the most common substitutes for the traditional Trinitarian language is to baptize in the name of the "Creator, Redeemer, and Sustainer," although this is an impersonal list of functions, each of which might, with equal authority, be assigned to any one or all three "persons" of the Trinity. For example, the prologue to the Gospel of John says of "the Word" (Christ) that "all things came into being through him" (John 1:3), identifying him with the act of creation, echoed in Hebrews 1:2, referring to Jesus, "through whom [God] also created the worlds." Psalm 104 links the Spirit with creation: "When you send forth your spirit, they are created; and you renew the face of the ground" (Ps. 104:30). The psalmist declares that Israel "remembered that God was their rock, the Most High God their redeemer" (Ps. 78:35), using "redeemer" in reference to the first person of the Trinity. The Letter to the Hebrews says of Jesus that "he sustains all things by his powerful word" (Heb. 1:3), which would entitle him also to be called "sustainer."

In a worldwide church that is fractured in many ways, it would seem to be a priority that, at the very least, each church ought to be able to recognize and affirm the baptism of all the others; such mutual recognition is placed in serious jeopardy should individual churches, ministers, or even denominations decide unilaterally to create new baptismal formulae without an ecumenical consultation that leads to consensus or, at least, consent. Bryan Spinks has suggested that the better approach to the dominance of male-gendered language might be to expand images for God so as to include those that are more typically associated with the feminine.

One possible example of the use of expansive language is "the formula suggested by James Kaye and adopted by the Riverside Church, New York: 'I baptize you in the name of the Father and of the Son and of the Holy Spirit, one God, Mother of us all'" (Spinks, *Reformation and Modern*, 159). Similarly, the baptismal service of the United Church of Canada provides, as one option, this blessing that directly follows the traditional Trinitarian formula: "May the blessing of the one God, Mother and Father of us all, be with you today and always" (*Celebrate God's Presence*, 348). While the Bible never directly names God as "mother," it does make use of explicitly feminine images for God, for example, "You forgot the God who gave you birth" (Deut. 32:18) and (God speaking) "I will cry out like a woman in labor, I will gasp and pant" (Isa. 42:14). God's speech in Isaiah 49:15 compares God to a nursing mother. The Riverside Church formula honors the classical Trinitarian language that all Christian churches recognize, while expanding it with an appropriate image that, set next to Father, Son, and Holy Spirit language, breaks the identification of God as male or female. Such a solution may not be acceptable everywhere, and certainly it is important that the ecumenical church continue to ponder the issues raised by language in hopes that a way forward may be found toward usage that is acceptable to all.

Baptism was understood and practiced in a Trinitarian way even before the Councils of Nicaea and Constantinople, and catholic Christianity in all its forms—Orthodox, Roman, Anglican, and

133

Protestant—has kept faith with the ancient, undivided church's baptismal practice as Trinitarian, even while differing about who is an appropriate candidate for baptism and how the rite should be done.

A hymn attributed to St. Patrick celebrates the Trinitarian themes. It is, appropriately, a hymn used both at baptisms and at ordinations, since baptism is an ordination to the corporate priesthood of the whole church.

> I bind unto myself the name,
> the strong name of the Trinity
> by invocation of the same,
> the Three in One and One in Three,
> of whom all nature has creation,
> eternal Father, Spirit, Word.
> Praise to the Lord of my salvation;
> salvation is of Christ the Lord!
> (*Evangelical Lutheran Worship*,
> #450, public domain)

The ecumenical creeds exhibit a Trinitarian form. The Apostles' Creed, the creed traditionally associated with baptism, has been included in baptismal liturgies both Roman Catholic and Protestant, often including the option of an interrogatory form.

Apostles' Creed	*Nicene Creed*
I believe in God the Father almighty, creator of heaven and earth.	We believe in one God, the Father, the Almighty, maker of heaven and earth, of all that is, seen and unseen.
I believe in Jesus Christ, God's only Son, our Lord, who was conceived by the Holy Spirit, born of the Virgin Mary, suffered under Pontius Pilate, was crucified, died, and was buried; he descended to the dead. On the third day he rose again; he ascended into heaven, he is seated at the right hand of the Father, and he will come to judge the living and the dead.	We believe in one Lord, Jesus Christ, the only Son of God, eternally begotten of the Father, God from God, Light from Light, true God from true God, begotten, not made, of one Being with the Father; through him all things were made. For us and for our salvation he came down from heaven, was incarnate of the Holy Spirit and the Virgin Mary

and became truly human. For our sake he was crucified under Pontius Pilate; he suffered death and was buried. On the third day he rose again in accordance with the Scriptures; he ascended into heaven and is seated on the right hand of the Father. He will come in glory to judge the living and the dead, and his kingdom will have no end.

I believe in the Holy Spirit, the holy catholic Church, the communion of saints, the forgiveness of sins, the resurrection of the body, and the life everlasting. Amen.

We believe in the Holy Spirit, the Lord, the giver of life, who proceeds from the Father (and the Son), who with the Father and the Son is worshiped and glorified, who has spoken through the prophets. We believe in one holy catholic and apostolic Church. We acknowledge one baptism for the forgiveness of sins. We look for the resurrection of the dead, and the life of the world to come. Amen.

(Texts from *BCW*, 64 and 65; versions by the English Language Liturgical Consultation; used by permission)

CHAPTER 5

The Spirit Clothes, Marks, Seals, Converts, Nurtures, and Incorporates

The word "spirit" and its adjectival form "spiritual" are attractive to many people for whom such language seems appealingly amorphous and unthreatening. The world has always been scandalized by the doctrine of the incarnation as well as by the claim that God has assigned a special role to the Hebrew people. "Spirit" would seem to bypass specific claims intimately related to Jesus of Nazareth or to the identity and mission of Israel, and to replace them with the language of a gentle and undemanding disposition of the heart, popularly known as "spirituality." However, "Spirit"—more specifically, the *Holy* Spirit—is neither so abstract nor so amenable to being attached to just any manifestation of the human religious impulse.

The New Testament witness is that the Holy Spirit is the biblical God in action, a force to be reckoned with. The Spirit is neither dependent on the material world nor resolutely separated from it. The Spirit is at work in sacramental ways, where water marks the boundary between one identity and another. The Spirit is at work in and through hands firmly laid on heads, with prayer. The Spirit is at work to strip us of one identity and clothe us with another. The Spirit converts, builds up, and strengthens faith. The Spirit seals and marks, laying a divine claim upon the recipient. It is the Holy Spirit who picks us up and then sets us down to take our place in the midst of a people who have been called and commissioned to a priestly role, rooted in God's covenantal promises and blessings. The Spirit works in different ways with different people, sometimes through personal decisions and sometimes through families and congregations that nurture and form and shape disciples from birth. The Spirit is at work in and through both individuals and communities at every stage of life: beginning, middle, and ending.

Laying On of Hands and the Gift of the Spirit

Acts 8:1b–17

Christian baptism has always been associated, in one way or another, with the gift of the Holy Spirit, as is evident in the stories of Jesus' baptism in all four Gospels, and as in Peter's sermon on the day of Pentecost, when he appealed to those in his audience to be baptized so that their sins might be forgiven "and you will receive the gift of the Holy Spirit" (Acts 2:38).

Acts of worship in the Old Testament were typically accompanied by gestures, whether by priests or worshipers, such as raising something up as an offering (Exod. 29:24), kneeling (Ps. 95:6), prostration (Deut. 9:18), bowing the head (Gen. 43:28), covering the head (2 Sam. 15:30), sprinkling (Lev. 4:6), lifting the hands in blessing (Lev. 9:22) or in prayer (Ps. 28:2). The laying on of hands is another of those ancient gestures, familiar in Old Testament times. One encounters it in Numbers, when God tells Moses that the Israelites should "lay their hands on the Levites" as part of a service of ordination (Num. 8:10), and in Deuteronomy, when Moses lays his hands on Joshua to pass his commission on from one servant of the Lord to another: "Joshua son of Nun was full of the spirit of wisdom, because Moses had laid his hands on him; and the Israelites obeyed him, doing as the LORD had commanded Moses" (Deut. 34:9).

In the New Testament, Jesus laid his hands on the children (Mark 10:16; 14:46; Matt. 19:13, 15) in a gesture of blessing, and he also laid hands on some whom he healed (Mark 5:23; 6:5; 8:23–25; Luke 4:40; 13:13). In the book of Acts, the church at Antioch commissioned Barnabas and Saul for a mission with the laying on of hands (Acts 13:3), and Paul cured a sick man with prayer and the laying on of hands (Acts 28:8). However, most often in the book of Acts, the laying on of hands is specifically identified as a

138

communication of the Holy Spirit. The problem, for those who love consistency, is that the laying on of hands with the intention of imparting the Spirit sometimes precedes baptism and sometimes follows it, and is described in both cases in ways that could lead to the opinion that baptism itself is not sufficient.

What can be said is that the gift of the Holy Spirit was associated with baptism "in the name of the Lord Jesus," but not always in the same sequence, and that the laying on of hands was sometimes, but not always, included either before or after the rite. We are not dealing here with a mechanical series of actions meant to produce certain results in a precise order. In fact, that sort of mechanical understanding of the gift of the Spirit is precisely what lay behind the rebuke of Simon Magus, who made an offer of cash in exchange for being given the "secret" that would enable him to reproduce what he had seen done by the apostles (Acts 8:9, 18–24).

> Now when the apostles at Jerusalem heard that Samaria had accepted the word of God, they sent Peter and John to them. The two went down and prayed for them that they might receive the Holy Spirit (for as yet the Spirit had not come upon any of them; they had only been baptized in the name of the Lord Jesus). Then Peter and John laid their hands on them, and they received the Holy Spirit. (Acts 8:14–17)

A severe persecution of Christians in Jerusalem had led to a dispersion of Christians "throughout the countryside of Judea and Samaria" (8:1b). Among them was Philip, who was a Hellenist (6:5), a member of a Greek-speaking group who were "the more radical Christians in terms of their relation to Jewish Temple worship" (Brown, *An Introduction,* 296). Philip preached the gospel to Samaritans, non-Jews. When the Jerusalem church learned that Philip had been making converts and baptizing Samaritans, they sent Peter and John to Samaria on a mission.

The Samaritan Christians "had only been baptized in the name of the Lord Jesus" (8:16). What are we to make of the "only" (Gk. *monon*)? After all, earlier in the same book Peter's sermon exhorted people to be baptized "in the name of Jesus Christ" (2:8). The "only" must refer not to some deficiency in the words that had been used to declare in whose name the baptisms took place but, rather, to some other omission, specifically, the gift of the Holy Spirit, a

139

problem remedied by the delegation from Jerusalem: "Then Peter and John laid their hands on them, and they received the Holy Spirit" (8:17).

Acts 8:14–17 does not mean to imply that there are two baptisms, one in water and one in the Spirit. The author of Acts has introduced Peter and John into the Samaritan picture in order to make the point that it was necessary for all the baptized to be linked to the Jerusalem church (8:14), which they effected in this instance through prayer and the laying on of hands. Before his ascension, the risen Lord had sent the apostles out to "be . . . witnesses in Jerusalem, in all Judea *and Samaria*, and to the ends of the earth" (1:8, emphasis added). "For some reason or another, it was essential to emphasize the inclusion of the semi-Jewish or 'heretical' Samaritans in God's people. So 8:14–17 brings out how, although the Samaria mission was initiated by others, it was incorporated into the mission with which the risen Christ charged his apostles" (Hartman, "Into the Name," 137).

This text accents the importance of coherent unity among all the baptized, a unity that has its origin in the apostolic community to whom Jesus gave his final evangelical commission. Traditionally, the word "apostolicity" has been used to denote authenticity, genuineness, the soundness of a community's faith. Some churches have held the belief that apostolicity derives from unbroken continuity in the laying on of hands from the apostles to bishops, and from them, to presbyters, down through the ages. History cannot sustain such a claim to unbroken continuity extending from the apostles to the twenty-first century, however. Certainly historical continuity has a role to play, since, for example, we rest on the many ways our forebears have reflected on the faith and lived it out, sometimes in comfortable circumstances and sometimes at a high cost to themselves. They must be included in the conversational circle as we, in subsequent generations, continue to learn from one another. Of course, desiring and striving for apostolicity is easier than being certain we have achieved it. Nevertheless, apostolicity is a goal that all the churches agree is the mark of authenticity, and ecumenical conversation and dialogue are one way that the churches seek to learn from and admonish one another to strive toward a faithful apostolicity in faith and morals. Communities that cherish their separateness as a badge of apostolicity, while withholding themselves from ecumenical give-and-take, are least likely to make a persuasive case for

140

apostolicity. Just as the Samaritan Christians needed to be in direct contact and communion with the first of the apostolic churches, in Jerusalem, today all need to be in contact and communion with one another, however that may be possible. Ideally, in time those recipical relationships might even be accompanied by a mutual laying on of hands, perhaps literal as well as metaphorical. The church of Jerusalem also needs the church of Samaria, because the Spirit is at work in both, and each has gifts (as well as admonitions) to bring to the other. The church of Jerusalem and the church of Samaria are both united in the apostolic tradition of holy baptism, in water and the Spirit, in the name of the triune God.

Acts 9:10–19

> [Ananias] laid his hands on Saul and said, "Brother Saul, the Lord Jesus, who appeared to you on your way here, has sent me so that you may regain your sight and be filled with the Holy Spirit." And immediately something like scales fell from his eyes, and his sight was restored. Then he got up and was baptized, and after taking some food, he regained his strength. (Acts 9:17–19)

These verses are part of a longer section that describes Saul, "still breathing threats and murder against the disciples of the Lord" (9:1), encountering Jesus on the road to Damascus, a dramatic meeting resulting in conversion accompanied by temporary blindness. In a vision, Jesus sent Saul to Ananias, a Christian who lived in Damascus. Ananias, led by a similar message from the Lord, reluctantly sought and found Saul and, calling him "brother," laid hands on him "so that you may regain your sight and be filled with the Holy Spirit." Then Saul was baptized.

The sequence of events in this case is not entirely clear. Although the intention of Ananias's unwilling mission is that Saul "be filled with the Holy Spirit," and although Saul's baptism followed the laying on of hands, the text does not tell us whether the Spirit was communicated directly in the laying on of hands or only following Saul's baptism. Apparently, establishing a sequence was not important to Luke, for whom the main point was that Saul, the former persecutor, was "filled with the Spirit" and that this spiritual gift was linked with baptism, a rite that included the laying 141 on of hands. "We need not speculate on some sort of detachment of the Spirit by the laying-on-of-hands from baptism. The two are mentioned here together to stress their unity rather than their separation" (Willimon, *Acts,* 77).

Acts 10:30–48 and 11:1–18

Cornelius, a Roman military officer who, though not a convert to Judaism, practiced almsgiving and prayer in accord with Jewish tradition, received a vision in which an angel directed him to send messengers to Joppa to summon Peter. At the same time, Peter had also experienced a vision, which he was struggling to interpret even as the three men Cornelius had sent reached him. Peter followed them to Cornelius's home in Caesarea, where he had gathered "relatives and close friends" (10:24). Peter spoke with them, describing his understanding of his own vision as one that obliterated the distinction between "clean" and "unclean" people.

At Cornelius's invitation, Peter began to address the gathering, bearing testimony to Jesus Christ: "He is Lord of all" (10:36).

> While Peter was still speaking, the Holy Spirit fell upon all who heard the word. The circumcised believers who had come with Peter were astounded that the gift of the Holy Spirit had been poured out even on the Gentiles, for they heard them speaking in tongues and extolling God. Then Peter said, "Can anyone withhold the water for baptizing these people who have received the Holy Spirit just as we have?" So he ordered them to be baptized in the name of Jesus Christ. Then they invited him to stay for several days. (Acts 10:44–48)

Responding to critics when he returned to Jerusalem, Peter defended his having baptized Gentiles, reporting to the Jewish believers the story of the heavenly vision and the summons to Cornelius's household, concluding with a description of his experience there. "And as I began to speak, the Holy Spirit fell upon them just as it had upon us at the beginning. And I remembered the word of the Lord, how he had said, 'John baptized with water, but you will be baptized with the Holy Spirit'" (11:15–16).

In this instance, the Holy Spirit was given *before* baptism of the new believers, and without mention of a laying on of hands. The detail that the Spirit preceded baptism feels right in the context of this narrative, since the whole matter of a breakthrough to the Gentiles lay not with human calculations, but with a divine initiative. When Peter had been puzzling over his vision, "*the Spirit* said

142

to him, 'Look, three men are searching for you. Now get up, go down, and go with them without hesitation; for I have sent them'" (10:19–20, emphasis added). Luke exhibits a special interest in the Holy Spirit, referring to the Spirit more frequently than any of the other Gospel writers, beginning with the narrative about the angel's annunciation to Zechariah, father of John the Baptizer, and continuing in the story of the annunciation to Mary. Luke mentions the Spirit more than twice as often in Acts—sixty-five times. For him, the Spirit is an active agent at work in the entire process of spreading the gospel and its reception (see Hartman, *"Into the Name,"* 135).

Baptismal practice in the early church was not uniform, but diverse. What is consistent is that all understood there to be a link between baptism and the gift of the Spirit. Baptism "with the Holy Spirit" (11:16) and with water, whether simultaneous or sequential, were two movements in a single action of incorporating persons into Christ and the community of the Spirit. "The baptism of the Spirit may precede or follow baptism with water, but the focal point of both is the invocation of the name of Christ, for it is in him that both baptisms find their unity" (Spinks, *Reformation and Modern*, 150).

Acts 19:1–7

It is puzzling, for those who prize consistency, that the book of Acts reports that baptism and the gift of the Spirit in those early missionary days do not always line up in the same predictable sequence, but it is also puzzling that the gift of the Spirit is sometimes linked with the laying on of hands and sometimes not.

> While Apollos was in Corinth, Paul passed through the interior regions and came to Ephesus, where he found some disciples. He said to them, "Did you receive the Holy Spirit when you became believers?" They replied, "No, we have not even heard that there is a Holy Spirit." Then he said, "Into what then were you baptized?" They answered, "Into John's baptism." Paul said, "John baptized with the baptism of repentance, telling the people to believe in the one who was to come after him, that is, in Jesus." On hearing this, they were baptized in the name of the Lord Jesus. When Paul had laid his hands on them, the Holy Spirit came upon them, and they spoke in tongues and prophesied— altogether there were about twelve of them. (Acts 19:1–7)

143

Luke suggests that these Ephesian disciples had been evangelized by Apollos, "an eloquent man, well-versed in the scriptures. He had been instructed in the Way of the Lord; and he spoke with burning enthusiasm and taught accurately the things concerning Jesus, though he knew only the baptism of John" (Acts 18:24–25). Priscilla and Aquila heard Apollos in the synagogue and "took him aside and explained the Way of God to him more accurately" (18:26). Probably aware of Apollos's deficiency, Paul had asked the Christians he encountered in Ephesus whether they had received the Holy Spirit when they became believers. They denied any acquaintance with the Holy Spirit. In consequence of further dialogue, Paul discovered that they had been baptized "into John's baptism," and he was led to explain the role John had played as one who had pointed to the one to come after him, Jesus. Then these disciples "were baptized in the name of the Lord Jesus," followed by the laying on of hands and the gift of the Spirit. The brief description of this phenomenon gives the impression that the newly baptized experienced something like the Pentecost charisms, probably including ecstatic speech and testimonies.

That these disciples were baptized a second time, this time "in the name of the Lord Jesus," indicates that Luke understood there was a significant difference between John's baptism of repentance and Christian baptism and that the difference was specifically linked to Jesus and to the Holy Spirit. Apart from this exceptional instance involving the omission of Christ and the Spirit, the older tradition of the church has been not to permit repeated baptisms, in the conviction that God's claim and God's promise in the sacrament are reliable and ought not be impeached, even if we are anxious about not having gotten the details quite right.

In the several accounts in the book of Acts describing baptism, the gift of the Spirit, and sometimes linking the gift of the Spirit with the laying on of hands, one finds a description of diverse practices. The scriptural background is not sufficient to make a case that there is a divine imperative behind any one practice, or even to make the case that the laying on of hands is essential to the giving of the Spirit, since it was not even mentioned in 10:44–48 or its parallel in 11:15–16.

144   In the course of time, a measure of consistency was achieved wherein the laying on of hands always *followed* baptism. At first,

it was the *episcopos*, the bishop, who normally presided over the entire baptismal rite, but the bishop was then the pastor of the local church rather than an ecclesiastical officer having responsibility for a diocese or regional body. In the Western (Roman) church, but not the Eastern, the laying on of hands became separated from the primary baptismal rite. When the bishop's jurisdiction became extended over a large geographical territory, he would complete the baptismal rite begun by the presbyters. This *episcopal* laying on of hands evolved into an entirely separate rite, indeed, a distinct sacrament, the sacrament of confirmation, which the Protestant reformers rejected as a sacrament, in part because it broke the sacrament of baptism into two parts.

Contemporary service books typically include the laying on of hands after the baptismal washing in water, following the model of the Eastern churches, which never separated this action from the baptismal rite; but in no case is this laying on of hands understood as "confirmation." One example is found in *Evangelical Lutheran Worship*. The rubric reads, "*Laying both hands on the head of each of the newly baptized, the minister prays for each:* Sustain <u>name</u> with the gift of your Holy Spirit: the spirit of wisdom and understanding, the spirit of counsel and might, the spirit of knowledge and the fear of the Lord, the spirit of joy in your presence, both now and forever" (*Evangelical Lutheran Worship*, 231). Note that the petition is that God "sustain" each of the baptized with the gift of the Spirit, not grant it, as though the gift had been withheld until this moment.

In early Christianity, the baptismal rite was perceived as a single and whole action, which could be and was understood in more than one way, but even amidst its diverse complex of meanings, it always had to do with the gift of the Holy Spirit, as had become evident in the telling of the story of Jesus' own baptism. Each of the separate movements that developed in addition to the original washing with water—whether washing accompanied by anointing before or after or both, or washing accompanied by laying on of hands before or after, or any combination of these—contributed to the total ecology of the rite as one in which the Holy Spirit that had fallen on the whole church fell also on the newly baptized. Each act—washing, anointing, laying on of hands—can play a role in helping those being baptized and the whole congregation to perceive what is not ordinarily perceptible to the eyes. Yet the separate actions, in

145

whatever combinations, form an ecology of the whole; they cannot be isolated from each other as though one action does one thing, and another action does something else. Each act interprets the whole rite in its own way, and thus serves a purpose.

The ancient gesture of laying on of hands takes another form in the typical gesture of the benediction, in which the person offering it raises hands with palms toward the congregation while pronouncing a blessing. This is a stylized laying on of hands, a gesture directed toward the assembly as a whole, recalling the laying on of hands and the gift of the Spirit associated with baptism. The physical act itself makes a statement, so it is best given facing the congregation rather than from behind them, as sometimes happens when the minister has already recessed with the choir.

Stripping and Clothing: Metaphor and Rite

Stripping and clothing are familiar New Testament images to describe the transformation expected in baptism. "As many of you as were baptized into Christ have clothed yourselves with Christ" (Gal. 3:27). The New Testament language of stripping off the old garments in order to be clothed in Christ is reminiscent of the Old Testament prophet, who records these as the words of a personified Zion, speaking for the people of Judah: "I will greatly rejoice in the LORD, my whole being shall exult in my God; for he has clothed me with the garments of salvation, he has covered me with the robe of righteousness" (Isa. 61:10).

The likelihood is that the New Testament language of putting off and putting on is both literal and metaphorical. Paul had written, "Put on the Lord Jesus Christ" (Rom. 13:14). The person to be baptized actually stripped off her or his own clothing and was baptized in the nude. Eventually the custom became widespread of reclothing the newly baptized person in a white robe. The practical need to divest oneself of everyday clothing before baptism served the metaphor. The ceremonial divestment and dressing in new clothes incarnated the metaphor in dramatic action, no doubt stamping upon the consciousness of the newly baptized and the community as a whole the fact that baptism was meant to be a movement from one identity to another.

146

Colossians 3:5–17

The baptism that marks a substantial change in our status before God is rooted in events that precede our personal participation in them: Jesus' death on the cross and his victorious resurrection. This is the gospel, the good news that serves as the context for the exhortations in Colossians 3.

> Put to death, therefore, whatever in you is earthly: fornication, impurity, passion, evil desire, and greed. . . . But now you must get rid of all such things. . . . Do not lie to one another, seeing that you have stripped off the old self with its practices and have clothed yourselves with the new self. . . . As God's chosen ones, holy and beloved, clothe yourselves with compassion, kindness, humility, meekness, and patience. . . . Above all, clothe yourselves with love. (Col. 3:5, 8–10, 12, 14)

Parents know from experience that exhortations are not likely to be effective, and anyone who has ever come up with a list of New Year's resolutions is aware that even when exhortations are self-directed, the results are equally likely to be disappointing. However, the apostolic letter, addressing those who have been baptized, recognizes that the Colossians have already come a long way and is pointing out how they might continue to mature in faith. They are no longer entirely in thrall to cultures that have formed them according to alien norms, but have been transferred to the jurisdiction of that One whose death they share, having died to those values and behaviors that are "earthly," that is, destructive, deceptive, and antagonistic to the true God. The apostle is calling for the baptized to live up to and into the new status into which their baptism has placed them, "seeing that you have stripped off the old self with its practices and have clothed yourselves with the new self, which is being renewed in knowledge according to the image of its creator" (3:9b, 10).

The image used to indicate leaving old ways behind is a vivid one: "you have *stripped off* [*apekdysamenoi*] the old self with its practices." The Greek verb translated "stripped off" is a form of the same verb (*apekdysei*) translated in 2:11 as "putting off" and also in 2:15 (*apekdysamenos*) in reference to Christ as having "disarmed" ("divested himself of") rulers and authorities. This divestment of a way of life is not about magic, as though the sacrament of baptism

147

could guarantee a change of character. Indeed, Adolf Hitler and Joseph Stalin had both been baptized. Yet neither is our baptism merely a pious wish for a godly life. In baptism, God has transferred us from one jurisdiction to another. We have been picked up and set down in a new context, and the context is Jesus Christ, manifested in the power of the Spirit at work in the body of Christ, which exhibits a corporate and communal presence in the world.

The exhortations—don't do *these* things (3:5, 7, 9), but *do* these things (3:12–17)—describe the communal norms of the body of Christ in the world. They serve as explicit statements of differences between the ways of death and the way of life. The community baptized into Christ understands itself to be one in which Christ is being formed as corporately it struggles to manifest God's reign in the midst of the contradictions that disfigure both society and individual members of it. Within the context of the church we encourage one another to cherish certain behaviors while distancing ourselves from others. Sexual license, [uncontrolled] anger, wrath, malice, slander, abusive language, lying: these belong to the old jurisdiction that owned us and does not easily let go of us, seducing us relentlessly and continuing to exert its pernicious influence. Compassion, kindness, humility, meekness, patience, thankfulness: these are what life in Christ looks like. Those baptized into Christ have been set into a context in which Christ may be formed in us as we share our pilgrimage together, encouraging one another, admonishing one another, teaching one another, and, no doubt, debating one another when issues arise that do not easily or immediately earn a consensus among the faithful.

Baptism is not magic but enacted prayer. It is not true that only the baptized are capable of making moral commitments, but baptism does matter, because it sets us in the midst of the church, the community of Christ, whose praise and prayer and common life are all about death and resurrection, Christ's and our own, and consequently about stripping off the old self and being clothed with the new. "Above all, clothe yourselves with love, which binds everything together in perfect harmony" (3:14).

Galatians 3:26–29

148

"As many of you as were baptized into Christ have clothed yourselves with Christ" (Gal. 3:27). Martin Luther, commenting on this verse, wrote that to put on Christ according to the Gospel means to clothe oneself with the righteousness, wisdom, power, life, and Spirit of Christ. By nature we are clad in the garb of Adam. This garb Paul likes to call "the old man." Before we can become the children of God this old man must be put off, as Paul says, Ephesians 4:22. The garment of Adam must come off like soiled clothes. Of course, it is not as simple as changing one's clothes. But God makes it simple. He clothes us with the righteousness of Christ by means of Baptism. . . . With this change of garments a new birth, a new life stirs in us. New affections toward God spring up in the heart. New determinations affect our will. All this is to put on Christ according to the Gospel. (Luther, *Galatians*, 147)

Luther's comment that "God makes it simple" is encouraging, and true in a sense, since God's graciousness comes to us as pure gift. Yet, it is not so simple to put off one "self" and put on another. It is a process, and usually a struggle, but God is in the process and in the struggle. Baptism points to the unearned gift and to God's engagement with us in the continuing effort to manifest it in our lives.

To have been "clothed with Christ" is to have put on a new identity. "There is no longer Jew or Greek, there is no longer slave or free, there is no longer male and female; for all of you are one in Christ Jesus" (3:28). Of course, ethnic and gender identities have not vanished, but those who have been "clothed with Christ" have been given a new identity that trumps other identities. Differences, whether of birth or of status, do not stamp some as of lower status and others as of higher, some as less worthy of respect and others more worthy, some whose voices must be excluded or muted and others whose voices are privileged.

Does Paul trace the moment at which the new identity is given to an objective event, Christ's death and resurrection, or to something that happens when someone makes "a decision for Christ"? The answer is both, though

> Paul's overwhelming stress falls on the momentous happening at the beginning of the Christian era when God acted decisively for the whole human race. . . . Christ's coming was an eschatological event. It was world-changing; it inaugurated the last times. Though not every individual has been aware of that event and its implications, the event is nevertheless true and impinges on the lives of all. . . . Baptism, then, is the occasion when the believer

149

by God's grace is drawn into that lordship with other believers and so "puts on Christ." (Cousar, *Galatians*, 84)

As late as ten years after World War II, the newspapers occasionally reported the discovery of surviving Japanese soldiers who had been living on their own in remote jungle and mountainous areas of the South Pacific for years, unaware that the war was over. In fact, the peace treaties had been signed, the imperial forces disbanded, and a new government established in Tokyo; yet, for each of the lone soldiers, it was as though there had been no peace. They continued to live on their survival skills every day, year after year: hiding, cautious, wary, suspicious, fearful, isolated, steering clear of human habitations, since other people represented a threat. In short, they lived as though they were in a state of war, whereas, though they did not know it, peace had already come. Similarly, it is quite possible for people to live in the world as though the new creation that has been manifest in Christ does not exist and we are still in a state of estrangement from God and one another, continuing to live behind the barriers that separate us by race, ethnicity, gender, condition, and tribal identities of all sorts. In baptism, we celebrate the peace that has already been established by God's action in Christ and that is now being made manifest in particular persons who are being "clothed" with him in the sacramental act.

Ephesians 4:17–32

The writer of the letter had established a context for understanding this passage earlier in the chapter, where he writes of the calling shared by all Christians, who are united in "one Lord, one faith, one baptism" (4:5). Then, taking off the gloves, he exhorts the Ephesians to repudiate the way "the Gentiles live, in the futility of their minds" (4:17). He insists that the Ephesian Christians must turn their backs on the culture that presses upon them from all sides, declaring, "You were taught to put away your former way of life, your old self, corrupt and deluded by its lusts, and to be renewed in the spirit of your minds, and to clothe yourselves with the new self, created according to the likeness of God" (4:22–24).

Surely there must have been aspects of pagan society that an observer might have admired and praised. If Paul's social analysis of the local culture in Ephesus seems one-sided, it is probably because he recognized that it is terribly difficult for people to separate

150

themselves from the dominant forces at work in any particular society, whether ancient or modern, Asian or American. Paul's interest was to strengthen the formation of a Christian counterculture that would be vigorous enough to overcome the insidious aspects of the dominant pagan culture that continued to exert pressure upon the little congregation in Ephesus. For the sake of the small Christian minority, it was necessary to mark the difference between old and new cultures in starkly contrasting terms in order to shore up their commitment to the formation of an alternative culture. In that Christ-shaped culture, members recognize themselves to have been clothed with a "new self, created according to the likeness of God in true righteousness and holiness" (4:24). Baptism was the transition point between one identity and another.

If the Christian minority community in Ephesus needed strong encouragement as it struggled to establish its identity in Christ, the need may be even greater for the church in North America, where one might presume by counting numbers that a Christian culture is dominant. In fact, many of the conventionally accepted values of contemporary North American culture result from Christian influence in centuries past. The confluence between specifically Christian values and secular ones, particularly when the latter have been shaped by direct Christian influence in earlier eras, can easily give the impression that Christian values and the values of the dominant culture are so nearly identical as not to require any substantial dissent. Certainly we Christians would be well advised not to interpret our host cultures, North American or other, exclusively in negative or stereotypical terms; but at the same time it is important for us to understand that we have reached a historical moment in which we must not imagine that the dominant culture can carry our Christian values for us or form our children in them. It is time for us to learn from our Jewish sisters and brothers how to think like a minority, in our case, intentionally thinking of ourselves as a people shaped by and from and into our baptismal identity, which includes stripping off that which we need to lay aside in order that we may be clothed in Christ.

Matthew 22:1–14

Matthew's parable about a wedding banquet a king had given for his son leads to a shocking ending when the host discovers a guest who had come to the festivities without a wedding garment. He was

151

thrown out into "outer darkness, where there will be weeping and gnashing of teeth" (v. 13). This treatment seems out of proportion to the faux pas of not showing up for the party in the proper dress, particularly when the guests were rounded up from here and there with no prior notice. So we, the readers, are more shocked than the king was. What was the nature of the man's offense? It has to be something more than taking advantage of the open bar too many times while casually dressed.

This parable about a wedding banquet should not be taken as though it were a first-century version of Miss Manners, offering suggestions for appropriate behavior when giving a party or when invited to one. Rather, it has to do with the difficult theme of judgment. The judgments seem harsh to us, but the very harshness sends the signal that something important is at stake here. The king is giving a wedding banquet for his son. The wedding banquet is one way that the New Testament characterizes the ultimate reign/ kingdom of God.

The parable appears at a point in Matthew's Gospel in which Jesus found himself in Jerusalem, approaching his final conflict with the authorities. Immediately preceding the parable, Matthew had reported that the chief priests and Pharisees "wanted to arrest him, but they feared the crowds" (Matt. 21:46). The context of the parable will help us understand sharp judgments in it.

The host of the wedding banquet exhibited enormous patience with those who had scorned his invitation, and, in case they had misunderstood, he sent out his emissaries a second time: "Everything is ready; come to the wedding banquet" (Matt. 22:4). This time, some of the invited guests turned their backs, while others went way beyond rudeness, responding to the emissaries with violence, even murder.

The king's response was to send his troops, destroy the murderers, and burn their city. Scholars believe that Matthew wrote his Gospel after the Romans had destroyed Jerusalem in 70 CE, so it is quite likely that his interpretation of the cataclysm was that the destruction of Jerusalem served as divine punishment upon those who had refused Jesus' invitation and the evangelical message of his disciples. However, Luke's Gospel may lead us to be skeptical of such an interpretation. When two of Jesus' disciples, indignant at Jesus' indifferent reception in Samaria, had asked him, "'Lord, do

152

you want us to command fire to come down from heaven and consume them?'" he rebuked them (Luke 9:54–55). The contemporary reader need not accept the interpretation of the Roman razing of the city as divine punishment, but rather see that point of view as a reflection of bitter disappointment by some Jews (including Matthew) that other Jews had not embraced Jesus as Messiah.

When the king in the parable had exhausted his anger, his next move had been to send out emissaries to invite anyone and everyone, without discrimination, to the banquet. In other words, God's invitation has been extended beyond the bounds of Israel, even to Gentiles. Those contemporary Christians who are Gentiles might, in retrospect, consider that it turned out to be providential that the greater part of Israel either turned away from Jesus or were indifferent to him, because the frustration of the (very Jewish) disciples at the unresponsiveness of their own community helped to motivate them to carry the gospel to non-Jews, crossing a boundary that they would not have crossed easily. They considered it providential, not in the sense that God *caused* most of Jesus' own people to respond either with hostility or indifference, but rather in the sense that God *made use of* the situation as it had evolved in such a way as to encourage the mission to the Gentiles. "So the wedding hall was filled with guests" (22:10), and that should mark a happy ending to the parable.

However, unlike its parallel (Luke 14:16–24), the Matthean parable continues further than the supposed happy ending. The king, having gone into the party to see his guests, encounters a man without a wedding robe (Matt. 22:11). We may presume that the man without a wedding robe is one of the guests invited when the intended guests refused to come—in other words, a Gentile. At this point, judgment shifts from Israel to the church. Matthew has indicated in other places in his Gospel that he is concerned that the infant church seems to include people of doubtful faith and commitment (e.g., Matt. 13:24–30), and in this parable the king's emissaries "gathered all whom they found, both good and bad." When the king discovered a guest without a wedding robe (baptismal garment), he was shocked and called upon his servants to throw the man out.

Baptism represents repentance. In Revelation, this message   153
was given to "the angel of the church in Sardis" (Rev. 3:1a):

> Remember then what you received and heard; obey it, and
> repent. If you do not wake up, I will come like a thief, and you will
> not know at what hour I will come to you. Yet you have still a few
> persons in Sardis who have not soiled their clothes; they will walk
> with me, dressed in white, for they are worthy. If you conquer,
> you will be clothed like them in white robes. . . . I will confess
> your name before My Father and before his angels. (Rev. 3:3–5)

The royal invitation has indeed been extended to everyone indiscriminately, but the appropriate response to it is more than just a willingness to enjoy the free food and drink; it includes stripping off everything that is inappropriate to the celebration and putting on what is appropriate. It may be that the first folks who were invited knew very well that if they were to come to the wedding banquet "they would have to put on a wedding garment, and they didn't want to. . . . The hard news is that, although everyone is invited, everyone has to show up wearing a wedding garment" (McKenzie, *Matthew*, 79, 80). In other words, none of us is fit for the kingdom/reign of God unless we are prepared to learn the customs of the place and commit ourselves to live by them.

A hymn for Holy Communion poetically evokes a profound spiritual change represented in a change of clothes. Just as the Lord Jesus divested himself of the divine privileges that he could rightly have held onto, the Spirit helps us to shed our old clothing in order that we may be clothed anew, in "joy and wonder":

> Now we join in celebration
> of our Savior's invitation,
> dressed no more in spirit somber,
> clothed instead in joy and wonder;
> for the Lord of all existence,
> putting off divine transcendence,
> stoops again in love to meet us,
> with his very life to feed us.
> (© Joel W. Lundeen, admin. Augsburg
> Fortress; used by permission)

While the parable underlines in stark and even intimidating terms the importance of repentance, it does not invite us to take any pleasure in the plight of those who do not repent. Our own continuing repentance may include a turning away from any suggestion of

Schadenfreude and turning toward the God for whom mercy is the last word. Alyce McKenzie generously suggests that "as we come [to the banquet], we are to bring those who weep in the darkness back to the banquet table where there is always room and nourishment for one more" (*Matthew*, 81).

Sealed and Marked

Set me as a seal upon your heart,
as a seal upon your arm;
for love is strong as death,
passion fierce as the grave.
          (Song of Solomon 8:6a, b)

Sealing was an ancient form of personal identification. A seal, made of a semiprecious metal or stone, might be worn on a cord around the neck or as a ring (*New Oxford Bible*, OT 968). In the Song of Solomon text, lovers identify so closely with one another that they share an identity, one as a seal upon the heart of the other.

Cyril of Jerusalem (315–386), taking the biblical word "seal" as equivalent to the branding of a flock of sheep, "drew upon the theme of Christ the Good Shepherd when he addressed the candidates for baptism: 'Come forward and receive the mystic seal so that the Master will recognize you. Be numbered in Christ's holy and faithful flock and he will place you at his right hand' (*Catechesis 1, 2*)" (Martos, *Doors*, 36).

Reformed Christians continued to regard the ancient image of "seal" as a reference to baptism, as one can discover in the Westminster Confession: "Baptism is a sacrament of the New Testament, ordained by Jesus Christ, not only for the solemn admission of the party baptized into the visible Church, but also to be unto him a sign and seal of the covenant of grace" (*The Constitution of the Presbyterian Church (U.S.A.), Part I, Book of Confessions*, 6.154). Anglicans make use of the image as well, as, for example, when the presiding bishop or priest lays on hands, marks with the sign of the cross, and says to each one baptized: "N., you are sealed by the Holy Spirit in Baptism and marked as Christ's own forever" (*BCP*, 308).

The New Testament does not ever use the word "seal" in an unambiguous identification with the sacrament, but it does use it in such a way as to suggest a relationship. Paul uses the word in reference to circumcision, which Abraham received "as a seal of the righteousness that he had by faith while he was still uncircumcised" (Rom. 4:11), and the Letter to the Colossians sees baptism as a kind of "spiritual circumcision": "In him also you were circumcised with a spiritual circumcision, by putting off the body of the flesh in the circumcision of Christ; when you were buried with him in baptism, you were also raised with him through faith in the power of God" (Col. 2:11–12). Clearly, New Testament references use "seal" unambiguously in speaking of the gift of the Holy Spirit.

2 Corinthians 1:21–22; Ephesians 1:13–14; 4:30

> But it is God who establishes us with you in Christ and has anointed us, by putting his seal on us and giving us his Spirit in our hearts as a first installment. (2 Cor. 1:21–22)

In a passage that briefly relates the story of their Christian initiation (Eph. 1:13–14), the letter to the faithful in Ephesus declares that the Christians there had been "marked with the seal of the promised Holy Spirit," with no explicit reference to baptism, but suggestive of it.

A seal on a document was designed to protect it from tampering, and so acted as a kind of guarantee that it was genuine. Paul and his associates Silvanus and Timothy have been anointed, that is, in this case, authorized and commissioned by divine command (2 Cor. 1:21), and evidence for this is that God has stamped his seal on them and given them his Spirit "as a first installment" on the ultimate certainty that the "glory of the Lord" (2 Cor. 3:18) will be revealed.

"Seal" is used in the epistles very much as it was used in the Gospel of John, in which Jesus, referring to himself as "the Son of Man," says, "For it is on him that God the Father has set his seal" (John 6:27), which may very well refer to Jesus' baptism, in which God provided a guarantee of Jesus' authenticity as God's Son in the descent of the Spirit and the voice from heaven.

Revelation 7:1–3; 22:3–4

156 One of the visions experienced by the seer John in Revelation provides reassurance that people of faith will be protected in a time of tribulation. An angel with the "seal of the living God" (Rev. 7:2)

called upon the four angels "at the four corners of the earth" to delay the damage they were preparing to bring upon the planet, saying, "Do not damage the earth or the sea or the trees, until we have marked the servants of our God with a seal on their foreheads" (Rev. 7:3; cf. Ezek. 9:4–8; Gen. 4:15). Those marked will be protected from the cataclysm.

In an eschatological vision of the *basileia* (the reign/kingdom of God), an angel assures the seer that, in the new creation, "nothing accursed will be found there anymore. But the throne of God and of the Lamb will be in it, and his servants will worship him; they will see his face, and his name will be on their foreheads" (Rev. 22:3–4). The "accursed" who will be excluded likely refers to the sorts of people named in the "vice lists" in Revelation, "the dogs and sorcerers and fornicators and murderers and idolaters, and everyone who practices falsehood" (21:8, 27; 22:15).

Brian Blount observes that

> the worshipers before the throne of God and the Lamb possess two especially important features. First, they have the privilege and ability to see God face-to-face. The implication is that they are closer to God than even Moses, who was only allowed to see Yahweh's back as it passed by him (Exod. 33:18–23). . . . Second . . . they will carry the identifying and protecting name of God on their foreheads. . . . [T]his "branding" is the reward for those who conquer, who witness faithfully to the lordship of God and the Lamb. (Blount, *Revelation*, 399)

A seal, as a mark of belonging, can be negative as well as positive. In the case of a slave, a collar or a brand is a highly visible marker that one is not one's own, heightening the dehumanization intrinsic to the institution. As used in the Song of Solomon, the seal is a joyful sign that indicates the way two lovers belong to one another. In the New Testament, it is most likely that the seal was meant to refer to the Holy Spirit, the gift of which served as a mark of authenticity, "the pledge of our inheritance toward redemption as God's own people" (Eph. 1:14), and as a sign that the bearer was under God's protection and would, in the *eschaton*, see God face to face. The seal, then, was not visible to the human eye. Of course, baptism in water was a tangible, physical sign of the action of the invisible Spirit, particularly as anointing and the laying on of hands served to interpret the rite.

157

Jane Parker Huber's baptismal hymn includes the language of the seal, relating it to God's covenant, a sign of which was in Israel circumcision and in the church "spiritual circumcision" or baptism (Col. 2:11).

> Wonder of wonders, here revealed;
> God's covenant with us is sealed.
> And long before we know or pray,
> God's love enfolds us every day.
> (© 1980 Jane Parker Huber, Presbyterian
> Publishing; used by permission)

Conversion, Catechesis, and Baptism

When we presume we live in a society that is predominantly Christian, it is easy to imagine that those who come to the church as potential members already have a general grasp of the biblical story, including the story of Christ in his incarnation, ministry, death, and resurrection, and that they know about the sacraments. Many congregations, still working with paradigms designed for an earlier era, provide a few classes for inquirers focused on the history and character of the denomination, the organization of the local parish, and various opportunities for discipleship and service. However, it does not take much probing to discover that many of those who approach the church have only the vaguest notion of the Christian faith and frequently need to unlearn much of what they imagine they do know.

In the last few decades, following the lead of the Roman Catholic Church's development of the Rite of Christian Initiation for Adults (RCIA), several denominations have reintroduced a form of the fourth-century catechumenate. A catechumenate involves engagement with Scripture, theological reflection, and mentored introduction to practices of the faith such as prayer, stewardship, and service. It is geared toward reaching a moment, determined by the readiness of the catechumens, for baptism and first communion (or other acts of welcome for those who have already been baptized).

158   Understanding the faith is not merely an intellectual matter but includes an intellectual dimension, that is, knowing the story and

being able to reflect on it theologically and having some grasp of how the church's worship embodies what it believes.

The early third-century Syrian *Didascalia Apostolorum* gives evidence for prebaptismal catechesis: "When the heathen desire and promise to repent, saying 'We believe,' we receive them into the congregation so that they may hear the word, but do not receive them into communion until they receive the seal and are fully initiated" (Johnson, *Rites*, 42). Once those who declare themselves to have been drawn to the faith have been exposed to the word for some period of time, they are baptized (receive the seal) and so incorporated into the covenant people.

When the New Testament describes conversions to Christian faith, the descriptions have to do with adults who presumably have made a choice. We read of encounters in which an apostle proclaimed the risen Christ, resulting in a response of faith. But what happened between the initial proclamation and the response that led to Christian initiation, that is, baptism? New Testament conversion stories, like many others of its narrative pieces, tend to be abbreviated, hitting the main points without supplying the details about which readers centuries later would like to know more. In later generations, certainly, it is beyond dispute that various catechetical processes developed to fill out the evangelical story and fortify the convert's budding faith before the actual baptism. The *Didache*, or *Teaching of the Twelve Apostles*, from the late first or early second century, begins with six chapters that outline the faith in the form of instruction meant to precede baptism, with chapter 7 focusing on the rite of baptism itself.

The liturgical season of Lent developed as a time in which to prepare catechumens for baptism at Easter. Such a process of preparation was in existence by the third century at least, and in the fourth century it was elaborated to meet the need occasioned by a huge influx of catechumens after the peace of Constantine. It is also clear that, in Jerusalem at least, catechesis continued *after* the initiatory rites, in the form of the so-called mystagogical catechesis, which focused on explaining the initiatory rites (which included first communion) to those who had just experienced them. As for the New Testament period, accounts suggest that at least a minimal sort of catechesis occurred, sometimes before baptism, sometimes after, sometimes both before and after. It is reasonable to conclude that instruction must have included some interpretation of the rite of baptism.

Acts 2:40–41; 8:12–13; 8:26–38; 10:44–48; 16:11–15; 16:25–36; 18:1–11

Most of the "conversion" stories appear in the book of Acts. The first is the account of Peter's preaching on the first Christian Pentecost, resulting in a huge number of people responding to the sermon by asking for baptism, "about three thousand persons" (Acts 2:41). Presuming that this happened all in one day, it is hard to imagine that any instruction could have been provided before the new converts were baptized; so it would appear that their only introduction to the risen Lord would have been Peter's sermon. However, the very brief description of this momentous event points to postbaptismal catechesis: "They devoted themselves to *the apostles' teaching* and fellowship, to the breaking of bread and the prayers" (2:41, emphasis added).

When Simon, who had been practicing magic in Samaria and drawing the amazed attention of the people, heard Philip preaching "the good news about the kingdom of God and the name of Jesus Christ," he believed and was baptized, like many others in the area (8:9–13). Acts suggests no time frame, so it is possible to imagine that Philip may have been preaching to the Samaritans over a period of time, perhaps even an extensive period, before he began baptizing Samaritan converts. If there was any prolonged time for instruction before people were baptized, Luke does not feel a need to tell about it. However, it is certainly safe to suppose that there was some sort of postbaptismal catechesis and formation, since "after being baptized, [Simon] stayed *constantly with Philip* and was amazed when he saw the signs and great miracles that took place" (8:13, emphasis added). Of course, a few verses on, we discover that Simon needed more conversion than he had experienced to that point (8:14–24)!

Philip plays the leading role in another conversion story when "an angel of the Lord" led him to take the wilderness road from Jerusalem to Gaza, where he encountered a court official from Ethiopia, whose responsibility was to serve his queen as treasurer of her kingdom. It is possible that this high official was a Jew; if not, he certainly had had some introduction to Jewish faith and practice, because he "had come to Jerusalem to worship and was returning home" (8:27), and furthermore, while traveling in his chariot, he had been reading Jewish Scripture, specifically, Isaiah 53:7–8. Led by the Holy Spirit, Philip approached the man in his chariot and asked whether he understood what he was reading. The man indicated a need for guidance, and Philip sat down with him and proceeded to interpret the prophetic text in terms of Jesus (8:32–35). The Ethiopian official asked for baptism, and Philip baptized him.

In this case, it is hard to see that there was time for any but the most minimal prebaptismal catechesis. However, it is significant that the Ethiopian already had at least an introduction to the Jewish Scriptures and was familiar with Jewish worship, in which he had participated in Jerusalem. He brought with him a level of acquaintance that provided a context that prepared him for the evangelical testimony to Jesus and laid the ground for him to respond in faith. In that sense, the process of his formation in Christian faith had begun even before he first heard about Jesus.

The story of the conversion of another man who was certainly a Gentile, Cornelius, indicates that he, though not a formal convert to Judaism, had been practicing that faith: "He was a devout man who feared God with all his household; he gave alms generously to the people and prayed constantly to God" (10:2). "God-fearers" is a familiar designation for Gentiles who had felt themselves drawn to the God of Israel and who practiced aspects of the Jewish faith while stopping short of outright conversion. Cornelius and the apostle Peter had been brought together by visions that each had experienced separately, and Peter proclaimed the gospel to him and his "relatives and close friends." Much to the surprise of Peter and his Jewish traveling companions, the Holy Spirit was poured out on Cornelius and those gathered with him, resulting in an ecstatic phenomenon, "for they heard them speaking in tongues and extolling God" (10:46). Peter "ordered them to be baptized in the name of Jesus Christ" (10:48). Like the Ethiopian, Cornelius had been prepared by his familiarity with and practice of Jewish prayer and almsgiving. Being immersed in Jewish ways, he too had begun a process of formation in faith before ever having heard the gospel. After he and his friends and relatives were baptized, "they invited [Peter] to stay for several days" (10:48). It would be surprising had those several days not included intense postbaptismal catechesis.   161

A Gentile woman, Lydia, described as "a worshiper of God," had heard the gospel for the first time when Paul and Silas visited the city of Philippi where she lived. They had found her among a group of people who had gathered near the river where there was a place of prayer (16:13). The description "worshiper of God" probably means that she, like Cornelius, and possibly the Ethiopian, was a sympathetic practitioner of basic elements of Judaism. "The Lord opened her heart to listen eagerly to what was said by Paul" (16:14), with the result that "she and her household were baptized" (16:15). Again, Luke provides no time frame to indicate whether all this occurred on the same day or over a period of time. It may well have been that Paul and Silas had spent considerable time with the group that habitually gathered in that place customarily used for prayer. After the baptism, Lydia invited Paul and Silas to stay at her home, which would imply time for conversation that served as postbaptismal catechesis.

Also in Philippi, Paul and Silas got in trouble with the authorities after a complaint by the owners of a slave girl that Paul had ruined their business after exorcising her. A mob accused them of disrupting Roman religious customs, which was against the law, with the result that Paul and Silas were stripped, beaten, and thrown into jail, their feet in stocks (16:16–24). During the night a violent earthquake caused the prison doors to open and the chains to be unfastened. When the jailer woke up, he was prepared to kill himself out of shame that his prisoners had escaped, but Paul and Silas intervened, which led him to beg them, "Sirs, what must I do to be saved?" (16:30). They replied, "Believe on the Lord Jesus, and you will be saved, you and your household" (16:31; NRSV here translates the Greek *epi* as "on," perhaps following the KJV), after which "they spoke the word of the Lord to him and to all who were in his house" (16:32). Then "he and his entire family were baptized without delay" (16:33).

It appears that at least a minimum of catechetical instruction preceded the baptism of the jailer and his household, since Paul and Silas "spoke the word of the Lord" to him and his household. If we take the account literally, it would seem that all this happened in the middle of the night. We might suppose that Paul and Silas did not leave Philippi without connecting the new converts with one another, who presumably continued to build up one another in faith. The Letter to the Philippians is evidence that a vital congregation grew up in Philippi.

According to Acts, Paul must have spent a stretch of time in Corinth, where he worked as a tentmaker (Acts 18:3). In Corinth, Paul made a convert of a fellow Jew, Crispus, "the official of the synagogue." Crispus "became a believer in the Lord, together with all his household; and many of the Corinthians who heard Paul became believers and were baptized" (18:8). Interestingly, though Paul apparently personally baptized very few, he himself later wrote to the Corinthians that he himself had baptized Crispus (1 Cor. 1:14). Luke tells us that Paul had spent some time in Corinth before seeing results of his teaching and preaching: "Every Sabbath he would argue in the synagogue and would try to convince Jews and Greeks" (18:4). He did not receive a favorable response from Jewish people, and so, indignantly, he resolved to "go to the Gentiles" (18:6). He visited the house of Titius Justus, a "worshiper of God" like Cornelius and Lydia, and possibly the Ethiopian. Titius Justus's house "was next door to the synagogue" (18:7). Filling in the blanks left by Luke, it is fair to presume that Paul had spent some time in conversation with Titius Justus and that Crispus, since he was a neighbor of the synagogue, somehow had joined in. In any case, it appears that Paul over time had cultivated people who were Jews, Gentiles, or Gentiles sympathetic to Judaism, resulting in "many" being baptized. What we see in Corinth is no doubt a prebaptismal catechesis that took a considerable investment of time and patience. Since, after receiving a message from the Lord, Paul remained in Corinth for a year and a half "teaching the word of God among them," it is clear that there was also plenty of time for postbaptismal catechesis.

As early as the third century, there had developed in some parts of the church a period of prebaptismal formation that might last as long as three years, at least in Rome. Typically, by the fourth century, those who wished to be baptized at Easter entered a period of more intense preparation a few weeks before. The lengthy period of preparation (catechumenate) had long disappeared by the time of the sixteenth-century Protestant Reformation. For centuries, nearly the entire population of Europe had been baptized in infancy, making a prebaptismal catechumenate obsolete. The patristic scholar Erasmus of Rotterdam (1466–1536) proposed reviving the catechumenate, but, taking into account the contemporary situation, catechesis would follow rather than precede baptism. The Protestant

163

Reformers welcomed this and set out to recover the link between baptism and a systematic program of postbaptismal catechesis. In 1523, "both Luther and Zwingli began to hold regular catechetical instruction for the youth of their respective churches" (Old, *Shaping*, 182–83). Luther, along with Martin Bucer (in Strasbourg) and John Calvin, prepared catechisms for the instruction of the young. In Geneva, Sunday afternoons were devoted to the gathering of children and youth in the church building for what today we would call Christian education.

How important is it that people today understand, for example, the multilayered meanings of the sacrament of baptism? Louis-Marie Chauvet insists, "It is clear that we cannot (and we ought not) equate the understanding of the liturgy with an intellectual comprehension" (Chauvet, "Are the Words . . . Worn Out?" 31). Ritual studies make it clear that a rite and its meaning are not two separate things that have to be brought together by the concentrated intellectual effort of each worshiper, but that the meaning is, in fact, embedded in the rite itself as it is experienced. Nothing is more likely to kill a ritual than explaining what it "means" while it is in progress. If the rite as practiced is not self-explanatory, then something is lacking in the rite. Explaining a rite creates a certain distance from it and causes us to step back and consider the rite as observers rather than participants. For this reason, when explanation accompanies the ritual action, it is counterproductive. Yet no ritual action can be self-explanatory without some familiarity with the context in which it is embedded. A newcomer, attending a Christian service for the first time as a courtesy to neighbors whose child is being baptized, is not likely to be able to intuit the meaning of the rite without knowing at least something of the Christian story. It is not likely that the words accompanying the rite will be sufficient, heard only once and in an unfamiliar setting with its many distractions, or that the meaning of the ritual actions will be self-evident. In this day of biblical illiteracy, even members of the church may require help in discovering how the rite relates to the biblical story as a whole, particularly to the story of Jesus, who was baptized, crucified, rose, and ascended with the promise that he will come again.

164   There is value in church people being able to recognize and even articulate some of the multivalent meanings of, for example, baptism and develop a perception of how it relates to the gospel as a

whole, with all its implications for the church and for our lives. But when is the appropriate time to begin learning about all this? Certainly not as a running didactic commentary during the rite itself. Many churches provide some kind of instruction for young people preparing to make their first profession of faith or for adults preparing for their own baptism or the baptism of their children; yet, in spite of these efforts, sacramental illiteracy persists in the church along with biblical and theological illiteracy. Cyril of Jerusalem and others like him were perhaps right to spend considerable time in *postbaptismal* catechesis. Working with people after baptism to help them reflect on and find words for what they experienced in the rite itself (or experienced as they observed the baptism of others) might lead to a deeper and more personal engagement with the rite and, more importantly, with the Lord who meets us in the rite, and enable the baptized to live up to and into their baptism with more intention and conscious resolve, while providing them with a language to talk about it. It is possible to teach *from the liturgy* as well as to prepare people for it.

When those who preach bring a sacramental sensibility and curiosity to texts for preaching, they often discover relationships that might not otherwise have been evident. For example, the Naaman text or the story of the crossing of the Jordan can be preached without any reference to the sacrament of baptism, but there is no question but that they can also serve to illumine aspects of the sacrament.

Other opportunities for catechesis occur outside of the worshiping assembly. For example, a church might schedule a time annually to gather the families who have brought a child for baptism in the year past, along with sponsors or godparents if there are such. The baptisms can be remembered and celebrated, stories and photos shared, a candle lighted, and a pastor, educator, or other church officer may moderate a discussion related to a baptismal text. The discussion might lead to mutual suggestions and encouragement, as parents and the church think together about the ongoing process of forming discipleship in their baptized children.

A similar gathering might be offered for adults baptized in the past year, with the discussion directed toward sharing experiences of the newly baptized persons as they have grown in faith and experienced challenges to that growth, and reflecting together on strategies for deepening discipleship in the year to come.

Where baptisms in a congregation are rare, a congregational gathering for a meal might center around telling baptismal stories. If baptismal records are kept in print rather than electronically only, the printed record can be displayed. Those present can be invited to tell where and when they were baptized and to describe baptismal certificates or mementoes if they have them. Those in leadership can use the occasion to explore a dimension of baptism that may not be familiar to most, making use of one of the many texts related to baptism. Some of the texts, vows, promises, and prayers used in the baptismal liturgy can be shared with each group as a beginning point leading both to a particular biblical text and to a consideration of how they relate to the ongoing life of the baptized.

Incorporation into a Community

1 Corinthians 12:12–26; Galatians 3:28; Ephesians 4:3–6

For just as the body is one and has many members, and all the members of the body, though many, are one body, so it is with Christ. For in the one Spirit we were all baptized into one body— Jews or Greeks, slaves or free—and we were all made to drink of one Spirit. (1 Cor. 12:12–13)

The Holy Spirit, at work in and through our baptism, unites us with Christ and with his "body," and, mixing the metaphors, the same Spirit becomes the communal drink—eucharistic wine?—the diverse body shares. Richard Hays observes that the comparison of various communities with a human body was a familiar rhetorical device in the ancient world, but that it was "ordinarily used to urge members of the subordinate classes to stay in their places in the social order" (Hays, *First Corinthians*, 213). For example, one understood to have been born a "foot" or a "leg," so to speak, ought not to aspire to be a "head." By contrast, the apostle Paul is using the image of a human body "to argue for the need of *diversity* in the body . . . and, at the same time *interdependence* among the members. . . . Thus, he employs the analogy not to keep subordinates in their places but to urge more privileged members of the community to respect and value the contributions of those members who appear to be their inferiors, both in social status and in spiritual potency" (Hays, *First Corinthians*, 213). To honor the diversity of

166

the body is also to honor the Holy Spirit, who makes use of our baptism to form a single body out of many separate parts.

The issues of unity and diversity continue to challenge the contemporary church. The argument Paul makes in 1 Corinthians 12 is part of his intention to address the issue of divisiveness that has been caused by differences between those who make use of the gift of speaking in tongues in public worship and those who do not. The apostle is wary of the power that a presumption of spiritual superiority has to strain relations in the church, whether spiritual elitism is claimed by those who do not manifest the gift of tongues or by those who do. That issue as such presented itself again particularly in the 1970s during the so-called charismatic renewal that extended beyond Pentecostal denominations to so-called mainline churches.

Spiritual elitism, however, may be manifested in many ways. In every religious conflict, both sides presume that they occupy the moral, theological, and reasonable high ground and find it very easy to look down upon the opposition with contempt. Conflicts over the status of baptized persons who are homosexual or over the role of women in ordained ministry, as well as churches and church-based groups that posit radically different ways of reading Scripture with respect to reproductive issues, offer abundant temptations to spiritual elitism. Theological conflicts, particularly those that have an impact on public policy, such as the struggles over the appropriateness of teaching creationism or intelligent design in the public schools or over how closely a church ought to identify with a particular political party, offer similar temptations for each side of the conflict to make scathing judgments of the other.

To all of us who find ourselves in any way engaged with these and other conflicts, Paul has addressed his affirmations that, as different as we may be, we are nevertheless "baptized into one body." Paul uses the image of body both metaphorically and realistically, treating the church as Christ's body ontologically. The implications of it would require us to take our union with each other in Christ with great seriousness. Differences are important and we should sort them out as though they do indeed matter, including engaging in strenuous debate. However, for Protestants particularly, it has proven far too easy to treat our oneness in Christ as no more than a watered-down figure of speech, as though we could claim a kind of "spiritual" unity that is not affected by the actual breaking of communion with one another. The public media carry the stories of our

167

various schisms, each justified on the grounds that the parent body has lost the true faith, is no longer faithful to the Bible, doesn't love Jesus Christ as much as the breakaways do. When it is not a matter of schism, sins against the body of Christ can as easily be a matter of relegating certain of the baptized to an inferior status, so that they are not eligible to be seriously considered for church office.

Even in the first century, when divisiveness and mutual scorn had already made an appearance in the apostolic church, the apostle was concerned enough to plead with the faithful.

> I therefore, the prisoner in the Lord, beg you to lead a life worthy of the calling to which you have been called, with all humility and gentleness, with patience, bearing with one another in love, making every effort to maintain the unity of the Spirit in the bond of peace. There is one body and one Spirit, just as you were called to the one hope of your calling, one Lord, one faith, one baptism, one God and Father of all, who is above all and through all and in all. (Eph. 4:1–6)

Schism can be painful, but it also manifests a troubling side of human nature that takes pleasure in righteous indignation. While mutual excommunication is hurtful, it also puts opponents out of sight, making us more comfortable as each side retreats behind its barriers. Both schism and mutual excommunication lead to an unjustifiable pride at having shaken off those whose faith and integrity seem inferior to our own. Our baptismal calling to be reconciled to one another is hard, but it is not optional.

Baptism, then, might serve as a reproach—a reminder that our union with one another in Christ is not simply the comfortable unity of those who are in sympathy with each other on the issue of the day, but also an uncomfortable unity that binds us ontologically to those with whom we may not be in particular sympathy: "Jews or Greeks, slaves or free." We are baptized into a community whose life is nourished by "one Spirit," and that cannot be sustained apart from that Spirit, in whom we are, for better or worse, one people.

Our obligations to our partners in the covenant extend further even than the community of the baptized. In fact, baptism may serve as a bridge that unites us with Israel. The apostle declared, "As many of you as were baptized into Christ have clothed yourselves with Christ. There is no longer Jew or Greek, there is no longer slave or free, there is no longer male and female; for all of

168

you are one in Christ Jesus" (Gal. 3:27–28). The verse that follows implies that baptism unites us not only with other Christians, but also with Israel: "And if you belong to Christ, then you are Abraham's offspring, heirs according to the promise" (Gal. 3:29). In the same chapter of Galatians, Paul had declared that those who believe are descendants of Abraham, adding, "And the scripture, foreseeing that God would justify the Gentiles by faith, declared the gospel beforehand to Abraham, saying, 'All the Gentiles shall be blessed in you'" (Gal. 3:8). Christians participate with Jews in God's solemn but joyful vocation to become a people whose mission must serve to bless "all the families of the earth" (Gen. 12:3). That mission cannot be served effectively when we cannot manage to sustain a covenanted relationship with one another.

Baptism is not a private act between God and the person being baptized, and it is never separated from membership in the church. While it certainly has a singular and personal dimension, baptism is always into a community, the body of Christ. The image of the church as body of Christ certainly includes each particular congregation of the church, but it also embraces the whole company of the baptized throughout all the world, as well as the church of all times, past, present, and future. For this reason private baptisms are inappropriate, and even when for grave pastoral reasons a baptism cannot take place in the midst of a congregation, representatives of the church ought to accompany the presiding minister. The generosity of the Spirit might also become more visible if it were to become commonplace for churches to send representatives to be present when neighboring churches of other denominations are celebrating the sacrament of baptism.

The *Book of Services* for the United Church of Canada includes this declaration and congregational welcome: "In the name of Jesus Christ, N. (and N.) *has/have* been received into the holy catholic church, the body of Christ in the world" (*Celebrate God's Presence*, 354).

Appropriate Candidates for Baptism

Every church—Catholic, Protestant, or Pentecostal—baptizes adult converts, with ample precedent in the New Testament. First-generation Christians will, of necessity, be persons who have

169

personally responded to the gospel in faith. Conflicts about who may be appropriate candidates for baptism emerge with respect to the second generation, that is, children born to Christian parents. The New Testament offers no explicit example of the baptism of infant children of Christian parents, but neither does it offer an example of the baptism of an adult (or one otherwise judged to be of an "accountable" age) offspring of a Christian parent. The New Testament may be judged to be silent about the second generation, and that silence has made room for conflict.

Some have believed that the New Testament references to household baptisms at least suggest the possibility that children of new converts may have been baptized along with everyone else in the household. For example, in Philippi, Lydia "and her household were baptized" (Acts 16:15); and in the case of the Philippian jailer, "he and his entire family were baptized" (Acts 16:33). One might presume that mention of a "household" would extend to more than a spouse but might well include children and/or servants and possibly their children. Even if no children were involved, the fact that servants or extended family were included indicates that the faith of the householder was decisive for the whole household, whatever the level of their personal knowledge of the faith or their disposition toward it.

Defenders of infant baptism often point to the account of Jesus welcoming the children: "Let the children come to me, and *do not stop* them; for it is to such as these that the kingdom of heaven belongs" (Matt. 19:14, emphasis added). There is in fact good exegetical support for that view, since the verb translated here as "stop" (*kōlyete*) is elsewhere associated with baptism. The same verb is used in the account of Philip and the Ethiopian when he says, "What is to *prevent* (*kōlyei*) me from being baptized?" (Acts 8:36), and in the story of Cornelius's household, where Peter asks, "Can anyone *withhold* (*kōlysai*) the water for baptizing these people?" (Acts 10:47), possibly indicating that Matthew's account of Jesus' use of the verb reflected baptismal language even in the first century. In Peter's sermon on the first Pentecost, he declared, "For the promise is for you, *for your children*, and for all who are far away, everyone whom the Lord our God calls to him" (Acts 2:39, emphasis added). Nevertheless, the lack of an explicit reference to offspring of believers of any age leaves the matter of the baptism of the second generation in the New Testament period unsettled.

170

Of course, since the Enlightenment, there has been a growing confidence in the view that each individual creates his or her own religious identity without any obligation to family, community, or the larger culture, and therefore must be encouraged to make autonomous decisions about religious faith. Indeed, this view has become embedded in the reigning plausibility structure in the West, although it is not as widespread among African Americans or observant Jews. A new parent with this perspective vows not to take his child to church (or synagogue) in order to leave the child free to "make up her own mind when she grows up." Of course, while the child is indeed theoretically free to do just that, the fact remains that she will make up her own mind after spending her growing years immersed in a household culture (and larger social culture) that repeatedly sends the message that it does not much matter whether one practices a religion or not, certainly not any particular religion. In other words, the parent's desire to remain impartial has the effect of forming offspring in a culture of indifference at best and, beyond indifference, skepticism. Neutrality is not really neutral.

Societies not so influenced by Enlightenment sensibilities have a very different understanding of the individual and the way that individuals form identities. Persons form identities in the contexts of the communities to which they belong or to which they have been exposed, whether the emergent identity is one that affirms or denies the values of the formative communities. People in biblical times knew that intuitively; in post-Enlightenment times, it must be learned with the help of psychological and sociological observation.

The presumptions of people in ancient times about the relationships between the generations and about the ways identities are formed and perpetuated cause us to consider that decisions about the second generation in the New Testament period may not have been made as people in post-Enlightenment societies would make them. First-generation Christians of Jewish background would likely have been formed to believe that children share the religious identity of their parents. Jewish boys, of course, were circumcised on the eighth day, incorporating them in this specific way into the covenanted people of Israel. With that background, it might have seemed natural to these parents that their own children should be incorporated into the community of Jesus Christ, through whom the covenant had been extended to include believing Gentiles.

171

André Benoit cites the example of Jewish proselyte baptism. Benoit says, "One could bring small children to proselyte baptism; they became Jews at the same time as their parents. But, at the age of majority, these children had the option of renouncing Judaism without being considered renegades" (Benoit, *Le Baptême*, 16, my translation from the French). In other words, they were in the community with the option of going out, rather than out with the option of coming in. It may be that, when the time came for the church to address the issue of a second generation, it followed a similar paradigm, rather than expecting the norm to be for the offspring to attempt to repeat the experience of the first generation. Even more likely is that the issue of the status of the second generation was addressed in different ways in different places or circumstances, with a fairly uniform practice developing only slowly. Irenaeus (first half of the second century) affirmed that "Christ came to save all [human beings] by himself: all, I say, who through him are reborn in God: infants and children, youths and adults, and the elderly" (Searle, "Infant Baptism Reconsidered," 395).

Maxwell Johnson notes that "Origen is a witness to the existence of infant baptism in the third century. Such a practice, he writes in his *Commentary on Romans*, was 'received from the apostles' themselves. While this, of course, is impossible to prove, the fact that Origen sees infant baptism as an 'apostolic custom' certainly points to it as a long standing tradition" (Johnson, *Rites*, 59).

Cyprian of Carthage, who was martyred in 248 CE, also staunchly defended infant baptism. Johnson quotes Cyprian's *Epistle* 64, in which he reports the decision of a recent synod: "Dearest brother, this was our opinion in council, that by us no one ought to be hindered from baptism and from the grace of God, who is merciful and kind and loving to all" (Johnson, *Rites*, 67).

A Special Commission on Baptism of the Church of Scotland offers biblical examples that, while not specifically about baptism, can be perceived as relevant to baptism. "We can be sure that [Christ] does act in Baptism and will act precisely as He acted during his ministry in Judea and Galilee, sometimes requiring *prior faith*, sometimes acting through *the faith of a parent or even master*, and sometimes *without any prior response* to His Word of re-creation and blessing of peace" (Spinks, *Reformation and Modern*, 149, emphases added).

The Gospels report several examples of situations in which Jesus heals someone whose faith is unknown. One of the most striking is the case of the paralytic brought to Jesus by his friends. Mark notes that Jesus forgave the sin of the paralytic, ordered him to stand up, and sent him home when he saw *"their* faith"—not the paralytic's (Mark 2:1–12 and parallels).

Even more striking are narratives in which Jesus acts to heal someone when there is no evidence that anyone at all has any prior faith in him. While teaching in a synagogue on the Sabbath, Jesus saw a woman "with a spirit that had crippled her for eighteen years." Without being asked by the woman, or a friend or bystander, Jesus "called her over and said, 'Woman, you are set free from your ailment,' whereupon she stood up straight and began to praise God" (Luke 13:10–13).

While none of these stories directly addresses baptism, they do make it clear that Jesus' ability to transform persons and alter their circumstances does not always require faith as a prerequisite. The example of the friends carrying their paralyzed friend to Jesus is a powerful example of how the faith of others may play a decisive role. Many who practice the faith have discovered that, in circumstances that lead to one's own faith burning low, the faith of others holds us up. When we are too distracted, depressed, hurt, or anxious to believe, others believe for us until we are strong enough to stand on our own. When we are suspicious or disgusted, the community offers its faith for us to lean on. Most of us have shared in providing support at some times and at other times have been supported.

Similarly, when parents bring a child for baptism, their faith and the faith of the community in which they and their child are embedded is the context for the formation of the child. The child herself, like the woman in the synagogue (Mark 2), is the beneficiary of God's love and power as they are and will be manifested, apart from any decision or initiative on the child's part. In the case of the child, that love and power are channeled through the community whose life she shares. Even in the case of an adult who is ready to make a profession of faith, the community of faith is the critical context for supporting that profession, sustaining it, and deepening it, relying on the power of the Spirit at work in the local church as well as the church universal. Even those whose primary introduction to the faith may have been through reading Scripture

173

all alone have in fact met the community and its Lord through that company of writers, preachers, storytellers, scribes, and teachers who created our Bible, established the canon, and handed on the sacred writings through the generations.

None of the churches disputes the fact that baptism and faith are related. Alexander Schmemann, the twentieth-century Orthodox theologian, points out that "the essential question about faith in its relationship to the sacrament is: *what* faith, and even more precisely, *whose* faith? And the equally essential answer to this question is: *it is Christ's faith*, given to us, becoming our faith and our desire" (Schmemann, *Of Water*, 67). He distinguishes between the faith of the convert, who hears the call and sets out on the journey of discipleship, and the faith into which we grow as Christ is formed in us over time. The church baptizes the new convert on the basis of "personal faith," but in the case of children, the church baptizes on "the promise and confession of those members of the Church— parents or sponsors—who have the power to offer their child to God and to be responsible for his growth in the 'newness of life'" (Schmemann, *Of Water*, 69). Even the faith of the new convert is in need of communal nurture if it is to survive and grow and mature— a need not too different in kind from that of the infant or child whose parent(s) nurture her in faith from birth onward.

Mark Searle's analysis is similar to Schmemann's.

> Baptism is the deliberate and conscious insertion of the child into the environment of faith, which faith is the faith of the Church, which in turn is the faith of Christ himself. If the Church did not continue to live by the pattern of Christ's own faith in its dying and being raised to life it would cease to be the Church. Such existential faith constitutes the identity of the Church and the identity of the family as domestic church. It is into this faith that the child is baptized when it is baptized in the faith of the Church. (Searle, "Infant Baptism," 400)

It is God who takes the initiative to call us into the royal priesthood that is the church. In the case of adults making a first profession of faith and coming to baptism, what is most immediately visible is the response of faith. In the case of a child of a family of the church, the fact that the child comes empty-handed highlights that God may call us before we are even capable of speech, much less capable of knowing anything about God or articulating God's

174

call or our own response. God's call comes in more than one way and by means of a variety of circumstances, but one way, surely, is to call us via the primary context of our lives, a believing family and the church in which that family is embedded. What Jesus said to the first disciples is relevant in every case, old or young, adult or child: "You did not choose me but I chose you" (John 15:16).

The World Council of Churches document *Baptism, Eucharist and Ministry* is intended to outline a basic ecumenical consensus about these subjects. It includes a warning about what it calls "indiscriminate baptism": "In many large European and North American majority churches infant baptism is often practiced in an apparently indiscriminate way. This contributes to the reluctance of churches which practice believers' baptism to acknowledge the validity of infant baptism; this fact should lead to more critical reflection on the meaning of baptism within those majority churches" (*BEM*, 7).

Indiscriminate baptism is, for example, baptism of the children of parents who have never been related to a church or who have only a past relationship. Such baptisms may be sought to satisfy another member of the family (usually a grandparent), out of a sense that it is the respectable thing to do, for superstitious reasons, or simply as a way of celebrating the birth of a child (Byars, "Indiscriminate Baptism," 36). In such cases, it is not reasonable to trust that the child will be formed within either a faithful family or in the community of faith. No doubt God loves all sorts of children, so baptism is not a matter of separating out a special class of children who have exclusive claim to that love; rather, baptism is the sign of a child of the covenant being inserted into Christ's corporate priesthood. The key is the reference to a "child of the covenant." The responsibility of the church is to take reasonable measures to assure that a parent who brings a child for baptism is faithful to her or his own covenantal commitments, that is, that the parent is still able to make an honest profession of her or his own faith, is a member of a particular congregation, and is willing to be responsible for making and following through on solemn promises to nurture the child, with the help of the church, toward a personal profession of faith.

The witness of Baptists and others who practice believers' baptism should serve as a solemn warning to the churches practicing infant baptism that it is not appropriate to do so in the expectation that the common culture can form Christian faith in children. For infant baptism to be justifiable, it is essential that it take place within a context that may reasonably be expected to support an intentional formation in faith and discipleship. This implies that churches look for pastoral ways to celebrate childbirth apart from baptism when the context for formation in faith is not present, and that they commit themselves to attentive and systematic follow-through with families whose children have been baptized.

Bryan Spinks encourages an intriguing practice that can enhance the life of the congregational community as it celebrates the sacrament of baptism. Without intending any embarrassment to the parents or exerting pressure, he suggests that when parents bring a child for baptism, they might be "given an opportunity within the service to say what their hopes are for their child in baptism" (Spinks, *Reformation,* 208).

Another practice that can make baptismal practice richer and more personal is the use of a baptismal garment. The traditional "baptismal gown" sometimes passed down in families from one child to another is a version of the ancient white robe. Many churches still observe (or commend) the practice of presenting the newly baptized with new clothes. For example, the *United Methodist Book of Worship* carries this rubric: "New clothing is sometimes presented to those just baptized, particularly in the case of infants, as a symbol that we 'have put on Christ' (Galatians 3:27) as one would put on new clothing. Such clothing is traditionally white, suggesting the 'white robes' in Revelation 7:9–14. Words such as these may be used: 'Receive these new clothes as a token of the new life that is given in Christ Jesus'" (*UMBW,* 91).

Spinks remarks, "In baptism it is not so much that we confess Christ as that he confesses us before the Father. We are presented before God as subjects of his saving activity, and are initiated into a mutual relation between the act of the Spirit and the response of faith" (Spinks, *Reformation,* 150).

Baptism embodies so many layers of meaning that it can be too much to attempt to express every one of them in every baptismal service. Depending on the liturgical season, the age and circumstance of the candidate(s), and the life of the particular congregation, some themes may be highlighted as seems appropriate. Hymns can help do this, as, for example, Ronald Cole-Turner's "Child of Blessing, Child of Promise," which accents the Spirit, the sign, the seal, and the need to learn to listen for God's call:

176

Child of blessing, child of promise,
Baptized with the Spirit's sign,
With this water God has sealed you
Unto love and grace divine.

Child of God, your loving Parent,
Learn to know whose child you are.
Grow to laugh and sing and worship,
Trust and love God more than all.

Crossing Over: Baptismal Witness at a Time of Death

Thomas G. Long writes about how his research into the Christian funeral caused him to change his mind:

> At the beginning of my work on this project, I would easily have agreed with what has become a virtual consensus among those who write about Christian funerals: the essential and overriding purpose of the funeral is to provide comfort for the grief-stricken. . . . I have gradually come around to the conviction that this consensus view is deeply flawed and has done much to weaken and diminish the Christian funeral today. Yes, funerals provide consolation to those who mourn, but they do so as a part of a much broader work involving the retelling of the gospel story, the restoration of meaning, the reaffirmation of the baptismal identity of the one who has died, and the worship of God. (Long, *Accompany Them with Singing*, xiv)

Pastors know how powerful local customs are at the time of death and are grateful for those that truly minister to the grieving, particularly when local customs are respectful of the faith of the church. However, even local customs of longstanding are frequently being displaced by improvisations shaped by popular culture or commercial interests. One may be forgiven for having doubts about the value of burying the dead wearing a Denver Broncos sweatshirt or designing a unique service featuring the deceased

177

person's love for a certain brand of beer. In the first decade of the new century, a Roman Catholic diocese in New England found it necessary to discourage strongly the singing of "O Danny Boy" at requiem masses, which had apparently become common.

However dear our loved one is, and however many stories may be told as proof of his or her virtues, the fact is that we are all sinners, even if not always notorious ones, and we are all ultimately dependent on God's grace. The funeral can be a strong testimony to that grace, in Scripture, sermon, and prayer, and in rite. Long reminds us that a "Christian funeral is a continuation and elaboration of the baptismal service," which is in fact the foundation of the funeral service and a vivid testimony to the grace upon which we depend (Long, *Accompany*, 81). Baptismal language, with its images of death and resurrection, can play a significant role in setting the death of a particular person within the context of the biblical story and the church's testimony.

Martin Copenhaver reports his experience as a pastor when he was called upon to perform a funeral service for a member of his UCC congregation whose wife was Jewish. He consulted a book that described various religious traditions and how a guest might participate in them. He writes,

> The funeral section of the book on Jewish practices is thick and explicit. . . . Then, out of curiosity, I turned to the page that deals with the traditions of my denomination. Under the heading of funeral practices there is this question: "Are there mourning customs to which a friend who is not a member of the United Church of Christ should be sensitive?" And this is the answer: "No. Local, ethnic, and cultural customs are more relevant than any particular religious tradition of the church." That statement, although not entirely accurate, was just true enough to make me wince. (Copenhaver, "Back to the Future," 4)

The church has in its treasury of traditions practices that, because they are God-centered rather than centered on personal habits, preferences, and idiosyncrasies, ironically possess more healing power than improvisations of the moment. Whether a particular church typically makes use of a service book, either directly or as a resource, or does not, it is nevertheless possible to draw upon the wisdom that the book serves to hand on.

178

Even in an era in which it is possible to express one's sympathy to the bereaved via an entry in an electronic guest book, many still find it of value for family and friends to gather before and after the funeral to offer mutual support and gestures of friendship, and to pray together. The *Book of Common Prayer* provides a prayer for such a gathering that includes explicit baptismal images: "Wash *him* in the holy font of everlasting life, and clothe *him* in *his* heavenly wedding garment. *Into your hands, O Lord, we commend our brother (sister) N*" (*BCP*, 465).

While baptism marks a spiritual death and resurrection, it is also a promise that even our very real mortality will not be the last word. Many funeral services in the contemporary service books of the several denominations make an explicit reference to baptism. *Evangelical Lutheran Worship* is typical in its provision of a thanksgiving for baptism, including a reading of the Romans 6 passage. Our baptism is made complete in our dying, since in our deaths we claim baptism's promise of union with Christ in his resurrection. The *Book of Common Worship* includes a prayer that offers thanks for one who has died, "whose baptism is now complete in death" (*BCW*, 921). *The Book of Common Prayer* commends to God "our brother (sister) N., who was reborn by water and the Spirit in Holy Baptism. Grant that *his* death may recall to us your victory over death" (*BCP*, 498).

Many churches follow the tradition of covering the casket with a pall, the color of which is white, the liturgical color used at Easter, each time in honor of the resurrection. The white pall is reminiscent of the white baptismal garment. As the pall is placed on the casket, the person presiding may say (drawing from Gal. 3:27):

For as many of you as were baptized into Christ
have clothed yourselves with Christ.

In *his/her* baptism N. was clothed with Christ;
In the day of Christ's coming,
he/she will be clothed with glory.

(*BCW*, 912)

Some churches make use of a paschal candle, lighted from Easter Day to Pentecost in celebration of the resurrection, lighting it also at baptisms and at funerals or memorial services, signaling the relationship between the celebration of the Lord's resurrection, baptism, and the hope of our own resurrection represented in the completion of our baptism in death. The lighted candle may be carried into the church as the coffin is brought in, and/or stationed near the head of the casket once it has been placed in the church.

The funeral services in both the *BCP* (497) and the *BCW* (922) include in the prayers "Our *brother/sister* was washed in baptism and anointed with the Holy Spirit; give *him/her* fellowship with all your saints."

Even in a service that makes no use of any of the liturgical books, it is both possible and fitting to make use of baptismal images in readings from Scripture, the sermon, and the prayers. White Bible markers and paraments mark the connection with Easter and the promise of the resurrection. In one church, an artist in the congregation designed a baptism banner that normally hung on a wall of the church but was suspended above the font at baptisms and could be placed in the same prominent position during a funeral, as a visual reminder of the link between baptism and our union with Christ in his death and resurrection.

The old gospel song "Shall We Gather at the River" has baptismal associations as well as associations with the Old and New Testament passages that offer the image of abundant waters as a mark of the *eschaton*, the new Eden, as well as evoking, in one stanza, an image of the baptismal garment.

> Shall we gather at the river, where bright angel feet have trod,
> with its crystal tide forever flowing by the throne of God?
>
> Yes, we'll gather at the river, the beautiful, the beautiful river;
> gather with the saints at the river that flows by the throne of God.
>
> Ere we reach the shining river, lay we ev'ry burden down;
> grace our spirits will deliver, and provide a robe and crown.
> (Robert Lowry, 1826–99; public domain)

The Sacrament of the
Lord's Supper

CHAPTER 6

Do This

You cause the grass to grow for the cattle,
    and plants for people to use,
to bring forth food from the earth,
    and wine to gladden the human heart,
oil to make the face shine,
    and bread to strengthen the human heart.
                    (Ps. 104:14–15)

The psalmist celebrates gifts for which it is appropriate to be grateful, among which two in particular stand out: wine, which makes the heart glad, and bread, which makes the heart strong. The New Testament identifies Jesus as, metaphorically, bread and wine:

> This is my body.
> This is my blood.

Like bread and wine, Jesus both makes the heart glad and strengthens it, for which we are thankful. Gratitude is key to understanding the Christian Eucharist: gratitude for God's good creation; gratitude for Jesus Christ, and our redemption in him, both present and future; and gratitude for the Holy Spirit, by whom the risen Christ becomes present to us and for us. The Eucharist itself (from the Greek, *eucharistein*, "to give thanks"), is the pulsing heart of our assemblies for worship. By it and through it, alongside the preached Word, God calls us to a new way of seeing the world—one that supports us in sustaining a eucharistic life wherever we are.

183

A eucharistic life is one that cultivates gratitude in such a way that it trumps resentment, disappointment, bitterness, jealousy, prejudice, and indifference, along with every other negative way of perceiving our lives and the lives of those around us. Gratitude is a disposition that can be learned. It is a way of being in the world that we can cultivate in ourselves and encourage in others. The church is meant to be the communion of those who, in Christ, support one another in a eucharistic approach to life.

Eucharistic living does not intend to deny or minimize the heartache and injustices that so frequently stamp a crosslike shape upon our lives and the lives of our communities. Heartache and injustices are real, and they are bitter. We see it all and lament it all, and yet by faith, in prayer and in action, those who strive to live a eucharistic life say: Nevertheless. Nevertheless, God is for us, not against us, and not for us only, but for all the families of the earth. In the days of sunshine and in the days of storms, God is God, and for that we are thankful.

If the Christian life is eucharistic life, then it follows that the "breaking of bread" in our assemblies for worship is not an esoteric rite, set off from our lives in the larger society. Rather, it informs our lives in the world, shaping and reshaping them both individually and communally.

The Eucharist, Lord's Supper, or Holy Communion gratefully holds up before God the remembrance of Christ's death on the cross, calling upon the covenantal promise of a new creation, no longer characterized by death or by tears.

—The church's Eucharist must faithfully embody the gospel, as the apostle Paul and the Gospel writers certainly understood, both for the well-being of the faithful and for the integrity of the church's engagement with the world. For this reason, they were not averse to criticizing eucharistic practice wherever it risked distortion.

—Eucharistic life is life in community. It is life that is open to and expectant of the presence of the risen Christ, and open to and expectant of being really present one to another and of the church being really present in and to society for the sake of the ancient vocation shared with Israel, to seek the blessing of all the families of the earth.

—A eucharistic life is not always optimistic, but always hopeful. If we impartially calculate the odds of things turning out in a way that will satisfy our best expectations, our assessments may not lead to optimism. The Christian life, as eucharistic life, is one that rests not on calculating the odds but on God's promise of a new creation—one that we can imaginatively characterize as a huge reunion banquet, a table set for all peoples. It will be a homecoming in which ancient separations and animosities will be left decisively behind. The Eucharist rehearses what the *basileia* is going to look like and so sustains us in our hope and strengthens us to live into it even now.

During Lent, a group of people in one church covenanted together to begin meals in their own homes with the familiar opening dialogue of the Great Thanksgiving:

The Lord be with you.
And also with you.
Lift up your hearts.
We lift them to the Lord.
Let us give thanks to the Lord our God.
It is right to give our thanks and praise.

In that simple way of initiating grace at mealtime, they joined the prayer at their own tables with the eucharistic prayer that unites the whole church. Life is—or can be—eucharistic; and every meal can be a rehearsal for eucharistic life.

In the eighteenth century, the Society of Friends (Quakers) rebelled against eucharistic practice in the churches with which they were familiar. From their point of view, those who attended worship in the "steeple houses" were going through the motions, not expressing a thanksgiving that was truly from the heart. The Friends decided that true worship required no particular form (although they soon settled on a form of their own), and sacramental worship was not necessary, since every meal was a sacramental occasion.

No doubt there is some truth in that perspective. Every meal is, at least potentially, a sacramental occasion. However, it is more likely that Christians will perceive their everyday meals as sacramental when sustained by the church's eucharistic meal as a continual paradigm and reminder of the sacramental dimension of all of life. The larger church may be grateful to the Society of Friends for reminding us that the Eucharist is not simply a ceremony that

185

has meaning within the place of assembly. Rather, it sketches out for us a whole way of living.

The church's Eucharist was itself shaped by a variety of meals whose participants might have taken to be "ordinary." Indeed, under the influence of the devout party of Pharisees, even regular Jewish meals were understood to be what we might call "sacramental"—eating and drinking before God. Their festive meals provided an essentially doxological model of blessing and thanksgiving that set a more or less consistent pattern for a prayerful table. The meal protocols common to both Greco-Roman and Jewish practice at the time called for a "mixed cup" (water mixed with wine) to be presented after guests had finished eating. In the Greco-Roman banquet setting, the mixed cup signaled the beginning of a time for drinking and entertainment. At a Jewish meal, however, the mixed cup became an occasion for the blessing of God (Lathrop, *Holy People*, 187). Paul describes the mixed cup as "the cup of blessing" (1 Cor. 10:16).

After the festive Jewish meal, the host presented the last cup of wine, over which he pronounced a *birkat ha-mazon*, a grace after meals. The Hebrew *birkat* derives from a root that means "to bless." The structure of the *birkat ha-mazon* was to begin with a blessing, such as "Blessed art Thou, O Lord our God, King of the Universe, Who feedest the whole world with goodness, with grace, and with mercy." Thanksgiving followed, such as, "We thank Thee, O Lord our God, that Thou hast caused us to inherit a goodly and pleasant land, the covenant, the Torah, life and food." Finally came supplication: "Have mercy, O Lord our God, on Thy people Israel, and on Thy city Jerusalem, and on Thy Temple" (Talley, "From Berakah to Eucharistia," 86).

The shape of eucharistic prayer in the church evolved from this Jewish table practice—specifically, the early *birkat ha-mazon*. It provided a structure that served Christian prayer very well, particularly in that its threefold form could be made to serve prayer in a Trinitarian mode. In the East, the Orthodox shape of eucharistic prayer, particularly in its West Syrian form, typically took this shape:

Praise to the Father	(Preface)
Thanksgiving for Christ and our redemption in him	(Post-Sanctus or Anamnesis)
Supplication for the sending of the Spirit	(Epiclesis)

One result of the liturgical renewal movement of the late nineteenth century and the twentieth has been that many churches have moved toward a common pattern of eucharistic prayer, one that departs both from the Roman model (the Canon of the Mass) and from Reformation models. Eucharistic prayers in Protestant and Anglican service books have typically followed, more or less precisely, the ancient West Syrian, or Antiochene, model that developed in the Eastern church. Since Vatican II, the new eucharistic prayers that may be substituted for the traditional Roman Canon have also been strongly influenced by the Antiochene model.

The Antiochene eucharistic prayer is a single prayer with a Trinitarian shape. The prayer first praises God for the creation and for redemptive acts in Israel; then offers thanksgiving for Jesus Christ; and, finally, offers petition that the Holy Spirit may bless both the assembly and the gifts of bread and wine. The first movement of the prayer is called the Preface. For example,

> Blessed are you, strong and faithful God.
> All your works, the height and the depth, echo the silent music of
>   your praise.
> In the beginning your Word summoned light,
>   night withdrew,
>   and creation dawned.
> As ages passed unseen, waters gathered on the face of the earth
>   and life appeared.
> When the times at last had ripened and the earth grown full in
>   abundance,
>   you created in your image man and woman, the stewards of all
>   creation.
> You gave us breath and speech, that all the living might find a voice
>   to sing your praise, and to celebrate the creation you call good.
> So now, with all the powers of heaven and earth,
>   we sing the ageless hymn of your glory . . .
> *Holy, Holy, Holy Lord* . . .
>   (Prepared by the International Committee on English in the
>   Liturgy, in the Presbyterian *Book of Common Worship*.
>   Great Thanksgiving E, 142; used by permission)

The Eucharist, with its taking, thankful blessing, breaking, and giving, and certainly also in our communal eating and drinking, is a way of remembering. We remember Christ's death and the covenant renewed in his death and resurrection. We also remember in

187

a special way, holding up before God the promises made in Christ and praying for their fulfillment in the *basileia*. In the sacrament, we eat and drink what the Spirit gives us in Christ, our paschal lamb.

That We May Remember

Eucharistic prayer, rooted in the *birkat ha-mazon*, is the way the church follows the Lord's own example of giving thanks over the bread and cup. The earliest of the so-called institution narratives, from the apostle Paul, hands on the tradition that the meal is rooted in thanksgiving, and that the cup in particular serves as a sign of the new, or renewed, covenant.

1 Corinthians 11:23–33

> For I received from the Lord what I also handed on to you, that the Lord Jesus on the night when he was betrayed took a loaf of bread, and when he had given thanks, he broke it and said, "This is my body that is for you. Do this in remembrance of me." In the same way he took the cup also, after supper, saying, "This cup is the new covenant in my blood. Do this, as often as you drink it, in remembrance of me." For as often as you eat this bread and drink the cup, you proclaim the Lord's death until he comes. (1 Cor. 11:23–26)

Paul's account precedes in time the institution narratives cited in the Synoptic Gospels. The apostle declares that the narrative and the commands attached to it have been "received from the Lord," which one could take to mean that they had been received by divine inspiration, perhaps in a vision similar to his encounter with Jesus on the road to Damascus (Acts 9:1–9). More likely, he means that he had received it from the tradition already present in and "handed on" in the community. The Latin equivalent of the Greek verb translated "handed on" (*paredōka*, v. 23) is in its infinitive form *tradere*, in which one can easily discern the roots of the English word "tradition." What Paul had received, he also "traditioned" to the Christians of Corinth.

188

The Greek verb translated "betrayed" is another version of the same word, *paredidoto*, so that a more consistent translation would be "on the night when he was *handed over*, he took a loaf of bread." Richard Hays calls attention to the fact that Paul had used the same verb in Romans 8:32 (also 4:25): "He [God] who did not withhold his own Son, but *gave him up* (*paredōken*) for all of us" (Hays, *First Corinthians*, 198). The use of the English word "betrayed" to translate *paredōka* would seem to refer to Judas's treachery, but Paul may well mean that it was *God* who had handed Jesus over "for our sins." In other words, it is God's providential action that called Jesus to bear the divine presence into the accursed places, the hopeless places, where cruelty and indifference combine to crucify the innocent and where there can be no hope for anyone apart from the grace and mercy made manifest in the cross.

The sequence of verbs in verses 23–24—"took" (*elaben*), "had given thanks" (*eucharistēsas*), "broke" (*eklasen*)—is found throughout the New Testament as a signal to the reader that a text should be heard eucharistically, as, for example, in the feeding of the multitudes (Mark 8:6) and the risen Lord's appearance to the travelers on the road to Emmaus (Luke 24:30). The bread is identified as representative of Jesus' body, which is to be understood not as a biological substance but, rather, as a manifestation of his person.

"Do this," Jesus says, "in remembrance of me." It is the *doing* that is the remembrance: taking bread, giving thanks for it, breaking it, and consuming it. This is not a summons to an introspective attempt to visualize the passion of the Lord, as though the effectiveness of the "remembrance" rested on each believer's success in psychologically traveling backward in time and being appropriately moved. The *actions* of the meal are the remembering, rather than an individual effort by each participant to focus on it cognitively or emotionally. In this respect, the Lord's Supper is similar to the Passover, in which the focus also falls on certain things specified to be *done* for the sake of remembering: "This day shall be a day of remembrance [*zikarron*] for you" (Exod. 12:14).

Paul hands on the tradition that Jesus took a cup "after supper." The apostle reports Jesus' saying that the cup is "the new covenant in my blood." This must have had a startling effect among the guests at such a meal. They would have understood a reference to the blood of the covenant, but astonished by Jesus' identifying it with his own blood.

189

At Sinai, Moses erected an altar and also twelve pillars "corresponding to the twelve tribes of Israel" (Exod. 24:4). Representatives of the people "offered burnt offerings and sacrificed oxen as offerings of well-being to the LORD" (Exod. 24:5). Moses divided the blood from the sacrificial animals, dashing half of it against the altar. Then he read the book of the covenant to the people, and they pledged to keep God's law. In response to their solemn vow, "Moses took the blood and dashed it on the people, and said, 'See the blood of the covenant that the Lord has made with you in accordance with all these words'" (24:8).

When, in the tradition that Paul hands on, Jesus identifies the cup as representing "the new covenant" in his blood, he does so against the background of the ritual by which God, through Moses, had sealed with blood the covenant made at Mount Sinai. It is striking to consider the Exodus text, in which Moses dashed the blood of the covenant on the people, alongside Jesus' identification of the cup as "the new covenant in my blood," and both of these in juxtaposition to the cry of the assembly when Jesus appeared before Pontius Pilate. When Pilate said, "I am innocent of this man's blood; see to it yourselves," the crowd is said to have answered, "His blood be on us and on our children!" (Matt. 27:24–25). One might understand this as saying more than the crowd assembled or even Matthew had understood at the time, that is, that there is continuity between the covenant to which Exodus witnesses, and the "new" covenant, made manifest in Jesus' death. The blood of the covenant covers even those who cry out for his death.

Raymond Brown, quoting the promise of a "new covenant" in Jeremiah 31:31, points out that "'new' has the connotation of 'renewed'": "Through the death and resurrection of Jesus, therefore, Christians believed that God had renewed the covenant with a fresh dimension; and they came to understand that this time the covenant reached beyond Israel to include the Gentiles in God's people" (Brown, *An Introduction*, 3, 4).

In time, hostility between the Jewish and Christian communities led to the view that a "new covenant" implied that the original covenant was obsolete. However, the apostle Paul does not support such a view. Referring to his own people, he writes, "They are Israelites, and to them belong the adoption, the glory, the covenants, the giving of the law," etc. (Rom. 9:4), and adds, "It is not as though the word of God had failed" (9:6), and "the gifts and the calling of God are irrevocable" (11:28). The "new" covenant is the old one expanded, and the sign of it is the blood not of a sacrificial animal,

190

but of Christ himself, who pours out his very life, emptying himself, "obedient to the point of death—even death on a cross" (Phil. 2:8).

Paul uses the focus on the Lord's Supper as a proclamation of Jesus' death to root the meal in that pivotal revelatory moment. Given the opportunity, we mortals would likely design a different God than the one who rules the universe—probably a God more likely to satisfy our short-term expectations. Jesus opens his arms on the cross to accept the free-floating rage of a humanity disappointed at the way the world works. He does not return human resentment or anger or pass it on. In the crucified Jesus, God both shares with the whole human race the desolation of the cross-shaped places and loves those who do not love God. Paul's pointing the eucharistic assembly to the Lord's death serves to remind the church that Jesus' cross is the very sign of a love that does not keep score of wrongs, but embraces the enraged and the disappointed as well as those who protect themselves by keeping at a neutral distance. The meal proclaims the Lord's death, a fact that is not incidental to the gospel story, but is at the very heart of the way God's character and disposition toward us have been revealed in him.

The Pauline institution narrative has three temporal dimensions: past, present, and future. It turns to the past: "on the night when he was betrayed." It embraces the present: "Do this." It looks to the ultimate future: "until he comes." The church's Eucharist today is rooted in the past and yet, trusting in the experience of generations, also relies on the promise that the Lord will become present in the meal. At the same time, the Eucharist anticipates the manifestation of the Lord's rule throughout the whole creation, of which the Lord's Table provides a foretaste. It is the future, eschatological dimension that is frequently muted or overlooked, even though the new service books are careful to point to it, following the example of ancient eucharistic prayers. (See chapter 9.)

That God May Remember

The second, Post-Sanctus (or Anamnesis) movement of the tripartite Great Thanksgiving includes the institution narrative in the body of the prayer, recalling the Lord's exhortation to do this "in remembrance." In many churches, the words "Do this in remembrance of me" appear on the front of the altar/table, or on the cloth that covers it. Certainly, this is consistent with New Testament exhortations that the faithful remember what they had already been taught. "The first duty of the apostle with respect to a community from the moment it was founded is to recall the faithful to that in which they have shared and already know—or ought to know" (Dahl, "Anamnesis," 75, my trans.). The point, of course, is not just to keep the history straight, but rather, that the gospel they have received be formed in them, in thought and action. That is straightforward enough. Yet our Enlightenment-saturated culture conditions us to understand these words, "in remembrance," too simply, as though they are meant to point to the Eucharist as a sort of audiovisual reenactment that is intended to remind us of Jesus and his passion.

The Greek word translated as "remembrance" is *anamnēsis*. The equivalent Hebrew word is *zkr*. The Old Testament uses variations on the word "remember" or "memorial" (*zikarron*) in a more nuanced way than simply as a means of jogging our memory of a past event. In fact, "in remembrance of me" may equally refer to the eucharistic action as a prayer for *God* to remember the passion of the Lord.

There are many Old Testament precedents in which an appeal is made for God to remember. For example, when Israel in the wilderness had become dismayed at Moses' long absence and had fashioned the golden calf, Moses responded to God's subsequent wrath. Moses pleaded for the people, reminding God of God's own covenant. He implored God, saying, "Remember [*zkr*] Abraham, Isaac, and Israel, your servants, how you swore to them, 'I will multiply your descendants like the stars of heaven, and all this land that I have promised I will give to your descendants, and they shall inherit it forever'" (Exod. 32:13).

According to Nils Dahl, "When God 'remembers the covenant,' that means that he intervenes and acts in conformity with it" (Dahl, "Anamnesis," 72, my trans.). In response to Moses' prayer, "the Lord changed his mind about the disaster that he planned to bring on his people" (32:14).

Moses' prayer of intercession, writes Max Thurian, is

the same intercession that the Church makes in the Eucharist, when it presents to God the crucified Christ, that [God] may remember in our favour the New Covenant established on the cross, and that [God] may remember it in the present personally for each sinner: "Remember Christ crucified," the Church must say, "because it is in Him alone that all has been accomplished for the salvation of sinners; remember him who said "Do this for my memorial," and apply to us this day the blessings that His death has procured for us. (Thurian, *Eucharistic Memorial*, 30)

Another example of a similar supplicatory prayer is that of the psalmist who pleaded with God, "Remember [*zkr*] your congregation, which you acquired long ago, which you redeemed to be the tribe of your heritage" (Ps. 74:2). And also, "For their sake he [God] remembered his covenant, and showed compassion according to the abundance of his steadfast love" (Ps. 106:45).

A visible object or other sign may also serve as a summons for God to "remember," a reminder of a promise made. At the end of the Noah story, God sets the bow in the clouds and promises to remember the covenant. "When the bow is in the clouds I will see it and remember [*zkr*] the everlasting covenant between God and every living creature of all flesh that is on the earth" (Gen. 9:16).

Isaiah announced that God had appointed "sentinels" (prophets) whose work it would be to call God's attention to promises made.

> You who remind the LORD,
>   take no rest,
> and give him no rest
>   until he establishes Jerusalem
> and makes it renowned throughout the earth.
> (Isa. 62:6b–7)

It is not, of course, as though God has a faulty memory and relies on human beings to be sure that nothing of crucial importance will be forgotten. Remembering before God resembles the way one person reminds another how, in their youth, they had pledged to one another that some day they would take a special trip together or share a home. Neither has forgotten, but they relish rehearsing the promise as they implicitly renew it and continue to anticipate the time of its fulfillment. Similarly, to hold up before God's "remembrance" the passion of the Lord is both to share the

193

bond that the precious memory represents and to remind God of the promise implicit in the death and resurrection of the Lord, that is, the covenantal promise of the new creation, the *basileia*, the reign of God that is yet to come, the eschatological consummation.

Brevard Childs's study of memory in Israel concludes that God's "remembering is not conceived of as an actualization of a past event in history; rather, every event stems from the eternal purpose of God. . . . God's memory is not a re-creating of the past, but a continuation of the selfsame purpose. . . . [God's] memory includes both the great deeds of the past as well as his continued concern for his people in the future" (Childs, *Memory and Tradition*, 42).

What God has done in the past is a clue to what God will do in the future and, more than a clue, a pledge. The dominical command, "Do this in remembrance of me," is surely a summons to the church to hold fast to Jesus and his saving death discernible in the eucharistic action by faith, but it is more than that. Before God, Jesus' death is not just a past event; it plays a role in God's eternal purpose. The praying church holds it up for God's "remembrance" as its prayer that God's purpose may be realized now. Susan Briehl's hymn, "By Your Hand You Feed Your People" includes this refrain, that links the passion of the Lord with the promise of a new creation:

> Christ's own body, blessed and broken,
> cup o'erflowing, life outpoured,
> given as a living token
> of your world redeemed, restored.
> (Briehl, © 2002 GIA Publications, Inc.)

Give Thanks, Eat, Drink

It is not known whether those who wrote the Synoptic Gospels knew Paul's institution narrative from 1 Corinthians or had received it from a source they held in common. However, the main points of the narrative are the same and represent a tradition that was already authoritative or that the Gospels themselves contributed to making generally authoritative in the church.

Mark 14:17–26; Matthew 26:20–30

When it was evening, he came with the twelve. And when they had taken their places and were eating, Jesus said, "Truly I tell you, one of you will betray me, one who is eating with me." . . .	When it was evening, he took his place with the twelve; and while they were eating, he said, "Truly I tell you, one of you will betray me." . . .
While they were eating, he took a loaf of bread, and after blessing it he broke it, gave it to them, and said, "Take; this is my body." Then he took a cup, and after giving thanks he gave it to them, and all of them drank from it. He said to them, "This is my blood of the covenant, which is poured out for many. Truly I tell you, I will never again drink of the fruit of the vine until that day when I drink it new in the kingdom of God." (Mark 14:17–18, 22–25)	While they were eating, Jesus took a loaf of bread, and after blessing it he broke it, gave it to the disciples, and said, "Take, eat; this is my body." Then he took a cup, and after giving thanks he gave it to them, saying, "Drink from it, all of you; for this is my blood of the covenant which is poured out for many for the forgiveness of sins. I tell you, I will never again drink of this fruit of the vine until that day when I drink it new with you in my Father's kingdom." (Matt. 26:21, 26–29)

The two Synoptic Gospels both begin with a reference to "the twelve," not an insignificant number, since it evokes the twelve tribes of Israel, reminiscent of the covenant event at the foot of Mount Sinai, when Moses built an altar and "set up twelve pillars, corresponding to the twelve tribes of Israel" (Exod. 24:4). Mark and Matthew are telling us that the new community, beginning with the twelve disciples whom Jesus had called, parallels God's chosen people, Israel. These two Synoptic institution narratives follow Paul's account in 1 Corinthians 11 fairly closely. Like the Pauline narrative, Mark and Matthew use the word "covenant" in reference to the cup, although without the adjective "new."

The Mark and Matthew texts conclude with an eschatological message, that Jesus will not drink this cup again until the coming of the "kingdom," with his death implied but not specifically mentioned, while a similar eschatological reference in the Pauline narrative identifies the acts of eating "this bread" and drinking the cup

195

explicitly as a proclamation of "the Lord's death until he comes" (1 Cor. 11:26).

The reference to the cup has a double meaning, one having to do with the literal cup in Jesus' hand, and the other having to do with a metaphorical "cup" that points to his suffering and death. When James and John asked that they might sit at Jesus' right and left hands in the *basileia* (kingdom), he asked them, "Are you able to drink the cup that I drink, or be baptized with the baptism that I am baptized with?" (Mark 10:38). Likewise, during Jesus' agony in Gethsemane, he prayed, "Father, for you all things are possible; remove this cup from me" (Mark 14:36).

Mark and Matthew differ in reference to the blood of the covenant; in Mark it is simply "poured out for many," while Matthew adds "for the forgiveness of sins." The phrase "blood of the covenant" evokes the memory of the blood of the sacrifices that Moses dashed on the people as "the blood of the covenant" (Exod. 24:8). Jesus declares that the cup is "my blood of the covenant, which is poured out for many for the forgiveness of sins" (Matt. 26:28). His words identify a profound connection between Jesus' death and the forgiveness of sins. Christ turns with love toward those who crucify him and toward all the rest of us who consent to and even participate in the daily crucifixions taking place all around us.

Love is costly. Anyone who has ever fallen in love or loved a child knows that love is costly. Whoever has loved the church, or their country, or some institution or cause to which they have devoted their lives knows that love is costly. To love is to open oneself to the possibility of disappointment and profound heartache. Someone we love does not love us back, or disappoints us, or betrays us. Our country does not embody the virtues it has claimed as its own. The church becomes obsessed with the trivial. We lose the business, or the cause fails. Love always risks pain. That may be why some forms of Eastern religion exhort us to find freedom from pain in a profound detachment. However, in the cross, the God revealed in Christ is anything but detached. The gospel that discovers its center of gravity in the cross is a powerful affirmation that love—attachment to other people in all their contrariness and neediness and in spite of their capacity to injure us—is more important than protecting ourselves from hurt and disappointment. Love is what life is all about, even though it is surely costly to the lover.

In the eucharistic meal, the self-risking, self-emptying, open-hearted love of Jesus Christ becomes our food and drink. He does not give us what we deserve, but embraces us in spite of the ways we strike out against God and one another. His life, poured out in a love that is often rejected, is the good news that God's forgiveness is strong enough and persistent enough to hold on to us in spite of ourselves. In the eucharistic meal we eat and drink this good news of God's covenantal pledge, and our subsequent release.

At a Passover meal, the custom is to sing the Hallel ("Praise") psalms (Pss. 113–118) as a unit after the *birkat ha-mazon*. Both Mark and Matthew end their narratives of the meal with the report, "When they had sung the hymn, they went out to the Mount of Olives" (Mark 14:26; Matt. 26:30), in keeping with this practice. One of the Hallel psalms includes the words, "I will lift up the cup of salvation and call on the name of the LORD. . . . I will offer to you a thanksgiving sacrifice and call on the name of the LORD" (Ps. 116:13, 17).

Luke 22:14–23

> When the hour came, he took his place at the table, and the apostles with him. He said to them, "I have eagerly desired to eat this Passover with you before I suffer; for I tell you, I will not eat it until it is fulfilled in the kingdom of God." Then he took a cup, and after giving thanks he said, "Take this and divide it among yourselves; for I tell you that from now on I will not drink of the fruit of the vine until the kingdom of God comes." Then he took a loaf of bread, and when he had given thanks, he broke it and gave it to them, saying, "This is my body, which is given for you. Do this in remembrance of me." And he did the same with the cup after supper, saying, "This cup that is poured out for you is the new covenant in my blood." (Luke 22:14–20)

Luke's institution narrative mentions two cups, one to be shared among the "apostles" at the beginning of the meal, with an eschatological reference, and the other "after supper," representing the "new covenant in my blood." A Jewish festive meal began with the drinking of a cup of wine as the guests arrived, with other cups following at intervals, so the cup Luke mentions as "after supper" (v. 20) is the mixed cup, the "cup of blessing" (1 Cor. 10:16).

Parallels between Luke and 1 Corinthians 11 are obvious. Jesus *gave thanks* for the bread, the equivalent of *blessing* it. In Luke the

197

bread is his body, "which is given for you," paralleling Paul's "for you." Luke also includes, in the same position as in Paul's account, "Do this in remembrance of me." The cup after supper is "the *new* covenant in my blood" in both Luke and 1 Corinthians 11.

Although the words of institution are not always found in the earliest eucharistic prayers, they have become part of the eucharistic tradition in both the Eastern and Western churches. In the Roman tradition, the institution narrative became so important that it came to be understood as absolutely essential to the "consecration" of the bread and wine. As late as the fourteenth and fifteenth centuries, a series of papal decrees declared the institution narrative to be the moment in which consecration, understood as transubstantiation, took place. Both Luther and Calvin, while adopting new forms of eucharistic prayer different from the Roman Canon, accented the importance of the words of institution to the extent that their role risked overshadowing other aspects of the prayer, thus appearing to narrow the eucharistic "consecration" to this one essential, reminiscent of the Roman tradition.

Meanwhile, in the Eastern church, the accent fell not on the words of institution, but on the epiclesis, the supplication that the Holy Spirit might bless the people and the gifts of bread and wine. Orthodox interpreters have held the opinion that it is the epiclesis, not the institution narrative, that is essential to consecration.

Contemporary liturgists, whether Eastern or Western, make the point that it is not appropriate to isolate one part of the eucharistic prayer as essential, as though everything else is dispensable, should some circumstance intervene to cause the time available to be limited. As Alexander Schmemann put it, "The sacramental character of the Eucharist cannot be artificially narrowed to one act, to one moment of the whole rite. . . . All parts and all elements are essential, are organically linked together in one sacramental structure. In other words, the Eucharist is a sacrament from the beginning to the end and its fulfillment or consummation is 'made possible' by the entire liturgy" (Schmemann, *Liturgy and Tradition*, 82).

Schmemann's argument is that the whole liturgy, from the moment in which the people enter the place of assembly to the moment when they are dismissed, *is* the eucharistic liturgy. The reading of Scripture and preaching of the gospel, for example, are integral to it. But certainly that portion of the liturgy that is specifically devoted to the Eucharist will include the entire eucharistic prayer, which is both Trinitarian and narrative in its structure, as well as the action at the altar/table, and must not be limited just to the institution narrative or just to the epiclesis.

Eucharist and Passover

All three Synoptic Gospels identify Jesus' last meal with his disciples as a Passover meal (Mark 14:12–16; Matt. 26:17–19; Luke 22:15), although it is also identified as "the first day of Unleavened Bread," which, according to Leviticus, is observed on the day *after* Passover (Lev. 23:5, 6). Neither the Gospel of John nor the apostle Paul identifies it as a Passover meal. Interpreters have endlessly debated, without reaching a level of certainty, the question of whether to trust the Synoptics or John as more accurate historically.

The fact that all four Gospels situated Jesus' Last Supper with his disciples in the season of Passover points to the Jewish festival as important background against which the meal needs to be understood. All four Gospels intended to make the theological point that Jesus' impending death would be for the world the central saving event that the exodus event had been for Israel. The chief theological reason for highlighting the exodus/Passover connection could be a common expectation that the Messiah would come at Passover. Even today, the Passover *Haggadah* includes prayer for the coming of the Messiah. One version includes this traditional prayer near the end of the Seder: "May the Merciful One grant us the privilege of reaching the days of the Mashiach [Messiah] and the life of the World to Come. He is a tower of salvation to His king, and bestows kindness upon His anointed, to David and his descendants forever. He who makes peace in His heights, may He make peace for us and for all Israel; and say, Amen."

Exodus 12

> The LORD said to Moses and Aaron in the land of Egypt: This month shall mark for you the beginning of months; it shall be the first month of the year for you. Tell the whole congregation of Israel that on the tenth of this month they are to take a lamb for each family. . . . Your lamb shall be without blemish. . . . You shall keep it until the fourteenth day of the month; then the whole

assembled congregation of Israel shall slaughter it at twilight. They shall take some of the blood and put it on the two doorposts and the lintel of the houses in which they eat it. They shall eat the lamb that same night. . . . I will strike down every firstborn in the land of Egypt. . . . The blood shall be a sign for you on the houses where you live: when I see the blood, I will pass over you. (Exod. 12:1–3, 5–8, 12b–13)

Instructions follow for the celebration of the meal. Important to the Exodus account is the description of the use of the blood of the slaughtered lamb (either a sheep or a goat), which was to be smeared on the lintel and the two doorposts of the Israelites' houses. Moses ordered the people to remain indoors until morning, because during the night, the Lord would "pass through the land of Egypt" and "strike down every firstborn in the land of Egypt, both human beings and animals; on all the gods of Egypt I will execute judgments" (12:12). The blood on the houses of the Israelites would serve to protect them from this sweeping divine judgment: "When he sees the blood on the lintel and on the two doorposts, the Lord will pass over that door and will not allow the destroyer to enter your houses to strike you down" (12:23).

After the night had passed, with its terrible holocaust of the firstborn, including Pharaoh's own, Pharaoh called for Moses and Aaron and told them to take their people and go. They could take their flocks and herds with them as well, and, poignantly, he asked them to "bring a blessing on me too!" (12:32).

Now, under pressure from the traumatized Egyptians, the people were pressed to leave quickly. "So the people took their dough before it was leavened" (12:34). The night in which the firstborn of Egypt were taken was remembered in Israel as a "night of vigil": "That same night is a vigil to be kept for the Lord by all the Israelites throughout their generations" (12:42). Verses 43–50 report the Lord's instructions with respect to participation in the meal by foreigners, slaves, hired servants, and so forth, probably because a "mixed crowd" left Egypt with the Israelites (12:37–38). This section includes the instruction that the Passover lamb must be eaten indoors, "and you shall not break any of its bones" (12:46). The narrative records the instruction, along with directions that no bone of the lamb should be broken, that the meal should be eaten with "unleavened bread and bitter herbs" (Num. 9:11; Exod. 12:8).

200

A feature of the Seder meal is a question traditionally asked by the youngest person present: "And when your children ask you, 'What do you mean by this observance?' you shall say, 'It is the Passover sacrifice to the LORD, for he passed over the houses of the Israelites in Egypt'" (12:26–27). The question provides the occasion for a response that became, in the Passover *Haggadah* used in the Seder liturgy, a lengthy narrative detailing God's redemptive action. Israel does theology by telling a story.

The Christian eucharistic prayer similarly makes use of a narrative dimension, modeled after narratives of God's work in Israel and in Jesus Christ, found in both the Old and New Testaments: for example, "A wandering Aramean was my ancestor . . ." (Deut. 26:5–9), and "The God of glory appeared to our ancestor Abraham when he was in Mesopotamia . . ." (Acts 7:2–50). The second movement of the eucharistic prayer, called the Post-Sanctus or the Anamnesis, exhibits the narrative form even as it gives thanks. It begins with gratitude for God's covenant, implicitly evoking Noah, Abraham and Sarah, and all their descendants, and then for Jesus Christ, the living bread. Then it recalls his ministry, death, resurrection, and ascension.

All holy God, how wonderful is the work of your hands!
When sin had scarred the world,
  you entered into covenant to renew the whole creation.
As a mother tenderly gathers her children, as a father joyfully
    welcomes his own,
you embraced a people as your own and filled them with longing for
    a peace that would
    last and for a justice that would never fail.
Through countless generations your people hungered for the bread
of freedom.
  From them you raised up Jesus, your Son,
    the living bread, in whom ancient hungers are satisfied.
  He healed the sick, though he himself would suffer;
    he offered life to sinners, though death would hunt him down.
  But with a love stronger than death, he opened wide his arms
    and surrendered his spirit.
  On the night before he met with death, Jesus came to the table
    with those he loved.
  He took bread and praised you, God of all creation.
  He broke the bread among his disciples and said:

201

Take this, all of you, and eat it. This is my body, given for you.
When the supper was ended,
he took a cup of wine
and gave thanks to you, God of all creation.
He passed the cup among his disciples and said:
 Take this, all of you, and drink from it.
This is the cup of the new covenant sealed in my blood
for the forgiveness of sin.
Do this in remembrance of me.
Gracious God,
as we offer you our sacrifice of praise and thanksgiving,
we commemorate Jesus, your Son.
Death could not bind him,
for you raised him up in the Spirit of holiness
and exalted him as Lord of creation.
  (*BCW,* Great Thanksgiving E, prepared by the International
     Committee on English in the Liturgy, 143–44)

   The narrative embedded in eucharistic praying served, in turn, as the paradigm for the ecumenical creeds. The so-called Apostles' Creed and the Nicene Creed both mimic the prayer's Trinitarian shape as well as making use of the narrative form.

   Understood as a Passover Seder, the Synoptic institution narratives show Jesus in the role of the host who presides at the meal. At the Seder, various foods represent aspects of Israel's exodus experience: bitter herbs represent the bitterness of bondage in Egypt; the unleavened bread recalls the haste with which the people left when Pharaoh told Moses that they were free to go. "An indispensable feature of the seder, then as now, was the interpretation of . . . various details of the meal, a responsibility that fell to the father of a household or to the host in a larger gathering. Jesus naturally assumed this role. Imagine the startled response of the disciples when the host, taking the *matzah,* made no mention of the ancient exodus but instead solemnly declared, 'This is my body'" (Hare, *Matthew,* 297).

   In the New Testament, Jesus' death is a pivotal redemptive moment, parallel to the exodus event for Israel. Luke's account of the transfiguration uses that very word when he tells how Moses and Elijah "appeared in glory and were speaking of [Jesus'] *departure* (*exodos*), which he was to accomplish at Jerusalem" (Luke 9:31, emphasis added). It would be a crossing over from one status to another: from bondage to freedom (exodus); from sin, alienation, and death to life (cross and resurrection).

John 13:1–30

The Gospel of John differs from the Synoptics in that there are in John no words of institution, and the last meal with Jesus' disciples is not a Passover meal, although it occurs close to the festival: "Now before the festival of the Passover, Jesus knew that his hour had come to depart from this world and go to the Father" (John 13:1). The date for Passover was 14 Nisan in the Jewish calendar, and the meal occasion in John 13 would have been on 12 Nisan, with the crucifixion on 13 Nisan, the "day of Preparation" (John 19:31).

The Gospel of John sends signals that Jesus can be understood as the Passover Lamb. The lambs would need to be slaughtered on the "day of Preparation." In Exodus, Moses gave directions to the people that they should slaughter the Passover lamb, then "take a bunch of hyssop; dip it in the blood that is in the basin, and touch the lintel and the two doorposts with the blood in the basin" (Exod. 12:22). John's account of Jesus' passion mentions that, when Jesus called out in thirst, the executioners "put a sponge full of [sour wine] on a branch of hyssop and held it to his mouth" (John 19:29). The detail is not simply an incidental one reported for the sake of a comprehensive account. Hyssop, rarely mentioned in the Bible, is a clear point of linkage with the blood of the Passover lamb.

In addition, although the executioners broke the legs of the other crucified men (19:31–32) to hasten death, they did not break Jesus' legs (19:33). John sums up the account: "These things occurred so that the scripture might be fulfilled, 'None of his bones shall be broken'" (19:36), recalling that the ordinance for Passover had forbidden the breaking of any of the bones of the paschal lamb (Exod. 12:46). William Propp speculates that the Passover lamb served as a stand-in for a healthy human being. That being the case, "it must be flawless and whole, with no bones broken" (Propp, *Exodus*, 438). Jesus, as the new paschal lamb, must also be "flawless and whole."

In his account of Jesus' baptism, John anticipates Jesus' death and interprets the meaning of it when he describes the Baptizer crying out, when he saw Jesus coming toward him, "Here is the Lamb of God who takes away the sin of the world!" (John 1:29). The book of Revelation frequently speaks of a Lamb in reference to Christ: for example, "Then I saw . . . a Lamb standing as if it had been slaughtered" (Rev. 5:6). The *Agnus Dei* ("Lamb of God, you take away the sin of the world . . .") has had a place in classical eucharistic liturgies, as, for example, in the UCC *Book of Worship* (51), where it may be sung or said during the people's communion.

Clearly, the early church understood the Eucharist in terms reminiscent of the theology of Passover, but did not understand it to be a reenactment either of the Seder or of the Last Supper. None of the Gospel writers or the apostle Paul shows any interest in the menu at the Last Supper, none mentioning either the lamb or the bitter herbs. The use of a *loaf* of bread does not square well with the stringent requirement that only unleavened bread (e.g., *matzah*) be permitted in the house at Passover. There is no evidence that the early church used unleavened bread in their Eucharists, and, in fact, the Eastern churches have never used unleavened bread (Lathrop, *Holy Things*, 26). Nor did the church attempt to replicate any of the other distinctive customs of a Passover Seder, most especially, by reserving it for only an annual observance.

It is well to recall that the four Gospels were not intended as biographies of Jesus, as though they were attempts to pull together a disinterested historical record of his life. Rather, the Gospel writers produced interpretations of Jesus' identity and vocation as well as his impact upon his followers, using sources that recalled, through a theological lens, his life, ministry, death, and resurrection. That all four Gospels place Jesus' death within the orbit of the Passover season is important for theological reasons, and their agreement on that detail suggests that he was indeed crucified at that time of the year.

In Greek, the word for Passover is *pascha*, which was used by the early Christians to describe the cycle of events from the events of Holy Week to crucifixion and resurrection. "For our paschal lamb, Christ, has been sacrificed. Therefore let us celebrate the festival" (1 Cor. 5:7). The *Book of Common Prayer* makes the link between Passover and the Christian *pascha* explicit in its eucharistic liturgy at the breaking of the bread: "Christ our Passover is sacrificed for us," with the response, "Therefore let us keep the feast" (*BCP*, 364).

204   The classic service of the Easter Vigil also reaffirms the ancient conviction that Jesus' dying and rising *is* the Christian Passover.

Sisters and brothers in Christ,
on this most holy night
when our Savior Jesus Christ passed from death to life,
we gather with the church throughout the world
in vigil and prayer.
This is the Passover of Jesus Christ:
Through light and the Word,
through water and the bread and wine,
we recall Christ's death and resurrection,
we share Christ's triumph over sin and death,
and with invincible hope
we await Christ's coming again.

        (*BCW*, 297, emphasis added)

The language of the vigil moves from a past event toward the ultimate, eschatological hope. The striking thing about the theological meaning of the Passover meal for Israel, in ancient times and still today, is that it has to do, at one and the same time, with a memory of past redemption and also with anticipation of a redemption yet to come. How does memory shape our anticipation? The character of God as One who hears the people's cries of distress and acts on their behalf provides more than a clue to the way God still works and will yet work. The Eucharist and the Passover have in common that both celebrate God's saving work in the past as a sign that God may be relied upon for future redemption. "The formal parallelism between the Jewish and Christian hope—both look to the past, both hope for the future—affirms the profound degree of solidarity which unites the two faiths together in a common testimony to God's final victory. Should there not then be a common sharing of God's joy which links the *seder* and the eucharist into common praise?" (Childs, *Exodus*, 214).

While Jewish and Christian theologies and liturgies have their own distinctive identities, at the same time there are deep resonances each with the other. For example, both Passover and Eucharist point to a present reality: that the transcendent God becomes an immanent reality as well, entering into the life of the world in redemptive ways, in the liberation of the Israelites and in the incarnation of the Lord who was crucified and rose again. The testimony of Christians is that God continues to become an imminent reality as the Spirit manifests the risen Christ in the Eucharist even now.

205

The Passover meal is also quite clearly the celebration of the redemption of a *people*—not just individuals. This is true as well for the Eucharist, the meal at the center of the Christian assembly. It is not a meal to be eaten alone, but a meal that sustains and nourishes a people who share a common journey and a common hope.

CHAPTER 7

When the Meal Goes Wrong:
Apostolic Critiques of Practice

The Bible has a great deal more to say about meals than it does about sex. Sometimes it warns against gluttony or drunkenness, but more often it mentions food and drink in positive terms, a blessing for which gratitude would be the most appropriate response. Food and drink sustain life, but they also serve as the centerpiece for festive occasions. One can certainly appreciate and enjoy a solitary meal, but a shared table implies a relative intimacy that draws one into a larger circle of *koinōnia*.

The more closely one examines the New Testament, the clearer it becomes that the community that Jesus gathered around him was a meal-keeping movement. Jesus himself reports the hypocritical accusations against himself as well as against John the Baptizer. In neither case did their critics believe that either John's or Jesus' meal habits squared with a religious vocation: "For John came neither eating nor drinking, and they say, 'He has a demon'; the Son of Man came eating and drinking, and they say, 'Look, a glutton and a drunkard, a friend of tax collectors and sinners!'" (Matt. 11:19).

Jesus' ministry as a whole can be understood as one of feeding the hungry. Mary's Magnificat includes the words "he has filled the hungry with good things" (Luke 1:53). In the Beatitudes as Luke records them, Jesus says, "Blessed are you who are hungry now, for you will be filled" (Luke 6:21).

207

Meals play an important role in the four Gospels and in other New Testament materials that describe the ongoing life of the church after the resurrection of the Lord. With whom shall we share a meal? This is an issue in Jesus' own time and in his ministry; and even in the nascent church, traditional religious and cultural dispositions continue to exert pressure on Christian practice. Even now, these many centuries later, the issue arises in different form, and the larger culture continues to have a role in driving the questions. What does it mean to belong to a body that is "holy" and "catholic"—that is, one that transcends barriers of class and ethnicity and even of theological and political opinion? How does the church tend its own boundaries—or should it even have boundaries? Should Communion be limited to the baptized? What do our sacred rites have to do with life outside the worshiping assembly? Particularly, what do our sacred rites have to do with the hungry and the poor? As in the early church, eucharistic practices continue to be appropriately subjected to critical scrutiny. The process of engaging these questions is not new, but has its origins in the New Testament itself. It is helpful to begin with a closer look at the social meaning of meals in the larger culture during the New Testament period.

Traditions of the Banquet in the Greco-Roman and Jewish Worlds

The Christian Eucharist, or Lord's Supper, grew out of Jesus' own meal practice, which exhibits the imprint of a Jewish culture in which meals matter. Jewish meals in the New Testament period reflect not only Old Testament precedents, but also festive meals as they had developed in a Hellenistic, Greco-Roman culture in which meals served a social purpose, often as a vehicle for signaling a particular status in society. Dennis Smith's exhaustive study provides a great many details (*From Symposium to Eucharist*). Jews had become familiar with Greco-Roman banqueting practices and, well before Jesus' time, had assimilated them into the ways they celebrated their own festive meals.

208   The typical pattern for festive meals, whether in a Jewish or Greco-Roman setting, began with servants removing the guests' shoes and washing their feet as they arrive (e.g., Luke 7:44; John

13:3–5). The fact that servants were available indicates that those who hosted such meals were people with the means to support such an expense.

English translations of the Gospels sometimes obscure practices of the period, such as the custom of reclining for a festive meal rather than sitting. Luke 7:36 provides an example. The NRSV reads, "and he went into the Pharisee's house and took his place at the table." The Greek verb for "took his place" is actually *kateklithē*, "reclined." Couches covered with pillows were provided the guests, who reclined on the left elbow, leaving the right hand free to eat. Tables were provided to be shared by the guests. Each couch was adequate for three diners. Most rooms set aside for banqueting accommodated seven, nine, or eleven couches. Wedding banquets included women, although in a separate room.

The banquet was most often, but not exclusively, hosted and attended by aristocratic males. The hosts were necessarily people of substantial financial resources, with large homes and multiple servants. After the washing of the feet and the diners taking their places on the couches, it was not uncommon for servants to anoint the heads of guests with perfumes (Mark 14:3). To be on the guest list itself indicated a certain status in the larger community, but the host also ranked the relative status of his guests by the way he placed them in the room. Evidence of this practice in Jesus' time can be found in his instructions about how to deal with ranking protocols when his followers find themselves invited to dinner. "But when you are invited, go and sit down [Gk. "recline"] at the lowest place . . ." (Luke 14:7–14).

Although it was condemned by moralists of the time, it was permissible for the host to serve a lower quality of food or wine to those he determined to be of a lower rank. "Thus the issue of status was a problem that had to be resolved at every meal, either by assigning positions according to some standard of ranking within society, thus inviting possible jealousies and hard feelings at what should be a pleasurable event, or by attempting to do away with rankings altogether" (Smith, *Symposium*, 44). Even when the host ignored a ranking system, some guests "would be insulted if they did not receive their due recognition."

Banquets served a variety of purposes, including marking birthdays and funerals, or as the meeting of a club, or for religious purposes. Prayers preceded the meal, as recorded, for example, in the

209

story of the feeding of the four thousand (Mark 8:6–7). In Greek practice, if meat were on the menu, it would have been sacrificed to a god. It was quite common for the meal to end with the singing of a hymn to one of the gods, a practice mentioned at the end of the institution narrative in both Mark (14:26) and Matthew (26:30).

Clubs whose meetings were centered on the banquet might be burial societies, trade guilds, or state cults of the gods. "Thus any group that sought to maintain its group identity tended to model itself on the clubs. Consequently both Christian and Jewish groups were often taken to be equivalent to religious clubs" (Smith, *Symposium*, 89).

Although festive Jewish meals conformed to the prevailing meal customs of the larger Greco-Roman culture, Jewish piety adapted the typical pattern of the banquet to fit their community's own distinctive religious beliefs and practices. For example, the Jewish meal ended with the chanting of the *birkat ha-mazon*. The Pharisees, who were particularly zealous about framing their meals in a proper religious context, were equally careful both about keeping the Old Testament dietary laws and about guarding the table so as to avoid association with any who might be considered impure. Eating with persons who could not meet purity standards would have the effect of compromising one's own religious purity.

In Greek contexts, the symposium (*symposion*, "drinking together") followed the banquet itself and involved everything from entertainment to philosophical discussion. "The standard entertainment was the flute girl . . . being included in virtually every pictorial representation of a symposium and mentioned in nearly every description. Since flute girls and other entertainers were traditionally the only women allowed at a Greek symposium in the classical period, they tended to be considered as little more than harlots, and it is likely that many of them were" (Smith, *Symposium*, 35).

Entertainment often took a sordid turn, but not always. There might be dancers, acrobats, and poetry readings, for example, as well as serious conversation, ethical debate, or prayers. "Even the use of a question-and-answer format and the motif of instruction are part of the symposium tradition" (Smith, *Symposium*, 150). Prominent Jews also hosted symposia, as for example the one to which a leading Pharisee invited Jesus, as told in Luke 14:15–24. In fact, Luke is particularly interested in meals, as evidenced by the fact that he has more than twice as many references to eating as any other Gospel. One of his favorite means of telling a story is to place it in the setting of a meal, which distinguishes this version of the story from its parallel in Matthew's Gospel (Matt. 22:1–14). In Luke's version, when Jesus is the table guest of a prominent Pharisee, Jesus tells a parable in the course of the conversation, after which, one of the dinner guests said to him, "Blessed is anyone who will eat bread in the kingdom of God!" (14:15). Clearly the other guests are watching Jesus closely. He has already spoken about meal practices, but the dinner guest has given him an opening he uses to tell a story about someone who had invited guests to a great dinner, only to have them back out at the last minute, making their various excuses. The host in the story then sent out servants to gather guests more or less at random. Jesus is taking advantage of the meal's symposium format to teach the other guests that the banquet "in the kingdom of God" will require a larger table, and that the guest list will be compiled rather differently than they are likely to expect.

After Jesus' death and resurrection, the earliest Christian communities continued to meet over a meal. Meal practices in the New Testament period were diverse; sometimes, for example, there would be Eucharist with a full meal (called an Agape meal, or lovefeast), which practice was most typical in the earliest years of the Christian movement. Sometimes, particularly as Roman authorities grew suspicious of religious associations, the meal was Eucharist alone, following no single paradigm. This is not surprising, since believing communities were often at a great distance from one another, and the means of communication were few. As Gordon Lathrop has noted, "Meals are always local events—with local food, local meeting places, local participants, local customs. Of course they are diverse, especially so in a time that had no particular instruments of extensive uniformity" (Lathrop, "Reforming Gospels," 196–97).

Christian meal practices, however, did not all develop in ways equally faithful to Jesus' ministry and the deepest insights of the gospel. The New Testament itself bears witness to apostolic efforts to criticize some of the meal practices of the church, not just for the sake of changing diversity to something nearer to uniformity, but for the sake of exhibiting more clearly the heart and core of the gospel as represented in the holy meal. The apostle Paul made one of the earliest of these critiques, based on information he had received about the meals of the Corinthian church, as a move toward reforming eucharistic practice.

1 Corinthians 11:17–23a

Now in the following instructions I do not commend you, because when you come together it is not for the better but for the worse. For, to begin with, when you come together as a church, I hear that there are divisions among you; and to some extent I believe it. Indeed, there have to be factions among you, for only so will it become clear who among you are genuine. When you come together, it is not really to eat the Lord's supper. For when the time comes to eat, each of you goes ahead with your own supper, and one goes hungry and another becomes drunk. What! Do you not have homes to eat and drink in? Or do you show contempt for the church of God and humiliate those who have nothing? What should I say to you? Should I commend you? In this matter I do not commend you!

For I received from the Lord . . . (1 Cor. 11:17–23a)

Corinthian practice needs to be understood against a background in which the nascent church is being defined in terms of unity. "Because there is one bread, we who are many are one body, for we all partake of the one bread" (1 Cor. 10:17). Wayne Meeks's study uses sociological terms to make the case that it was essential for the young community to establish strong boundaries for the sake of group solidarity (Meeks, *First Urban Christians*, 160). Since the inclusion of the Gentiles put an end to the use of Jewish purity laws in the church, it became necessary to establish new practices that testified to and solidified a communal relationship among believers in Jesus.

The apostle, in his critique of the Corinthians' meal practice, reports that he has heard of "divisions" [Gr. *schismata*] in the community. Paul may be using irony when he suggests in verse 19 that "factions" [Gk. *haireseis*] are necessary to expose the difference between those Christians whose faith is genuine from those whose faith falls short.

That there was a serious problem associated with meal practice in the Corinthian church is evident. Determining the exact nature of the problem is a bit more difficult. Certainly the banquet tradition in the dominant culture had a powerful influence even among the Christians, who must have taken it for granted, much

212

as we today take for granted the cultural constructs that are part of our everyday environment. The Greco-Roman banquet tradition was one characterized by an institutionalized system of social distinctions, even though there were, within the system itself, critics of blatant inequalities. While the Corinthian church probably did not include persons of great wealth, it did include people who were relatively well off financially and of some status in the larger community.

Paul is writing the letter to the Romans from the neighborhood of Corinth, and he sends greetings from Gaius, "who is host to me and to the whole church" (Rom. 16:23). Gaius is one of those whom Paul had baptized in Corinth, along with Crispus, who had been "the official of the synagogue" (Acts 18:8) and "the household of Stephanas" (1 Cor. 1:14–16). Stephanas was probably the leader of the delegation who brought Paul a letter from the Corinthians (1 Cor. 16:17), and Paul recognized him and his household for having "devoted themselves to the service of the saints" (1 Cor. 16:15). Those named, and perhaps others in the Corinthian congregation, enjoyed a certain social status in the city as well as in the church because of their relative wealth and position. Although they were not likely part of the local aristocracy, they were in a position to do things for the Christian group that other members of the church would not have been able to do.

Accustomed to the ways of doing things that were deeply rooted in their culture, these relatively powerful people may have perpetuated in the church's meal practices the ranking patterns typical of the banquet tradition. It was probably the case that the more affluent members provided the food for everyone and, following prevailing custom, served the best of everything to those whose social status was similar to their own. The result was that, while some at the community meal had a lot, others had little: "[O]ne goes hungry and another becomes drunk" (11:21).

Some, apparently, started to eat before everyone had arrived (v. 21). The difference in arrival times might be related to the fact that the more well-to-do were in control of their own schedules and were likely to enjoy leisure time in the evening, while those of the working classes could not get to the place of assembly until they had finished their daily obligations. Another possibility is that some members brought food with them, and began eating before the formal start of the meal. Paul reminds the Corinthians that, if

213

it were merely a matter of satisfying their appetites, they could eat and drink at home. "Or do you show contempt for the church of God and humiliate those who have nothing?" (v. 22)

Paul contrasts *kyriakon deipnon* and *idion deipnon*—"Lord's supper" and "your own supper" (vv. 20–21)—with the latter highlighting the individual and the individual's personal resources in such a way as to obscure or disfigure the communal nature of the assembly. Distinctions in social class may have been the primary influence in perpetuating the ranking standards of the larger culture in the Christian congregation, but it is possible that other ways of determining status played a role. It is likely that the life of the congregation itself offered ways of achieving status not related to social class or standing in the larger community. For example, it is evident that "spiritual gifts" such as glossolalia, speaking in tongues, might confer status. The apostle addresses issues related to tongue-speaking in 1 Corinthians 12. The issue of divisions and factions, then, may be more complicated than simple divisions between relatively richer or poorer.

The assembly took place in a private home, of course, such as the home of Gaius, who had served as host to the whole church. The dining room of a private home would accommodate only a limited number of people, particularly if they were reclining, as custom dictated. "Other guests would have to sit or stand in the atrium, which might have provided space for another thirty to forty people" (Hays, *First Corinthians*, 196). It would be surprising if the host had not chosen to be surrounded by those of similar status in the dining room, whether identified by social class or status determined by the church, while lower-status members, including slaves and freed persons, would be relegated to the larger space outside.

Whatever the circumstances that caused it, there is no mistaking that the eucharistic meal in Corinth had become an occasion for serious distortion of the gospel. Even if the offending practices originated in simple thoughtlessness—an unquestioned mirroring of the larger culture—the result was that some members of the church had been humiliated, which was a way of holding the church in contempt and, implicitly, also the gospel it was meant to embody.

214   In the course of Paul's expressing his dismay and indignation at developments in Corinth, he shares with them his "institution

narrative," the earliest in the New Testament (see chap. 6). In these few verses (11:23–26) he points directly to Jesus Christ and his saving death in order to direct the Corinthian Christians back to basics as a way of refocusing their practice of the eucharistic meal. He follows the narrative with admonitions.

1 Corinthians 11:27–34

> Whoever, therefore, eats the bread or drinks the cup of the Lord in an unworthy manner will be answerable for the body and blood of the Lord. Examine yourselves, and only then eat of the bread and drink of the cup. For all who eat and drink without discerning the body, eat and drink judgment against themselves. For this reason many of you are weak and ill, and some have died. But if we judged ourselves, we would not be judged. But when we are judged by the Lord, we are disciplined so that we may not be condemned along with the world.
>
> So then, my brothers and sisters, when you come together to eat, wait for one another. If you are hungry, eat at home, so that when you come together, it will not be for your condemnation. About the other things I will give instructions when I come. (1 Cor. 11:27–34)

The apostle warns the recipients of his letter that it is an offense against the crucified Lord to eat and drink "in an unworthy manner." He urges the members of the little congregation to examine themselves first, and then to eat and drink. Paul is not directing the Corinthians, or us, to engage in a strenuous effort at introspection. The charge is simple enough: look at your practice through the eyes of those who have suffered, or are at risk of suffering, humiliation.

Paul's charge has been misunderstood over the centuries, leading to unfortunate consequences. In the medieval church, it was taken as a warning not to commune until after having achieved a state of ritual purity. One was required to make a confession and receive a sacramental pardon so as to be in a state of grace before communing. As a consequence, communion came to be associated with penitence, and communion became a pious exercise for the few who were prepared. Both the communal nature of the Eucharist and a sense of joy in the Lord crucified and risen became obscured. Fewer and fewer felt worthy to commune, so that most typically only the priest(s) communed at Mass. Eventually the

215

Fourth Lateran Council (1215 CE) had to require Catholics to commune at least once a year, at Easter.

The Reformed tradition heard Paul's warning in a similar way, and in the Church of Scotland and other Presbyterian churches, lengthy preparatory services preceded Communion Sundays, and church elders visited parishioners to distribute tokens to those whom they determined to be in an appropriate spiritual state to commune. Again, the Lord's Supper became associated with strenuous penitential acts, as well as the expectation that communicants should demonstrate intellectual understanding of the sacrament before approaching the Communion table.

In other traditions, the Pauline warning caused church members to stay home on Communion Sundays or, if they went to church, to abstain from Communion, for fear that they might actually be "unworthy." Unfortunately, this misunderstanding persists among some church members even today. Paul intended none of this. In any case, never did he say, "Examine yourselves, and if you don't like what you find, don't eat the bread or drink the cup."

Similar misunderstandings have accrued in response to Paul's warning that it is spiritually necessary for those who eat and drink to discern the body. Those who fail to do that "eat and drink judgment against themselves." Many in the church have heard this as having to do with the way communicants perceive the elements of bread and wine, as though an orthodox belief in the appropriate sacramental theology is a requirement for a true Communion. However, Paul is not requiring intellectual assent to a theory about the bread and wine, but insisting that those who participate in the meal recognize that, in the eucharistic meal, those who share it are, in fact, the "body of Christ."

Victor Turner, a cultural anthropologist, has used the word "communitas" to describe a phenomenon that is associated with a worshiping community. "Communitas" occurs in tandem with what Turner calls "anti-structure." In other words, as people enter the worshiping assembly, they leave behind the various statuses that identify them in everyday life. The banker serves Communion side by side with the person who works in a nursery school; the professor and the person who works for the lawn service both hand out service bulletins and take up the offering. "The heart of worship lies in its being a communitas experience which is related dialectically and perhaps paradoxically to the world of structure but is distinctly and critically different from it" (Nichols, "Worship as Anti-Structure," 405).

When worshipers return to their regular lives, they assume once again the various statuses they temporarily leave behind when they enter the worshiping assembly, but the anti-structural experience nevertheless has a continuing effect on their perceptions of themselves and their vocation in the world. It is something like this that the apostle intends when he writes of "discerning the body." "Another way to put this would be to say that the *communitas* experienced in baptism, in which divisions of role and status are replaced by the unity of brothers and sisters in the new human, ought to be visible, in Paul's intention, in the Supper" (Meeks, *First Urban Christians*, 159).

Those who go to church every week may understand some of the difficulty of discerning the body of Christ in the people who assemble for worship. For the most part, they are the same people one sees at the ball game, the farmers' market, and the school dance. They exhibit all the usual characteristics of any group of people, some who are remarkably gracious and self-giving, and others whose concerns seem to be very narrow. One sees the confident and the uncertain, the fortunate and the broken, the folks whose company one seeks and those whose company one is inclined to avoid. The observer, even while a member of this ambiguous company, needs to look carefully to discern in this assorted group the body of Christ.

The task of discerning the body of Christ extends beyond those assembled in our own congregations on Sunday morning. It requires us also to discern the body of Christ as manifested in churches very different from our own, of which we perhaps even disapprove.

The value of the denomination, even in these days when denominations are declining, is that it links people in disparate places and circumstances with one another. A United Methodist in San Francisco and a United Methodist in rural Tennessee may experience the world quite differently, but in denominational decision making they are required to take account of one another, even when to do so is uncomfortable. Stand-alone, nondenominational congregations have no such obligation. This may make their internal lives easier, but living out their church life without having to

217

deal with Christians whose situations are different from their own may mean that it will be just a bit too easy to avoid Paul's injunction to discern the body.

Paul writes in verse 29 about judgment, a theme in great disfavor among most mainline Protestants. Yet a God who takes us seriously must be a God who holds us to a high standard. Judgment is a form of love and of grace, because the intention of God's judgment is not retribution but a stimulus to healthy change and a commitment to justice. The truth is that when we distort the gospel by treating one another shabbily in the very heart of our worshiping assemblies, there will be consequences. One reason we are so wary of talking about judgment is that it is so very difficult to know exactly how and where and when such consequences may be manifest. We are called to a very great modesty at just that point. But we are also called to be deeply aware that it matters to God how we learn to see one another and treat one another and shape the community that bears Christ's name, because the church is meant to be a sign to the world of God's blessing, rather than a sign that deeply rooted inequities and discrimination are instituted by heaven and endorsed by angels.

When Paul declares that the consequences of the Corinthians' distortion of Christ's meal has led to some among them becoming weak, or ill, or actually dying, he is supporting his warning of judgment, and following biblical precedents. In the Old Testament, God more than once warned the people not to forget the Lord lest they perish, "because you would not obey the voice of the LORD your God" (Deut. 8:20). Yet Paul may not have been as modest as he should have been when he presumed that one could draw a straight line between specific, observable outcomes and the Corinthians' misshapen eucharistic practice.

"But if we judged ourselves, we would not be judged" (v. 31). Richard Hays suggests that Paul is saying that it was the *community's* responsibility to exercise internal discipline so that defective and humiliating practices might be identified and rejected. Otherwise, God will judge us, "so that we may not be condemned along with the world" (v. 32).

A notable feature of the Corinthian situation is that the assembly for the meal included women, which in Greco-Roman banquet culture was rare, although not unique. Women prayed and prophesied in the assembly just as men did (11:4). The issue for Paul was not whether they should be present, but whether they were dressed appropriately (11:5–6). "The role of women in the Pauline movement is much greater and much more nearly equal to that of men than in contemporary [i.e., ancient] Judaism" (Meeks, *First Urban Christians*, 81). The communal meal also included masters, slaves, rich, poor, Jews, Gentiles. The eucharistic meal in Corinth was, in a sense, already countercultural. However, Paul's point is that it was *inconsistently* countercultural, in such a way that its very nature as a community stamped in the image of Christ was distorted, thus urgently requiring apostolic rebuke and correction.

The apostle's concern for the integrity of the community, as represented by equality in the communal meal, indicates his concern that the poorer members of the congregation not be humiliated. This attentiveness to the poor became, over time, deeply embedded in eucharistic practice. In the Jerusalem church, the apostles "prayed and laid their hands on" Stephen, Philip, Prochorus, Nicanor, Timon, Parmenas, and Nicolaus, ordaining them to an ecclesiastical office that involved the distribution of food (Acts 6:5–6). Justin, writing his *First Apology* in Rome about 150 CE, describes a Christian Eucharist when it had been separated from the full, communal meal; he reports that "the deacons bring a portion [of the Eucharist] to the absent." Then he adds, "Besides, those who are well-to-do give whatever they will. What is gathered is deposited with the one presiding, who therewith helps orphans and widows" (Jungmann, *The Mass*, 14).

In some places the practice developed of worshipers bringing bread and wine from their own tables to be used in the Eucharist. As they arrived at the place of assembly, they placed these gifts, representative of their own lives, on a table provided for them. When the moment arrived for the gifts to be set apart by prayer and distributed sacramentally to the congregation, church officers took a portion of the offerings of bread and wine to be presented to the presiding minister for this purpose. When the service was over, the bishop-pastor sent the surplus of the people's gifts to be distributed to the poor. The people also provided alms that were distributed in the same way and at the same time.

Today, many churches continue the practice of an offertory procession at the Lord's Supper, when members of the church take to the altar/table at least some of the bread and wine to be used in the celebration. Some include foodstuffs that members have brought from home to be distributed to food pantries, soup kitchens, or others in need of it. In order to make the link between the church's Eucharist and its concern for the poor even more vivid, some suggest that it be made known that the monetary offering (or collection) at the Eucharist is always designated for use solely for services to those whose need is greatest. In other words, monetary gifts for the support of the congregation—utility bills, furnishings, staff salaries, and so forth—although they certainly fall under the category of ministry, might be collected at another time or in another manner.

Joel Lundeen's hymn "Now We Join the Celebration" points to both the communal nature of the Lord's Supper and its implications as we serve our neighbors:

> Lord, we share in this communion
>   as one fam'ly of God's children,
> reconciled through you, our brother,
>   one in you with God our Father.
> Give us grace to live for others,
>   serving all, both friends and strangers,
> seeking justice, love, and mercy
>   till you come in final glory.
>   (© Joel W. Lundeen, admin. Augsburg
>   Fortress; used by permission)

The Challenge of Unity in Communion

1 Corinthians 10:14–33

> Therefore, my dear friends, flee from the worship of idols. . . . The cup of blessing that we bless, is it not a sharing in the blood of Christ? The bread that we break, is it not a sharing in the body of Christ? . . . Consider the people of Israel; are not those who eat the sacrifices partners in the altar? . . . You cannot drink the cup of the Lord and the cup of demons. You cannot partake of the table of the Lord and the table of demons. . . . So, whether you eat or drink, or whatever you do, do everything for the glory of God. (1 Cor. 10:14–16, 18, 21, 31)

220

The apostle Paul is challenging an easygoing approach to the eucharistic meal—one that is only about taking nourishment in friendly companionship, not taking seriously enough the depth of the spiritual relationships continually being formed and deepened in every eucharistic occasion. The Christians' communal meal is not to be undertaken casually, nor are community meals in the local pagan temple to be enjoyed thoughtlessly, as though nothing much were at stake.

Paul had already, earlier in the same chapter, reminded the Corinthians that, although the children of Israel "were baptized into Moses in the cloud and in the sea, and all ate the same spiritual food and drank the same spiritual drink" (1 Cor. 10: 2–4), "Nevertheless, God was not pleased with most of them, and they were struck down in the wilderness" (v. 5). The crafting of the golden calf serves as a warning: "Do not become idolaters as some of them did" (v. 7). In other words, the apostle was warning them to beware of the serious perils of any association with idols.

The banquet customs of the Greco-Roman culture were such that the menu at meals celebrated in religious settings frequently featured meat that had been sacrificed to one of the local gods. Christians invited to such a meal faced a dilemma of conscience: should they partake of the meal, or not? Paul addresses the question first in chapter 8, but takes it up again here. In chapter 8, the apostle acknowledges that idols have no real existence and that Christians believe in one God alone. However, for the sake of members of the church whose consciences might be wounded, Paul advises those who are more sophisticated to refrain from consuming meat associated with the cult of a pagan deity. In chapter 10 Paul has not changed his mind, but this time he approaches the question from a theological rather than an ethical perspective.

The cup and the bread, Paul insists, are means by which we share in Christ's blood and in his body; we are joined in some way to him and to his saving death and united with him and one another in covenant relation. Paul justifies this claim by referring to religious practice in Israel, where priests eat of the sacrifices of the altar. "Every male among the priests shall eat of it; it shall be eaten in a holy place; it is most holy" (Lev. 7:6). This act of eating joins the priests to one another and to the Holy One to whom the sacrifice has been offered. Paul warns that it is not possible to share in food sacrificed to a pagan god, even though they have no ontological reality, without some risk. He is no doubt thinking of Deuteronomy, in which Moses charges Israel: "They made him jealous with strange

221

gods. . . . They sacrificed to demons, not God, to deities they had never known, to new ones recently arrived" (Deut. 32:16a, 17). The apostle declares, "You cannot partake of the table of the Lord and the table of demons" (v. 21).

The quotation from the Song of Moses (Deut. 32) is an indictment of Israel's having fallen into idolatry in times past. The people whom God has chosen for special service turned to "demons," the deities of neighboring peoples, gods who were not God. The apostle did not believe that these "demons" actually existed as rival deities, but he "affirms the existence of a world of spiritual powers hostile to God, who are associated with pagan cultic practice. . . . Those who participate in the temple meals are becoming 'partners . . . with demons'" (Hays, *First Corinthians*, 169). The very word "demon" has a sinister ring to it. Biblical monotheism has an exclusive character and is not open to the sort of compromise that makes room for other gods, however accommodating the local religious culture may be.

Language about God being jealous or about demons seems distant from twenty-first-century thinking. We may find it easier to say it in another way, but spiritual eclecticism, while it appears to be broadminded and generous, can be dangerous. We may be reluctant to speak of demons, yet whoever is familiar with the history of the twentieth century should be able to recognize that there is such a thing as the demonic. The twentieth century, not so long past, is one in which the demonic surfaced more than once: witness only the Armenian genocide, the Holocaust, mass executions in the former U.S.S.R., and the Rwandan massacres. The demonic can masquerade as a political or a religious movement or surface in the midst of otherwise positive political or religious phenomena.

Many persons who do not describe themselves as people of faith, and certainly not as religious, prefer to define themselves as "spiritual." "Spiritual" can be healthy, and it can be profoundly unhealthy. When it is private and exclusive, shuns community, and erodes mutual accountability; when it is so open and undiscriminating that it is unwilling to search out and commit to necessary distinctions between good and evil, true and false; when it scorns discipline whether intellectual or spiritual, it can be dangerous. The God of biblical faith calls us into a covenant relationship that does not leave room for devotion to rival deities, whether in the form of ideologies secular or religious, or designer spiritualities. God will not share place on a shelf next to an idol or a whole pantheon of gods.

The little Christian congregation in Corinth, vastly outnumbered in a pagan culture, faced every day the pressure of trying to find its bearings in a world oriented to a different compass from its own. Having been immersed in the dominant culture from birth, and continuing to be exposed to it in every aspect of their lives, those who had put on Christ had to work consciously and conscientiously to negotiate their way through the minefields of everyday decisions that seemed as deceptively simple as what and where to eat. Paul understood that for them to do this successfully while remaining faithful to the gospel they had received, they needed to set some boundaries. Boundaries would support a sense of group identity and solidarity and serve as a constant reminder that they were working from a different blueprint than the wider society.

Boundaries are tricky things. We may understand how a tiny minority might need to get a firm grip on its identity in order to keep from being washed away in the overwhelming tide of the majority. It may be equally urgent for us, in twenty-first-century North America, to understand how to get a firm grip on our identity as Christians in a culture we have for generations taken to be especially our own, that is, a "Christian" culture. Since the 1960s it has become increasingly evident to those who are paying attention that the dominant culture cannot be so easily characterized as "Christian." It is, at one and the same time, stridently secular and earnestly "religious," and its religiosity takes many forms, some Christian, some not. Counting the numbers of Christians in comparison to Hindus, Jews, and atheists will not help us much to form a clear picture of our situation. The new shape of North American society requires a new thing of us, and the new thing also calls for us to think about boundaries.

On the one hand, we mainline Christians know that God has called us not simply for our own sake, but for the sake of the world. To believe that makes us suspicious of boundaries. Further, we have watched as some American Christians have heightened boundaries and used them as a barricade against the world. Businesspeople advertise in "Christian Yellow Pages." Large churches build "Christian Life Centers" with running tracks, fitness rooms, and basketball courts complete with their own leagues, as well as coffee houses, schools, grills, and bookstores. Theoretically, it must be possible in some instances to live one's whole life in isolation from the wider culture. Boundaries that serve as barricades have the feel of sectarianism, and the resulting isolation seems unhealthy.

On the other hand, churches that lack a clear sense of boundaries can seem as though they are too ready to embrace the spiritual, intellectual, and moral fashions of the larger culture, with such a weakened sense of identity that they are neither willing nor able to make critical distinctions based on a commitment to the gospel. When this is the case, Paul's theological summons to recognize and keep boundaries is particularly relevant.

Boundaries need not mean either fencing Christians in or keeping other people out. They serve, rather, to clarify who we are and whose we are. Who we are certainly must include living with respect for our neighbors, whatever their faith or lack of it, but respect is not the same as indifference. Indifference is the easy way, because it frees us from the difficult duty of sorting things out and making necessary distinctions. Indifference tempts us to meld into the larger society and embrace a generic religiosity, leaving us so bland that we make uncomfortable neither our neighbors nor ourselves. But without a specific sense of identity as disciples of Jesus Christ, we have nothing much beyond good intentions to bring to the greater society.

The identity that is ours by virtue of baptism is centered in Jesus Christ crucified, risen, and ascended, who is made manifest among us in Word and sacrament. The Lord's Supper, our eucharistic meal, is the meeting place where the community is nourished, strengthened, and sustained—a continual sharing in the blood of Christ and in his body, where we find ourselves, in him, "one body" (v. 17). From that identity we are, every day, both individually and corporately, working out what such an identity means as we live with and for others, pursuing God's call to be a blessing to all the families of the earth. Just as observant Jews in North America need to think through how to meet the challenges of keeping kosher in a society whose food preferences and meal habits pose a challenge, Christians need to take account of the challenges we face in a culture that is, in many ways, increasingly alien, in order to support one another as we work out strategies to meet these challenges.

"Open" Communion?

The question of boundaries and the transcending of boundaries raises a question about so-called open communion. Most churches other than Orthodox or Roman Catholic welcome to Communion all who are baptized, but an issue under discussion today is whether that welcome ought to extend also to persons who are *not* baptized. In churches that in recent decades have sought to reverse the long-standing practice of virtually excommunicating baptized children, the question has arisen as to whether *unbaptized* children in the parish should also be welcome to commune. In an era in which the church has become more sensitive to seekers, some have argued that to exclude unbaptized seekers from Communion is more or less equivalent to reestablishing the kind of purity boundaries that Jesus' own meal practices challenged.

Although the New Testament offers no definitive answer, it is possible for those representing both points of view to cite possible precedents. For example, on the one hand, when the apostle Paul was aboard ship just before the fateful shipwreck off the coast of Malta, Luke tells us that he had urged all aboard to "take some food" to give them the strength to survive. "After he had said this, he took bread; and giving thanks to God in the presence of all, he broke it and began to eat" (Acts 27:35). In this verse we note the familiar sequence of verbs associated with the Eucharist. Was Paul celebrating a Eucharist that included people who were not baptized, perhaps motivated by the dire situation in which they found themselves? Or was Luke only highlighting typically Jewish meal piety as Paul presided as host at what might have been the last meal for all of them?

On the other hand, Matthew's parable about the guest who was thrown out of the wedding banquet because he was not wearing a wedding garment can be understood as an argument for excluding the unbaptized from the Eucharist (Matt. 22:11–13). Matthew's liturgical interest in this addendum to the parable is indicated in the fact that the word translated "attendants" in the NRSV is *diakonoi* ("deacons") rather than *douloi* ("slaves"), as in 22:3, 4, 6, 8, and 10. As early as the patristic age, the wedding garment was understood to represent baptism. Matthew's Gospel shows evidence of his concern that the church included persons who were not repentant

225

(e.g., Matt. 13:24–30, the parable of the Wheat and the Weeds). Geoffrey Wainwright believes that the parable may be evidence of a controversy in Matthew's church over the question of whether baptism was necessary for the Lord's Supper.

Although the New Testament itself does not clearly identify a precise rule that either includes or excludes the unbaptized from the Eucharist, from as early as historians have been able to determine, baptism preceded Communion. When the catechumenate was in full flower, unbaptized persons present in the worshiping assembly were dismissed after the service of the Word. Indeed, as more uniform practices developed, first communion was clearly an integral part of the rite of baptism itself, the newly baptized being led into the eucharistic assembly directly from the baptistery.

When the issue of open communion came before the General Assembly of the Presbyterian Church (U.S.A.), a task force appointed to study the issue reported in a document called *Invitation to Christ*. They noted that persons on either side of the issue are able to make persuasive arguments based on their readings of Scripture. Those who favor an open table are inclined to accent the theme of reconciliation, rooted in Christ's death to forgive the sins of all, leading to the breaking down of barriers such as race, gender, and relative power and position in society. Those who advocate against an open table are more likely to accent the fact that God has called out a covenant community, which, while not identical with the *basileia*, must maintain a recognizable identity as a distinct, covenanted people whose work is to bear witness in the world to God's coming reign.

Geoffrey Wainwright would side with those who take the latter position. His view is that, since baptism is the sacrament of repentance and faith, baptism *before* Communion is important to safeguard the distinctiveness of the church. He argues that "every blurring of the church's edges is a threat, sometimes more serious than others, to its continuing existence as a covenant group able to celebrate the signs that summon the world to that kingdom of God which is, for people who freely accept it, salvation" (Wainwright, *Eucharist and Eschatology*, 166).

The PCUSA task force reached a conclusion similar to Wainwright's. They wrote: "In our review of the literature the biblical-theological rationales used by those in favor of and opposed to open table practice seem to suggest that the fullest range of meanings

226

of baptism and the Lord's Supper—both God's expansive love and forgiveness and the call to be a community of disciples, the body of Christ in the world—is preserved and embodied through the normative practice of baptism before Eucharist" (*Invitation to Christ*, 24).

Ministers and members of the so-called mainline churches find it difficult to support the drawing of boundaries that give even the appearance of excluding people, whether they be the unbaptized children of church members or onetime Sunday morning visitors who came to church because their neighbor's child was playing French horn on Easter Sunday. While no one is likely to doubt the church's obligation to welcome one and all to the church's Easter breakfast or its Wednesday evening meal, it is not unrealistic to be concerned that an unconditional invitation to the eucharistic meal can suggest such indifference to boundaries as may pose a severe threat to the church's covenantal identity. The apostle Paul was not opposed to boundaries as such, but the boundary in which he was invested was a boundary marked by being "in Christ," rather than a gender, tribal, social, or ethnic boundary.

Those who advocate that baptism precede participation in the Eucharist see a sharp enough distinction between a specifically Christian identity and the general culture, in its secular, religious, and "spiritual" versions, as to raise cautionary flags against an open rite that may give the appearance of sanctioning an indifferent religious eclecticism. Their point of view would be that commitment to Jesus Christ matters, whether made by one seeking Communion or by a parent who promises to nurture their child in faith, and such commitment has traditionally been embodied in various ways in the baptismal rite itself. If they are right, an "open" communion poses a clear risk of blurring the boundaries or even encouraging a kind of spiritual dilettantism.

However, from the point of view of its advocates, open communion is grounded in the confidence that grace carries with it no conditions at all—not even commitment—and that the unconditionally welcoming posture is less risky than any marking of boundaries. Those who hold this point of view may also believe that open communion is likely to win more souls than is clearly defining baptism as the threshold for admission.

The Presbyterian task force is not ready to depart from the baptism-first policy, but it points out that "there is a strong biblical

227

crosscurrent . . . that would seem to allow or even call for the disruption of . . . regular practices if and when those sacramental practices wrongly serve exclusionary purposes" (*Invitation to Christ*, 24).

Ideally, the question of who may commune would best be settled by the careful and structured deliberations of denominations and ecumenical bodies. In the meantime, pastoral sensitivity and discretion are essential. The one-time visitor who communes so as not to stand out is surely a different case from the seeker who presents for Communion more than once. Harold M. Daniels reports a note printed in one church's order of service: "We invite all who seek the real presence of Christ to share with us in Holy Communion. If you have not been baptized and wish to receive regularly, please speak with the minister about the process that leads to Baptism" (unpublished manuscript). The note clearly indicates that communing and baptism are intimately related, and that the relationship needs to be followed up, even while leaving discretion for the possibility that communing may, in some cases, precede baptism. Opportunities for misunderstanding are legion, which means that open and frequent interpretation of practice is necessary.

The apostle calls both the Corinthians and us to eucharistic practice that is taken seriously, one in which covenant unity with Christ and his church serve to keep us grounded. "All things are lawful" (1 Cor. 10:23) then, as the apostle says. Christians then and now are not forbidden from engagement with the larger society or from working out the terms for such engagement. Different persons and different churches will handle the boundary questions differently. "But not all things build up" (1 Cor. 10:23). "So, whether you eat or drink, or whatever you do, do everything for the glory of God" (1 Cor. 10:31). It might be added, let the churches continue to consult one another to report what they are discovering in their varied experiences, as well as to invite the counsel of sisters and brothers.

Paul leaves to the discretion of the members of the Corinthian church whether they accept an invitation to a meal in a pagan temple. The key, in Paul's time and our own, is to ponder whether what we do will have an effect more positive than negative. Does it "build up"? Does our sacramental practice build up the church? Does it build up its members in faith? Does it build up the witness of the

228

covenanted community? It is far easier to have a hard and fast rule and stick to it. Established custom has a useful purpose and should not be abandoned lightly—but it is certain that it will not prove adequate for the exceptional situation.

The Limits of the Law

Galatians 2:11–14

> But when Cephas came to Antioch, I opposed him to his face, because he stood self-condemned; for until certain people came from James, he used to eat with the Gentiles. But after they came, he drew back and kept himself separate for fear of the circumcision faction. And the other Jews joined him in this hypocrisy, so that even Barnabas was led astray by their hypocrisy. But when I saw that they were not acting consistently with the truth of the gospel, I said to Cephas before them all, "If you, though a Jew, live like a Gentile and not like a Jew, how can you compel the Gentiles to live like Jews?" (Gal. 2:11–14)

Although the text is not explicit, it is likely that the meals to which it refers are the communal agape meals of which the Eucharist formed a part before the two were separated by circumstances. The common meal was the heart of the Christian assembly. Peter's stature was such as to lead the other Jewish Christians in Antioch, including Barnabas, Paul's mission partner, to set up a separate table. As Paul perceives, and as Christians have experienced ever since, "separate but equal" arrangements are likely to separate us from God. He uses the Greek word *hypokrisis*—not "hypocrisy" as the NRSV translates it in verse 13. Rather, according to Charles Cousar, the word more frequently means "apostasy" or "defiance of God" (Cousar, *Galatians*, 48).

It is not possible to know exactly who persuaded Peter to abandon his customary practice (v. 14) and to revert to the conventional separation of Jew and Gentile. They may have been Jewish Christians, but Cousar is persuaded that the "certain people from James" were representatives from the Jerusalem church who were themselves under pressure back home from non-Christian Jewish nationalists (Cousar, *Galatians*, 47). In Judea, ethnocentric

229

nationalism exerted a powerful force, and the Jewish Christians in Jerusalem may well have felt that rumors of open-table practices risked drawing the wrath of the nationalists. If that were the case, James's representatives from Jerusalem may have prevailed upon Peter to avoid contributing to practices that could stir retribution against the mother church, vulnerable as they were. Peter's submission then might be understood as an act of charity, a compromise made to protect the Jerusalem church, which ultrascrupulous and militant Jews would have considered to be guilty by association with the breach of purity customs in Antioch.

Paul was able to see the issue in a larger frame. Compromise may be a virtue, but not if it undermines the very foundation of the church's unity. Later in the same letter, Paul will write to the Galatians that by virtue of their baptism "there is no longer Jew or Greek, there is no longer slave or free, there is no longer male and female; for all of you are one in Christ Jesus" (Gal. 3:28). If distinctions were introduced into the community on the basis of official "Jewishness" characterized by circumcision and keeping Jewish dietary and purity laws, this baptismal unity would be fractured. Gentiles did not need to become Jews to be Christians; and Paul was not willing to see introduced into the church an option short of compulsion, that is, those Gentiles who could bring themselves to become Jews as a means of membership in the church would do so, while Gentiles who did not feel compelled to do so would not. Such an option would not improve the situation, since there would still be two tables, two meals, two separate congregations.

The apostle has seen clearly enough that the issue at stake had to do not merely with the ability to compromise, if necessary, to protect the mother church in Jerusalem from implicit or explicit threats of hard-liners within or without, but also with the very theological and spiritual integrity of the gospel itself. The church is meant to be the first fruits of a new creation, a sort of tentative model of a reconciled humanity (2 Thess. 2:13; Jas. 1:18). If the gospel of reconciliation does not reconcile—if it leaves in place two where there should be one—it loses credibility: "If justification comes through the law, then Christ died for nothing" (Gal. 2:21).

In Galatians 2:15–21, Paul proceeds to contrast "works of the law" with "faith," a familiar theme in his writings. The problem is not the law itself. The problem is that sin is at work everywhere in everyone all the time, and sin finds an opening precisely where the zeal for righteousness is strongest. Those most committed to keeping the law are made vulnerable by their very earnestness—vulnerable to a form of hyperscrupulousness that can lead to smugness and a sense of being among a spiritual elite, who need to hold themselves at a distance to keep from being contaminated by the other.

Paul Meyer, discussing a similar argument in Romans, understands Paul's reasoning to be that

> the effect of *sin* on the genuinely religious person who looks to God's Torah for life has been to produce exactly its opposite, death. This is not because the law has not been obeyed or because there is something demonic about the law. It is not because looking to God's Torah for life is somehow a lower order of human religion. The transcendentally . . . demonic nature of sin is its power to pervert the highest and best in all human piety, typified by the best in Paul's world, his own commitment to God's holy commandment, in such a way as to produce death in place of the promised life. (Meyer, *The Word*, 71)

Here in Galatians, Paul contrasts the law specifically with life in the Spirit (Gal. 3:1–3). The Spirit was manifested among Gentiles who responded to the preaching of the gospel, and the Spirit created a new community that embraced Jew and Greek, slave and free, male and female.

The church today, as in all previous centuries, still has to sort out how to balance a proper respect for the law with a proper respect for the Spirit, who may lead us to weigh the law differently as contexts change. Those who pride themselves on a strict and uncompromising keeping of the law are on dangerous ground spiritually, while those who are proud of not taking the law too seriously are in equal danger. Not every issue that demands our attention has been directly and unequivocally addressed in Scripture, making it necessary for us to pray, analyze, discuss, reflect, and ponder together in hopes of being led by the Spirit to a consensus of the faithful, or at least to learning how to live with one another without a consensus. Paul's treatment of the conflict in Antioch makes clear enough, however, that the church's eucharistic meal brings together what in other contexts has been separated. Any meal practice designed to exclude any of Christ's disciples must be criticized and reformed.

Banquet and Counterbanquet

Gordon Lathrop suggests that New Testament reports of conflict over meal practices such as those in the churches of Antioch, Galatia, and Corinth indicate that disagreement was not rare: "Not all of these widely diverse ancient meals were worth continuing or emulating" (Lathrop, "Reforming Gospels," 199). One of the intentions of the four Gospel writers may very well have been to "reform the assembly-and-meal practices of the churches for whom the books were originally prepared" (Lathrop, "Reforming Gospels," 199–200). The evangelists resisted the churches' willingness to conform to dominant cultural models that governed communal dining, as exemplified, for example, in the *deipnon* of Herod.

Mark 6:21–29 in contrast with Mark 8:15

> But an opportunity came when Herod on his birthday gave a banquet for his courtiers and officers and for the leaders of Galilee. When his daughter Herodias came in and danced, she pleased Herod and his guests; and the king said to the girl, "Ask me for whatever you wish, and I will give it." . . . She replied, "The head of John the baptizer." (Mark 6:21–22, 24)

> And he cautioned them, saying, "Watch out—beware of the yeast of the Pharisees and the yeast of Herod." (Mark 8:15)

Although Greco-Roman banqueting practices influence both festive Jewish meals and the subsequent agape meals-cum-Eucharists of the earliest Christian communities, both Paul and the writers of the Gospels attempt to reshape received practices theologically and practically. Herod's birthday party is a banquet (Gk. *deipnon* and *symposion*) that exhibits characteristics typical of the dominant tradition. Although not described in detail, the traditional pattern is evident in the text.

As we have seen, the banquet guests are males of a certain social and cultural status. Their social relationship reinforces their working relationships. Herod needs them, and they need Herod. No women are present, except perhaps as servants or as part of the entertainment. The meal itself is finished by the time Herod's daughter (stepdaughter?) is called in to contribute to the entertainment (symposium) part of the celebration. Her role is parallel to that of the ubiquitous "flute girl" so often identified as a major

232

player in the symposium. Josephus calls the girl Salome, although Mark calls her Herodias, and some ancient texts of the Gospel call her "the daughter of Herodias." The occasion has been memorialized in folk legend by reference to her supposed "dance of the seven veils," the title at least suggestive of an erotic element. Of course, there is no way to know the age of the girl or young woman, or whether the dance was a chaste affair or something more provocative. In any case, her performance pleases Herod and his guests so much that he impulsively promises to grant her whatever she asks. The girl, uncertain what favor to request, leaves the scene to consult with her mother, who shrewdly takes advantage of Herod's (perhaps drunken) promise by asking for the head of John the baptizer "on a platter."

Herodias (Herod's wife) "had a grudge against" John (Mark 6:19), because John had rebuked Herod, questioning the appropriateness of their marriage, since she had previously been married to Herod's brother. She had pressed Herod to arrest John and now perceives the opportunity to realize her desire to see him dead. Herod, whose promise to the young woman had been witnessed by his guests, is in a bind. Whatever his plan for John, Herod now has no choice but to do for his daughter what he has promised. The symposium on the occasion of Herod's birthday banquet thus ends on a grisly note.

It is by contrast with Herod's banquet that we read Mark 8:15: "Beware of . . . the yeast of Herod." In the context of the feeding miracle described in Mark 8, the warning seems rather abrupt and even puzzling. However, it can be understood as a critique of Herod and his banquet and the way it represents and perpetuates social power. Jesus' own meals in Mark's Gospel reject the status-loaded cultural traditions. Jesus eats with tax collectors and sinners (Mark 2:16) and feeds the hungry multitudes. Later in the Gospel, in a context related to a question of status, Jesus put into words for his disciples what he had been practicing: "You know that among the Gentiles those whom they recognize as their rulers lord it over them, and their great ones are tyrants over them . . . but whoever wishes to become great among you must be your servant" (Mark 10:42–43). Of course, Jesus himself has taken this servant role. Mark is commending to his community a communal meal practice that runs counter to that of the dominant culture, the worst of which is demonstrated in Herod's birthday banquet.

233

Mark 7:24–30

Mark tells the story of a Gentile woman in desperate straits who knew Jesus by reputation and had heard that he was staying with someone in the area ("the region of Tyre"). The Syrophoenician woman's daughter "had an unclean spirit." It is impossible to know exactly what that means in twenty-first-century terms, but it is clear the daughter's behavior was disturbing and that it caused her mother deep distress. The mother "begged" Jesus to remedy the situation. Jesus at first rejected her pleas with sharp words that, significantly, evoked the image of a meal: "Let the children be fed first, for it is not fair to take the children's food and throw it to the dogs" (Mark 7:27).

It does not soften Jesus' words to know that banquet customs in the Greco-Roman world were to throw leftovers to the dogs wandering about the neighborhood. That image would have come readily to mind to Jesus as well as to Mark. Perhaps if he had considered his response more deliberately, Jesus would have tried to explain that he understood his mission to be directed toward Israel, the people with whom he shared an ethnic and historical identity, and he had up to that moment perceived no authority to extend it to Gentiles. Of course, it is quite likely that Mark (or his source) framed Jesus' response in precisely the abrupt and dismissive words of the text because they were vivid and made use of reference to a familiar practice, offering the opportunity to dramatize a sharp turning point in Jesus' ministry.

The Gentile woman swallowed any offense she might have taken at Jesus' choice of words. In fact, she turned it back by making use of the same image when she replied, "Sir, even the dogs under the table eat the children's crumbs" (v. 28). The remarkable thing is that the Gospel portrays Jesus as having been persuaded: "For saying that, you may go—the demon has left your daughter" (v. 29). As Jesus—and Mark's readers with him—began to conceive his divine mission in terms that required stretching the imagination toward perceiving a place even for Gentiles, he framed his change of mind in terms of a meal. One cannot begrudge those who gladly consume what "the children" have left over. The desperate mother might trust Jesus more than some of his own disciples managed to, anticipating the movement of the Spirit in and through Gentiles as the Christian movement unfolded. She needed the nourishment she knew he could provide, and was not above begging and enduring humiliation for it. Subtly yet vividly the Gospel of Mark presents us with an image of Jesus' expanding table, at which even those taken to be unlikely diners will be nourished.

Following the encounter with the Syrophoenician woman, Jesus turned toward the Sea of Galilee and found himself "in the region of the Decapolis" (v. 31), where the population included many Gentiles. After healing a blind man, Jesus fed a crowd of four thousand people. When Jesus asked the disciples how many loaves were available for feeding the hungry crowd, they replied, "Seven" (Mark 8:5), a number that typically served as symbolic of Gentiles, just as the number twelve signified Israel. Mark's use of the story of Jesus feeding the crowd of Gentiles serves to signal that Jesus' encounter with the Syrophoenician woman marked a turning point that led to an opening out of his ministry.

Luke 4:14–30

> But the truth is, there were many widows in Israel in the time of Elijah, when the heaven was shut up three years and six months, and there was a severe famine over all the land; yet Elijah was sent to none of them except to a widow at Zarephath in Sidon. (Luke 4:25–26)

When Jesus returned to Nazareth, his hometown, he addressed the people in the synagogue. Prophets are taken more seriously when we are not acquainted with their families, nor recall their child-hood. As the saying goes, familiarity breeds, if not contempt, then skepticism.

Jesus' sermon was not calculated to curry favor with the home folks. He recalls for them a Bible story they must have known but preferred not to think about too deeply. During a time of famine, the prophet Elijah had visited a widow who with her son was starving to death. Elijah had asked the woman for a piece of bread, but she had none to spare. He asked her to use her very last resources to make him just a morsel to eat and promised her, "The jar of meal will not be emptied and the jug of oil will not fail until" the famine ends (1 Kgs. 16:14). What startled the congregation in Nazareth was Jesus' homiletic interpretation of the 1 Kings text. He reminded them that there had been plenty of starving widows in Israel in those days, and the prophet Elijah was sent to none of them, but rather to a Gentile woman in Zarephath. Jesus further offended

235

by offering the Gentile woman as a model of faith, since she had responded to the prophet's plea even when she and her son found themselves at the very meeting point of life and death. Luke uses Jesus' sermon to point again to an opening out of Jesus' ministry.

Sinners at the Table

Luke 7:36–50

> One of the Pharisees asked Jesus to eat with him, and he went into the Pharisee's house and took his place at the table. And a woman in the city, who was a sinner . . . began to bathe his feet with her tears. . . . (Luke 7:36–38)

In Luke's account of the woman who anointed Jesus' feet and washed them with her tears, the Lord had accepted an invitation to dine with a Pharisee. Jesus went into the Pharisee's home and "took his place at the table" (Gk. *kateklithē*, "reclined"). His host, unlike the widow of Zarephath or the Syrophoenician woman, was not a Gentile but a member of a strict Jewish party, known for scrupulous observance of the rules of purity. A woman identified only as a "sinner" came into the dining room with an alabaster jar of ointment. Because of the way houses of the time were constructed, it would not have been terribly difficult for someone to make an unexpected entry. She could have entered by the door leading into an atrium that led to a dining room, both open to the sky. The woman, whose sins are not identified, washed Jesus' feet with her tears and dried them with her hair, and then anointed his feet with the ointment she had brought with her. Jesus' host took the fact that Jesus accepted the woman's ministrations as a sign that he could not be a prophet or "he would have known who and what kind of woman this is who is touching him" (v. 39).

Luke describes Jesus' teaching, which corresponded to the postmeal symposium. Beginning with a story about two debtors who both owed money—one a lot and the other only a little—Jesus asked his host which debtor would be most grateful, were the debt to be canceled. Simon (the host) responded, logically, that the one who would be most grateful would likely be the one who had owed the most.

Jesus then contrasted the actions of the woman with the indifference of his host, who had provided no water for Jesus' feet, and added, "You did not anoint my head with oil, but she has anointed my feet" (v. 46). Jesus concluded with a theological point: the woman, who was guilty of many sins, showed great love, because she had much for which to be forgiven. Then he said to her directly, "Your sins are forgiven" (v. 48), after which the other guests began to speculate about his authority: "Who is this who even forgives sins?" (v. 49).

Understood as a critique of ways that religious purity rules had ruled some people out and some people in, the words of Jesus turned them upside down. Some who have been out, will be in; some who have been in, will be out. The woman who would never have been admitted to the table of the pious turns out to be the one whom the Lord welcomes most effusively, while the pious host is exposed as one who "loves little." The *koinōnia* of the Lord's table, as Luke demonstrates, is meant to include those who have no credentials to offer except for their love for Jesus and their wish to turn their lives around, so as to be oriented toward him. If this *koinōnia* excludes anyone, it is those who are so proud of their moral successes that they harden their hearts against God and neighbor. Their overscrupulous bookkeeping denies the grace of the God who freely forgives the sins of those who repent.

Luke 15:1–2, 11–32

> Now all the tax collectors and sinners were coming near to listen to him. And the Pharisees and the scribes were grumbling and saying, "This fellow welcomes sinners and eats with them.". . . Then Jesus said, "There was a man who had two sons. . . ." (Luke 15:1–2, 11)

There is a certain risk, in reading the Bible, that we may decide the notorious sinners have an advantage not available to those who always play it straight. We are already familiar with the genre of novels, films, and plays that show the prostitute with the heart of gold in a far more generous light than the church treasurer. The parable of the Generous Father may broaden the picture a little.

The parable is about two sons, and it involves food. Two sons enjoy a secure living in the bosom of their family. The younger son, seeking adventure and independence, asks his father for his share of the estate he stands to inherit sooner or later, and the father decides to bear the offense of granting the son's request, which is tantamount to wishing the father dead. The younger son, living off what he has been given rather than earned, squanders it and loses everything. He is hungry, perhaps for the first time in his life, and remembers that even laborers on his father's farm "have bread enough and to spare" (v. 17). Then comes a dramatic homecoming. Throwing aside the reserve that one might expect of a man of dignified standing whose trust, in this case, has been abused, the father runs to his penitent son, embraces him, and calls for a party. Once again, it seems as though the one who did all the wrong things ends up with a reward.

The boy's older brother is deeply hurt, because he has played by the rules his whole life long, yet their father has never thrown a party for him. He is bitter, and his bitterness puts him in a position every bit as alienated as that of the younger son had been. There are many people in the church and outside it who have more in common with the older son than the younger. They obeyed their parents and teachers, didn't get in trouble with the law, were neither wild or rebellious. They didn't cheat in school, didn't take what belonged to someone else, respected authority, paid their taxes, and were faithful about making an annual pledge to the church and/or contributing to the United Way. They mentored Scouts, coached ball teams, and took casseroles to the sick and the grieving. But . . . for them there have been no banquets in their honor, no medals pinned on their collars. It feels as though they have been taken for granted, while the attention has gone to penitent miscreants, who are featured in newsmagazines and get invited to speak in churches and to Kiwanis Clubs. Bitter. So, where is the father in relation to his older son?

The contrast between the younger and older sons may seem to give the advantage to the younger, but the older has not in fact been left out. For one thing, living by the rules that kindle respect for other people and personal discipline is a reward of its own, even when it doesn't lead to one's being the person-of-the-week. In any case, the father's love for both sons embraces them, in, through, and in spite of their apparent indifference to him. And, although it may seem an afterthought compared to a party for all your friends, it really is no small thing to be one to whom the father says, "All that is mine is yours" (v. 31).

Read as a commentary on the church's (eucharistic) meal practice, one may understand the parable to characterize God as one whose love and embrace reach out to both the rebel and the one who has kept the rules, even if grudgingly. This God, who opens arms to us rather than simply waiting for us to find our way, is the God whose love is embodied in Jesus' practice of sharing a table with sinners. Jesus' welcome to all kinds of people serves as a blessing, both for those who have lost their way, and for those who have been fortunate enough never to have lost it. God's love, expressed in the celebratory meal, is enough to feed and nourish and strengthen Jew as well as Gentile, Pharisee and sinner too—those who come to themselves sooner and those who come to themselves later (v. 17).

Acts 2:42–47

> They devoted themselves to the apostles' teaching and fellowship, to the breaking of bread and the prayers. . . .
>
> All who believed were together and had all things in common; they would sell their possessions and goods and distribute the proceeds to all, as any had need. (Acts 2:42–43, 45)

The assembly that devotes itself to apostolic teaching, the holy meal, and the prayers is one that is imprinted with a commitment to any who are in need. This text is not a directive to society in general, ordaining any particular way of ordering an economy, although its deep concern for the needy must certainly be important to church communities as they consider their own social and political contexts. Acts 6 describes an increase in the number of believers, and mentions a "daily distribution of food" (6:1). The texts both describe the Jerusalem church's concern for the poor and remind us that those who are beneficiaries of the Lord's kindness must never forget those who are dependent on our sharing that kindness in tangible ways.

History records that the church's eucharistic assemblies, from early on, led from the place of assembly to the distribution of both alms and food to those who had need. Eucharistic theology in our own times is not only about whether something "happens" to the bread and wine, or how it may be appropriate to speak about the risen Lord's "presence" in the Eucharist, or about just how important

239

it may be to use the words of institution or include a proper epiclesis. Those issues are not insignificant, but of equal importance is a eucharistic theology that links the holy meal with the actual feeding and nourishment of the poor. If a church has a clear and orthodox eucharistic theology but no means of expressing a visible commitment to those who need the basic things to assure them of life and dignity, then that church's orthodoxy is in fact compromised. As a church ponders ways to reform its eucharistic practice in such a way as to make it larger, more vivid, and more faithful, concern for the poor needs attention, both liturgically and in shaping diaconal service, as well as in regular catechesis.

As Lathrop writes, "The Eucharist will not solve world-hunger, but it will make a meaningful sign toward the poor and the hopeless. Such is a reform we still—and continually—need. The Eucharist ought not be centered on us and our consumption. It is to be centered on Jesus Christ for the sake of the life of the world. And that center is a continually revealed gift" (Lathrop, "Reforming Gospels," 210).

In the Taizé community in France, the assembly sings while they commune. In the repeated chorus, it is as though the Lord Jesus himself is calling out to those who trust him, and even to the whole world:

> Eat this bread, drink this cup,
> come to me and never be hungry.
> Eat this bread, drink this cup,
> trust in me and you will not thirst.
> (© 1984 Les Presses de Taizé France;
> with permission of GIA Publications, Inc.;
> used by permission)

CHAPTER 8

Real Presence

Eating together is an act of intimacy. Whether a meal is eaten in silence or accompanied by animated conversation, it joins us to others in ways not easily put into words, but recognized intuitively nevertheless. The word "presence" may at least point us in the right direction. When we eat together, we become at some level more than ordinarily present to one another. Both Jews and Christians have testified that in some meals we are especially present to God, and God to us. Those whose spiritual formation includes a eucharistic meal have also sensed a call to be present to others who may be distant, indifferent, or even hostile now, but to whom God is calling out that they also might come from north and south, east and west, to sit at table in the *basileia*.

The eucharistic meal, the Lord's Supper, is intimately linked to the Lord's Day, the day of the resurrection, with its attendant promises. It is a meal that shapes our expectations and forms in us an identity in which rehearsing how to be present to God and to one another and to the stranger is key. The bread that nourishes us in this meal is at the same time both ordinary bread and bread "that came down from heaven."

Christians from early times have testified to their conviction that the risen Christ manifests his presence in the Eucharist or Lord's Supper. To affirm this is not to deny that Christ is present otherwise as well, but rather to say that the presence of the Lord is particularly focused, and typically experienced at a higher level of intensity, in the sacrament. The phrase used to communicate this conviction is "real presence," although the simplicity of the words conceals the fact that the nature and means of such "presence" has been a source of acute controversy in the history of the church.

> The fathers of the church had . . . spoken of a change in the bread and wine, and they referred to the change in a variety of terms: transmutation, transfiguration, transelementation, transformation. But their chief concern was not with explaining how the change was effected but with affirming that it did in fact occur. For this reason they were usually content to say that the change in the elements took place by the power of God. (Martos, *Doors*, 239)

The rise of scholasticism in the thirteenth century led to a desire by church leaders to provide a more careful description of what "real presence" meant. Hildebert of Tours was the first to use the term "transubstantiation," as a way of affirming that the substance of the bread and wine truly changed, even though their appearance did not. Thomas Aquinas developed the theory making use of Aristotelian philosophy, by which he offered a metaphysically based explanation of how the sacramental change occurred. The Fourth Lateran Council (1215 CE) endorsed the doctrine of transubstantiation, and it was strongly affirmed in the post-Reformation Council of Trent (1551). Clearly a benevolent intention informed the doctrine, to declare with assurance that believers could be confident of Christ's real presence in the Eucharist.

At the Reformation, many things once considered to be "settled" were unsettled. Martin Luther strongly affirmed "real presence," but denied transubstantiation. His position was similar to one that had been expressed by some pre-Reformation scholastics, called "consubstantiation." Consubstantiation, in its pre-Reformation version, meant that the body and blood of Christ coexisted in and with the bread and wine consecrated in the Eucharist. Luther did not use the term "consubstantiation" himself but added to the scholastic argument his understanding of the eucharistic implications of the ubiquity of the risen Christ. Wherever Christ is, he is present in his whole being, including his bodily as well as his spiritual presence. Luther was offended by the position of Swiss reformer Huldrich Zwingli, whose understanding can be characterized as "memorialist." For Zwingli, the accent fell on the church's act of remembering Christ and his sacrifice for us, rather than on his presence in the sacrament.

John Calvin, the reformer of Geneva, did not identify with any of these new or classical positions, but took one that in many respects is closer to that of the Orthodox. He affirmed Christ's real presence in the Eucharist but rested his argument not on any philosophical or metaphysical foundation but on the mysterious but trustworthy action of the Holy Spirit. Calvin wrote, "Now, that sacred partaking of his flesh and blood, by which Christ pours his life into us, as if it penetrated into our bones and marrow, he also testifies and seals in the Supper—not by presenting a vain and empty sign, but by manifesting there the effectiveness of his Spirit to fulfill what he promises" (Calvin, *Institutes*, 4.47.11, 1373).

The Eastern church has always strongly affirmed the real presence of the risen Christ in the Eucharist, but has refrained from tying that affirmation to any philosophical or metaphysical theory, choosing instead to speak only of the work of the Holy Spirit in the sacrament. While many Orthodox no doubt find themselves in accord with traditional Roman Catholic doctrine, they have not normally used the word "transubstantiation," or framed th.. eucharistic theology using that language. Alexander Schmemann is an articulate advocate of the classic Orthodox approach: "And so, the liturgy is accomplished in the *new time* through the Holy Spirit. It is entirely, from beginning to end, an *epiklesis*, an invocation of the Holy Spirit, who transfigures everything done in it, each solemn rite, into that which it manifests and reveals to us" (Schmemann, *Eucharist*, 222).

Today, the churches continue to exhibit diversity in eucharistic theology, from a traditional doctrine of transubstantiation at one end of the spectrum to a view at the other end of it as primarily a human pledge of fidelity to Jesus Christ, or even as a special kind of spiritual *koinōnia*. It remains true, however, that most churches affirm Christ's real presence in the Eucharist and that they have come to treat each other's eucharistic theologies more charitably than in earlier times, even though the traditional conflicts have not been altogether resolved. Yale theologian Hans Frei's view was that

243

the presence of Jesus Christ to faith is as unique and inconceivable as the resurrection from which it arises and the future summing up of all history to which it points. The contemporary mode of Christ's presence is indirect. It is not direct the way that it was during his earthly career, nor in the way that it will be again at the end of all things. . . . Yet even in this indirect and penultimate mode, his presence is nothing less than the mysterious and self-focused presence of God. . . . And just as Jesus Christ gives himself to sinners in physical form through his death, so he also gives himself to them as forgiven sinners in physical form here and now through the Sacrament. (Frei, *Theology and Narrative*, 254–55)

While "real presence" has traditionally referred to Christ, it can also be understood more broadly. The Eucharist is not a pious devotion for a few dedicated souls who scrupulously prepare themselves to commune, even though that is exactly what it appeared to be in Roman Catholic settings before Vatican II and often appears to be in many Orthodox parishes today, as Schmemann laments. The Eucharist is, rather, a communal act, a ritual manifestation of Christ's body, the church, in the world. God's salvation connects us to each other. There is no such thing as a solitary, isolated salvation, strictly between a single human being and God. Salvation is communal, even when circumstances cause us to be separated physically from one another.

"Real presence," then, refers as well to the need to be present each to the others and, as Christ was and is, to be present to those who are outside the boundaries for a variety of reasons. The eucharistic community is one that recognizes and honors God's call to be present to others who are separated from Christ and his church, whether "sinners," fairly or unfairly labeled, or those who are at the moment strangers to us and we to them. Jesus is the "bread that came down from heaven," and we are meant to be his diaconal servants, distributing the nourishment of the gospel to the hungry crowds. "Real presence," then, has a horizontal as well as a vertical dimension.

Old Testament Meals Eaten in God's Presence

244

"Real presence" is a doctrine articulated as such after the biblical period, but it was a phenomenon known to the experience of people as early as the Old Testament era. The altar, the focal point for worship in the Old Testament, was a place for sacrifices, presided over by priests who followed specific rules for preparing and offering them, whether animal or vegetable. Although some sacrifices were entirely consumed by fire, most were intended to be eaten (e.g., Lev. 8:31). Food and its consumption provided a link to the holy and occupied a place at the heart of Israelite worship, both before the centralization of the cult and after. It is not surprising, then, that meals exhibit a sacred dimension. God may become known in the sharing of a meal. "O taste and see that the LORD is good; happy are those who take refuge in him" (Ps. 34:8).

Exodus 18:1–12

> Jethro, the priest of Midian, Moses' father-in-law, heard of all that God had done for Moses and for his people Israel. . . . Jethro rejoiced for all the good that the LORD had done to Israel, in delivering them from the Egyptians.
>
> Jethro said, "Blessed be the LORD. . . . Now I know that the LORD is greater than all gods." . . . And Jethro . . . brought a burnt offering and sacrifices to God; and Aaron came with all the elders of Israel to eat bread with Moses' father-in-law in the presence of God. (Exod. 18:1, 9–12)

What is most striking about this text is the statement that Jethro, Aaron, and "all the elders of Israel" shared a meal *in the presence of God.* The Hebrew translated as "presence" is *lifne*, "in the face of." Exodus does not spell out what "in the face of" might mean. No doubt a certain measure of ambiguity is necessary, if only because modesty requires not pretending to be able to reduce a holy encounter to tidy explanations. Nevertheless, to speak of a meal consumed before God ("in the presence of God") is intriguing, because the testimony of the church from New Testament times has been that the risen Lord becomes present to the faithful in the Lord's Supper. In a text often interpreted eucharistically, Jesus said, "For where two or three are gathered in my name, I am there among them" (Matt. 18:20). To speak of a communal meal that takes place before the Holy One clearly did not originate with the Christian Eucharist. It was a testimony that could be made in Israel long before Christ.

A similar testimony may be found later in Exodus, after God has given the law to the people through Moses and they have sworn that "all the words that the LORD has spoken we will do" (Exod. 24:3). Moses then takes blood from sacrificed animals and splashes it on the people, calling it "the blood of the covenant." At that point, Moses, Aaron, two of Aaron's sons, and seventy elders of Israel "went up, and they saw the God of Israel" (24:10). "They beheld God, and they ate and drank" (v. 11).

Brevard Childs describes this as a covenant meal, "a eucharistic festival in which selected witness[es] celebrate the covenant sealing of vv. 3–8. The God of Israel has not become familiar or less awe-inspiring on account of the covenant, but a new avenue of communion has been opened to his people which is in stark contrast to the burning terror of the theophany in ch. 19" (Childs, *Exodus*, 507).

A meal that is, in effect, a "eucharistic festival," as Childs describes it, in celebration of the divine covenant, enjoyed in God's presence, might well serve as a template to help Christians describe their experience of the sacrament.

In a Deuteronomic text intended to serve the purpose of centralizing the cult, God forbids the practice of eating sacrifices in the various dispersed communities. The rationale behind this prohibition includes concern about abuses associated with worship practices at local shrines that had originally been devoted to Canaanite deities. "But you shall seek the place that the LORD your God will choose out of all your tribes as his habitation *to put his name there*" (Deut. 12:5, emphasis added). The people are instructed to carry their various offerings, sacrifices, tithes, donations, and the first-lings of their herds and flocks to the authorized shrine. "And you shall eat there *in the presence of the LORD your God*, you and your households together, rejoicing in all the undertakings in which the LORD your God has blessed you" (12:7, emphasis added).

Once again, a festive meal is said to be eaten "in the presence" of God. However concretely and specifically God's presence may have been perceived in a later period, after the construction of the temple, here Deuteronomy avoids saying that God is personally present at the central shrine. Deuteronomy understands God to dwell in heaven (26:15). Rather, God's presence is mediated through "his name." "Here we have a theologically very striking conception of the name, which is present at the shrine in almost material form, is regarded almost as a person, and acts as a mediator between Yahweh and his people" (von Rad, *Deuteronomy*, 90).

246

The image of "mediator" is striking. It is as though to speak of God's presence personally and directly evokes an experience so intense that it requires mediation to soften the encounter between the holy God and mortal beings, who cannot bear that presence straight on. In eucharistic theology, the epiclesis, or invocation of the Holy Spirit, may serve a similar purpose. God is *present*—yet it is a mediated presence, by the power of the Spirit. The classic Antiochene eucharistic prayer, Trinitarian in its form, reaches its climax in a specific petition for the Holy Spirit, an epiclesis. Here is an example from the Church of England:

> Pour out your Holy Spirit as we bring before you
> these gifts of your creation;
> may they be for us the body and blood of your dear Son.
> As we eat and drink these holy things in your presence,
> form us in the likeness of Christ,
> and build us into a living temple to your glory.
> (Common Worship. Eucharistic Prayer
G, 203, used by permission)

Some early eucharistic prayers have, instead of an epiclesis of the Spirit, an epiclesis of the Word. For example, an anaphora ascribed to Sarapion of Thmuis prays, "God of truth, let your holy Word come upon this bread, in order that the bread may become body of the Word, and upon this cup, in order that the cup may become blood of truth" (Johnson, "Archaic Nature," 86). The "name" in Deuteronomy 12:5 functions similarly. The Holy God of Israel, who is in "heaven," is nevertheless also present, in mediated fashion, in the place where this God chooses "to put his name there" (v. 5). The "name," like the Spirit, and like the Word, is the medium that serves to draw the divine presence near to the people, while softening the radical incommensurability between mere human beings and the Holy One.

The theme of sharing food with rejoicing appears again after the Babylonian captivity, when the exiles had returned to Jerusalem and were engaged in its reconstruction. The people had gathered into the square before the Water Gate, and the scribe Ezra had read to them "the book of the law of Moses" (Neh. 8:1). The people were so moved to hear the law of God that they wept. Nehemiah, the governor, along with Ezra and the Levites, declared the day to

247

be holy to the Lord. And Nehemiah said to them, "'Go your way, eat the fat and drink sweet wine and send portions of them to those for whom nothing is prepared.' . . . And all the people went their way to eat and drink and to send portions and to make great rejoicing, because they had understood the words that were declared to them" (Neh. 8:10, 12).

The several references to meals eaten before God (NRSV: "in God's presence") establish an Old Testament context that would inform the way Christians learned to describe their own eucharistic experience at the Lord's Table. A document from the World Council of Churches, attempting to formulate a consensus of several traditions, states that

> the eucharistic meal is the sacrament of the body and blood of Christ, the sacrament of his real presence. Christ fulfills in a variety of ways his promise to be always with his own even to the end of the world. But Christ's mode of presence in the eucharist is unique. . . . The Church confesses Christ's real, living and active presence in the eucharist. While Christ's real presence in the eucharist does not depend on the faith of the individual, all agree that to discern the body and blood of Christ, faith is required. (*BEM*, 12)

The whole action of the Eucharist has an "epikletic" character because it depends upon the work of the Holy Spirit (*BEM*, 13).

The Lord's Supper, or Holy Communion, is appropriately also called Eucharist—thanksgiving. It is a meal shared in joy and gratitude for God's redemption in Christ. It is far from the melancholy meal that has so often distorted eucharistic practice, both Catholic and Protestant. Old Testament precedents set the tone. The Deuteronomist, anticipating the end of the wilderness journey, reports that Moses and the elders charged the people to follow certain procedures when they shall have crossed the Jordan into the land of promise. They are to build an altar. "Then offer up burnt offerings on it to the LORD your God, make sacrifices of well-being, and eat them there, rejoicing before the LORD your God" (Deut. 27:6–7).

While historical study makes it evident that the Eucharist in the early centuries of the church was a celebration (a solemn celebration, but nevertheless a celebration), by the late medieval period the focus of the Eucharist in the Western church, but not in the Eastern, had shifted to a melancholy tone that focused on the

248

passion of the Lord and minimized his resurrection. The Protestant Reformers carried this melancholy tone into their own Eucharists even as they reformed the medieval Mass, and, for many Protestants even today, the Lord's Supper has something of the feeling of a funeral for Jesus. This is so, even though the texts in the several service books of the denominations have been shaped by resurrection and eschatological themes alongside the commemoration of Jesus' death. The texts and the rubrics that accompany them can easily be trumped by familiar practices that deserve scrutiny. (See Moore-Keish, *Do This.*)

When the Lord's Supper is understood primarily in terms of Christ's Last Supper with his disciples, the tone almost inevitably becomes somber. This is especially likely when the institution narrative occupies a place so prominent as to overpower the Great Thanksgiving (eucharistic prayer) as a whole. Focus on the Last Supper interprets that meal apart from those that took place during Jesus' ministry, including the feedings of the multitudes, and apart from meals with Jesus after the resurrection. When those meal traditions are permitted to contribute to the shaping of a church's eucharistic praying and practice, the Lord's Supper becomes a celebration of the Lord who was indeed crucified, but who is also risen. Of course, every celebration of the Lord's Supper will be shaded a bit differently, depending on the time and circumstances. On Maundy Thursday, or in a time of crisis or communal sorrow, it will be colored in a more somber tone than it will be on Easter Sunday or at the celebration of a wedding. Yet the sober and the joyful are always present in tension, neither permitted to obliterate the other.

Postresurrection Meals with the Lord

> [Peter said to those gathered in the home of Cornelius,] "They put him to death by hanging him on a tree; but God raised him on the third day and allowed him to appear, not to all the people but to us who were chosen by God as witnesses, and who ate and drank with him after he rose from the dead." (Acts 10:39b–41)

The New Testament witness is that the meal tradition did not end with the Last Supper, but persisted in the postresurrection community. When speaking of the risen Lord's "presence" in the eucharistic action, there is always the danger of saying too much or too little. Psychological language is too subjective, and metaphysical language tends to overreach. The Gospel writers make effective use of the narrative form to point to real presence.

Luke 24:13–50

Two of them were going to a village called Emmaus. . . . While they were talking and discussing, Jesus himself came near and went with them, but their eyes were kept from recognizing him. . . . Then beginning with Moses and all the prophets, he interpreted to them the things about himself in all the scriptures. . . . When he was at the table with them, he took bread, blessed and broke it, and gave it to them. Then their eyes were opened, and they recognized him. . . . They got up and returned to Jerusalem. . . . Then they told what had happened on the road, and how he had been made known to them in the breaking of the bread. (Luke 24:13, 15–16, 27, 30–31, 33, 35)

The story is a familiar one. The two people from the larger circle of Jesus' disciples are troubled and puzzled both by Jesus' crucifixion and by reports that some of the women have seen "a vision of angels who said that he was alive" (v. 23). Others have visited the tomb and verified the women's statements that his body was not there, but these travelers have experienced no special revelation. While they ponder this disturbing series of events, a third person joins them on the road and enters into their fevered conversation. The reader knows that this third person is Jesus, but the disciples don't recognize him. He responds to their bewildered account by engaging with them in a bit of Bible study, adding to their narrative summary of the situation his statement that Moses and the prophets should have led them to understand that the Messiah must suffer and then "enter into his glory" (vv. 26, 27).

The two travelers must be intrigued, because when they reach their destination, they implore the stranger to stay with them. It is late, after all, and night is approaching. Jesus, still incognito, serves as their guest, but also as their host: "When he was at table with them, he took bread, blessed and broke it, and gave it to them" (v. 30). The succession of active verbs posts the signal for eucharistic language: "took, blessed, broke, gave." "Then their eyes were opened, and they recognized him" (v. 31).

N. T. Wright observes that the first meal recorded in the Bible was eaten by Adam and Eve, who ate of the fruit of the one tree that

God had set off limits to them. The result of this unfortunate meal had been that "the eyes of both were opened, and they knew that they were naked" (Gen. 3:7). The meal at Emmaus is the reversal of the meal in the garden: "Their eyes were opened, and they recognized him."

"This, Luke is saying, is the ultimate redemption; this is the meal that signifies that the long exile of the human race, not just of Israel, is over at last. This is the start of the new creation. . . . This is the first day of the new week" (Wright, *Resurrection of the Son of God,* 652).

Whatever history lies behind Luke's telling of the story, the account also serves to describe eucharistic worship in the church as Luke knew it. When, in the assembly for worship, a presider takes, blesses, breaks, and gives the bread, and the community eats and drinks together, experience points to the likelihood that they will recognize the presence of the risen Lord in their midst. This recognition is certainly a gift of the Holy Spirit—not something for which human beings have a natural capacity or something that can be guaranteed just by following the rubrics. The testimony that comes from Luke's church has been repeated over and over throughout the generations, and is still the testimony of the church today. By the Spirit's power, people of faith are enabled to discern the presence of the Lord in the midst of the meal-keeping assembly.

Ironically, at the moment when the disciples' eyes are opened so that they are able to recognize who was at table with them, the Lord vanishes from their sight. There is a mystery here: not seeing, seeing, then not seeing; presence and absence. Luke reports that the two, having had this experience at the table, reflect ecstatically upon their discussion with Jesus on the road: "Were not our hearts burning within us while he was talking to us on the road, while he was opening the scriptures to us?" (v. 32).

Again, the way they reflect on their experience tells us something about the way Luke's church experienced the Word read and proclaimed: Hearts burning, the stranger's voice heard, he opening the Scriptures. The risen Lord, opening the Scriptures for the two travelers, has touched their hearts. While he links one thing with another, appealing to their reason, his words reach them all the way to their vital, thinking-feeling core. As Luke and his community 251 could testify, the word of the Lord encountered them at every level of their being.

With Luke, everything begins at Jerusalem and goes out from it. Nightfall notwithstanding, after the meal experience, the two disciples turn right around and rush back to Jerusalem to report to the eleven disciples and their companions. When the pair arrives in the city, they are startled to hear the report of the eleven disciples that the risen Lord has appeared to Simon (Peter), and they respond by reporting their own astonishing story about "what had happened on the road, and how he had been made known to them in the breaking of the bread" (v. 35).

At this point, the risen Lord appears among them. The text addresses the disciples' fear that they are seeing a ghost, that is, a disembodied spirit, but Jesus exhibits his wounded hands and feet in order to demonstrate that he is tangibly present. To reinforce the testimony to his physicality, the Gospel tells us that "They gave him [Jesus] a piece of broiled fish, and he took it and ate in their presence" (vv. 42–43). Much like the writer of John when he reports the appearances of Jesus behind locked doors in John 20, Luke means his readers to grasp the fact that the risen Lord cannot be understood in terms of familiar categories, like ghost or resuscitated corpse. The risen Lord is neither a disembodied spirit nor a reanimated dead body. He can appear among them suddenly and vanish from their sight; yet his wounds can be seen and touched, and he can eat a piece of broiled fish. The Lord's resurrection body is sui generis. There are no precedents, no other examples. The apostle Paul attempts in 1 Corinthians 15 what is ultimately impossible, that is, to put into human language and images what the resurrected self is like. One thing is clear: the resurrected body is not a disembodied spirit.

Neither Luke nor Paul wishes to explain the unexplainable, but only to bear testimony, perhaps having in mind Christians who claimed that Jesus could not have really suffered or died, and that he was essentially spirit rather than flesh. Muslims believe that the prophet Jesus did not die on the cross, but that he was replaced by an *eidōlon*, a sort of phantom double. Christian Science also denies that Jesus suffered or died, making the gnostic argument that the physical world and suffering are not real, but only the products of distorted thinking. The canonical Gospels take pains to testify to the true suffering and death of the incarnate Lord, who bears his wounds even in his resurrection body; it is nevertheless a body transformed by the power of God, in continuity with his earthly body, but not identical to it.

The remainder of Luke 24 reports the risen Lord saying that, as he had told them during his ministry, "everything written about me in the law of Moses, the prophets, and the psalms must be fulfilled" (v. 44). "Then he opened their minds to understand the scriptures" and charged them to bear witness "to all nations, beginning from Jerusalem" (vv. 45–48). The narrative ends with Jesus leading the disciples out of the city to Bethany, then lifting up his hands to bless them, then withdrawing from them and ascending beyond their sight, after which they return to Jerusalem.

The main point of Luke's testimony is that the risen Lord can and does become present to his people as the Scriptures are opened and as the meal is celebrated. It is not a matter of one *or* the other, but one *and* the other. The risen Lord becomes manifest to the community in the Scriptures opened, interpreted, and preached in the assembly; and in the meal in which eyes are opened to recognize and discern his presence. The two are similar and different, not identical but complementary. As Gordon Lathrop writes, "We need the meal side-by-side with the scriptures in order to understand what the scriptures are about" (Lathrop, *Central Things*, 48). What both are about is Jesus Christ, crucified and risen, seated at the right hand of the Father, interceding for us and the whole creation. He is our daily bread and our festive cup.

When pondering the question of Christ's "presence" among us, the dictionary will not help much. This sense of the risen Lord's presence in the assembled congregation is rooted in the experience of generations of worshipers. Presence cannot be precisely defined, certainly not as easily as the use of such concepts as "transubstantiation"; nor is it particularly helpful to resort to that vague adverb, "spiritually." However, Christian people for centuries have particularly identified a sense of Christ's presence in the Word and in the Eucharist. The Lord is present in human speech that becomes, by the Spirit, God's Word, penetrating mind and heart. He is present in actions of hospitality and promise expressed in wine and in bread broken, blessed, given, consumed, and internalized. Hearts burn, eyes are opened—not always on schedule, not always in the same way, not always overwhelming the sort of resistance that rises from indifference or skepticism. The presence is given for the hungry and thirsty self, whether it is registered and celebrated or not.

John 21:1–14

> Jesus said to them, "Come and have breakfast." . . . Jesus came and took the bread and gave it to them, and did the same with the fish. This was now the third time that Jesus appeared to the disciples after he was raised from the dead. (John 21:12, 13–14)

After the climactic events in Jerusalem, at least some of the disciples have returned to Galilee, and to the Galilean sea where they had first encountered Jesus. Even though Jesus had given the disciples a commission, sending them out equipped with the power of the Holy Spirit (John 20:21–23), it would not be surprising for them to take at least a little time apart to assimilate all of this, and what better refuge in which to do it than the familiar places and occupations of their earlier lives?

They were fishing at night, with no success. At daybreak, they caught sight of a figure on the shore, "but the disciples did not know that it was Jesus." They had not caught any fish. He gave directions as to where to cast their nets, and they were instantly rewarded with a huge catch.

When they came to shore, they found a charcoal fire with fish on it, and bread. "Jesus said to them, 'Come and have breakfast'" (v. 12). It is curious that, even though the Beloved Disciple has already identified Jesus as the figure on the beach (v. 7), the disciples were too intimidated to ask him directly to confirm his identity, "because they knew it was the Lord" (v. 12). Richard Leach's hymn rehearses the disciples' return visit to the Sea of Galilee.

> The empty-handed fishermen,
> The net that fills when cast again:
> Who shows abundance with a word?
> None dare to ask; it is the Lord.
>
> There's breakfast waiting on the shore,
> with bread and fish upon a fire.
> Who stands and welcomes, feeds, and more?
> Who dares to ask? It is the Lord!
>
> (Richard Leach, © 1994, Selah
> Publishing Co., Inc.; used by permission)

They dared not ask—curious, yet one can imagine both knowing and not knowing, sensing who it must be, and yet afraid of whatever small chance there might be that they could be disappointed. One can imagine being elated and still not wanting to spoil the moment by demonstrating yet one more time how slow they were to catch on, or being fearful of being perceived as presumptuous by asking Jesus to produce his credentials.

No one asked. The answer to their unasked question came when "Jesus came and *took* the bread and *gave* it to them, and did the same with the fish" (v. 13). Here are two of the telltale verbs that point to eucharistic action. John's manner of telling the story brings to mind the same Gospel's account of the feeding of the five thousand. In John's description of that occasion, "Jesus took the loaves, and when he had given thanks, he distributed them to those who were seated; so also the fish" (John 6:11).

In this Galilean resurrection scene, one may discern at the end of John's Gospel what had also been indicated at the beginning, in the story of the wedding at Cana. The message is that where Jesus is found, there is an abundance, whether of wine (John 2:1–11) or of food (in John 21, bread and fish).

Understood eucharistically, the Gospel pictures the risen Lord as the host of the meal, and there is more food than the seven plus their host can possibly consume. The theme of abundance points to the Lord's Table as a welcoming place, where there is nourishment sufficient for all who are hungry, and to the *basileia*, God's ultimate reign, which, like Eden, will lack for nothing. The book of Revelation supplies a snapshot of that eschatological abundance, when the river of the water of life will support the tree of life, "with its twelve kinds of fruit, producing its fruit each month" (Rev. 22:2).

The appearances of Jesus to disciples in his postresurrection body continued only for a time, concluding with his ascension. However, the apostolic church met regularly for a meal in which they were present to the Lord and to each other, and he to them, on the day that they called "the Lord's Day."

Lord's Day and Lord's Supper

Acts 2:42; 20:7

They devoted themselves to the apostles' teaching and fellowship, to the breaking of bread and the prayers. (Acts 2:42)

On the first day of the week, when we met to break bread, Paul was holding a discussion with them. (Acts 20:7)

Since the New Testament writers supply few details, it is often necessary to work backward from patterns and practices that are better documented in the second century to attempt to form a picture of the earliest period. In Justin Martyr's *First Apology*, which he composed in Rome about 155 CE, Justin wrote a brief description of Christian worship for interested persons who were unfamiliar with it (Thompson, *Liturgies of the Western Church*, 9). He writes,

> On the day which is called Sunday, all who live in the cities or in the countryside gather in one place. And the memoirs of the apostles or the writings of the prophets are read as long as there is time. Then, when the reader has finished, the president, in a discourse, admonishes and invites the people to practice these examples of virtue.... [W]hen we have finished the prayer, bread is presented, and wine with water; the president likewise offers up prayers and thanksgiving according to his ability.... The elements which have been "eucharistized" are distributed and received by each one; and they are sent to the absent by the deacons. (Justin Martyr, *First Apology*, 67)

In the period of the New Testament, practices were still in a process of development, and one may safely presume that they were not uniform. Nevertheless, from very early on it is clear that the new Christian communities were meal-keeping congregations, and that they assembled for the common meal on the first day of the week, Sunday, which came to be called the Lord's Day (Rev. 1:10). The first day, Sunday, was the day of the resurrection, but it was also the day of Jesus' ascension, the day of the first Pentecost, and possibly the day of his coming again. An early Syriac document rehearses the communal memory in a form that could be used liturgically:

256

> On the first day of the week let there be service, and the
> reading of the holy Scriptures, and the oblation:
> because on the first day of the week
> our Lord rose from the place of the dead,
> and on the first day of the week
> he arose upon the world,
> and on the first day of the week
> he ascended up to heaven,
> and on the first day of the week
> he will appear at last with the angels of heaven.
>
> (Wainwright, *Eucharist and Eschatology*, 97)

It is conceivable that the early Christians might have decided to celebrate the Lord's Supper annually, following the example of Passover. Or since the meal proclaimed the Lord's death, one might imagine a logic that would lead to observing it on Thursday, in honor of the Last Supper, or even Friday, in acknowledgment of the crucifixion. Alternatively, it might have been linked to the Jewish Sabbath, if only for the sake of convenience, since that was already established as a day set aside for communal worship. They chose none of those options.

Sometimes one hears it said that the Christians "changed" the Sabbath from Saturday to Sunday, but that is not the case. The first-generation Jewish Christians continued to observe the Sabbath as they always had, but added to it a weekly assembly of believers in Jesus on the first day of the week. The first day, our Sunday, would have been an ordinary working day, of course, so that the meeting of the Christians would likely have been after sundown on what we would call Saturday evening. Since Jewish practice considered a new day to begin at sundown, Saturday evening would be counted as the beginning of the first day of the week.

From early on, the day of the Christian assembly on the first day of the week was also called the "eighth day," signifying the conviction that the day of resurrection marked the inauguration of a new age, beyond the time-keeping represented by the seven-day week. If the Sabbath represents a celebration of the creation, after which God rested, then the Lord's Day represents a celebration of the new creation, vividly manifested in the resurrection of the Lord, with its implicit promise of a transfigured creation. Both the Lord's Day and the Lord's Supper were eschatological in nature,

257

and so the two are inescapably joined together. The Lord's Day recurred weekly, with the very fact that this was the church's day of assembly serving as testimony to the resurrection and the eschatological promise, and the Lord's Supper was at the heart of the weekly meeting.

> The meeting is called a meeting on the eighth day because it opens toward what cannot be reached simply by more days like those of the seven-day weeks we have known. In the meeting on the first day there is an opening toward the day beyond days, toward the last day of God. . . . That meeting has always meant . . . the encounter with the risen one and so with the end of death and the endless cycles of loss. . . . The eighth day is the beginning of a new creation. (Lathrop, *Holy Things*, 40)

Lord's Day and Lord's Supper were joined together from as early as we can determine. The meal, which proclaimed the Lord's death until he comes, was celebrated on a day that pointed to the resurrection of the Lord. Is the Lord's Supper about Jesus' death or his resurrection? As the postresurrection appearances of Jesus make clear, the risen Jesus is also and always the Jesus who bears his mortal wounds, even after the resurrection. At the same time, the crucified Jesus is always the risen Jesus, and ever shall be. The Lord's Supper is about the crucified Jesus and the risen Jesus, both together. Like the Passover, a celebratory festival whose origins nevertheless included the sorrow of the deaths of the firstborn, the Lord's Supper is a celebratory meal, because it can never be separated from the risen Lord who brings us over from death to life.

The first day or eighth day—the Lord's Day—was the day of assembly for a communal meal, and this practice must have begun very early. As early as 50 CE or shortly after, the apostle Paul testifies to the practice when he criticizes the Corinthians, because, "when you come together, it is not really to eat the Lord's supper" (1 Cor. 11:20). Luke, describing the first Pentecost with its many converts, recalled, "They devoted themselves to the apostles' teaching and fellowship, to the breaking of bread and the prayers" (Acts 2:42).

The communal meal, called an agape or lovefeast, in some cases certainly preceded discussion, teaching, preaching, or testimony, following the model of meal-symposium that prevailed everywhere

258

in the Greco-Roman world. The book of Acts describes Paul's visit to Troas: "On the first day of the week, when we met to break bread, Paul was holding a discussion with them; . . . he continued speaking until midnight" (Acts 20:7). At some point, the churches abandoned the community meal, perhaps because of the sort of difficulties that led to Paul's critique of the Corinthians, or perhaps because the Romans, suspicious of private gatherings, outlawed "dinner clubs." "The famous letter of Pliny gives evidence that by about the year 110 the Roman authorities in Asia Minor had banned the evening meals of the Christians as dangerous and immoral 'clubs'" (Lathrop, *Holy Things*, 44).

By the time of Justin Martyr's written report, the pattern had changed from a full communal meal, shared in the evening, to a ritual meal, probably in the morning. The order has evolved as well, from an order in which the common meal may have come first, followed by discussion, teaching, and so forth, to an order in which Scripture readings and discourse by the presiding officer came first, following the model of the synagogue, with the Eucharist following. The pattern would have been (1) "synagogue" service (of the Word), followed by (2) eucharistic meal.

This pattern, or *ordo*, became the norm in both East and West. In the medieval church, that part of the service that focused on the proclamation of the Word became less important and less diligently pursued. Both Luther and Calvin lobbied for the restoration of the service of Word and Eucharist as the weekly norm, but they were both overruled by circumstances—Calvin sooner than Luther. In Calvin's case, the Geneva city council overruled him. They had been accustomed to communing only once annually, at Easter, and were intimidated when imagining weekly Communion. Luther enjoyed more success, but it was not long lasting, with weekly Communion reduced within a century of his death, largely due to the influence of Enlightenment rationalism. In the eighteenth century, John Wesley was committed to a service that included weekly Communion, but, as with his predecessors, circumstances intervened to prevent its realization. Wesley was loathe to leave the Church of England. The Methodist movement did not understand itself to be a church with power to ordain, with the result that they lacked a supply of ordained ministers, and Wesley was not willing that non-ordained persons should preside at the Eucharist.

By the twentieth century, the typical pattern for Protestant worship was a service of the Word as the weekly norm, with Eucharist occasionally, usually at least quarterly. By the mid-twentieth century, the principal morning service for Episcopalians was Morning Prayer, perhaps with a weekly Eucharist in the early morning, often without music. By the dawn of the twenty-first century, it was far more typical for Episcopal churches to have as their principal service one that included both Word and Eucharist; and Lutherans were not far behind. In the meantime, other churches have evolved toward a monthly service of Word and Eucharist, although some observers argue that the greatest enemy of weekly Eucharist is monthly Eucharist—presumably because, after the evolution of the frequency of Holy Communion from four times a year to twelve times, it is easy for complacency to set in. Progress seems sufficient enough to reduce a sense of urgency and so permit resting on the relatively new status quo.

The earliest known norm was to link Lord's Day and Lord's Supper, and the sixteenth-century Reformers and Wesley would without a doubt be disappointed that the two continue to be so frequently separated. Calvin in fact used the word "defect" to describe the Lord's Day without the Lord's Supper. The absence of the eucharistic meal, which so mysteriously yet so intimately embodies Christ's presence to the worshiping assembly and our presence to one another, resembles the situation of being invited to dinner, only to discover that no meal will be served.

The Generous Table

Mark 2:15–17; Matthew 9:10–13; Luke 5:29–32

And as he sat at dinner in Levi's house, many tax collectors and sinners were also sitting with Jesus and his disciples—for there were many who followed him. When the scribes of the Pharisees saw that he was eating with sinners and tax collectors, they said to his disciples, "Why does he eat with tax collectors and sinners?" When Jesus heard this, he said to them, "Those who are well have no need of a physician, but those who are sick; I have come to call not the righteous but sinners." (Mark 2:15–17)

Sometimes Jesus extended an invitation to sinners, and sometimes they sought him out for a meal. In either case, he was present to them. In this text, Jesus has just invited Levi ("son of Alphaeus") to follow him. In the parallel passage in the Gospel of Matthew, the same person is identified as "a man called Matthew" (Matt. 9:9). In Luke's version of the story, Levi has given a banquet in honor of Jesus. Having been a tax collector himself, it is not surprising that Levi (or Matthew) invites other tax collectors to the meal.

Tax collectors were despised by the local population because they served the Roman occupiers, often against the interests of their own people. Fred Craddock reminds us that there were "poll taxes, road and bridge tolls, taxes on merchandise, and what we could call property taxes" (Craddock, *Luke,* 77). It was understood that the chief tax collectors in a district, who divided the work among others who worked for them, would collect considerably more than they owed the government, thus lining their own pockets.

It was not simply a matter of opinion whether someone was a "sinner" or not. "It was a term for those whose breach of the Mosaic law was known in the community, their violations having been formally or informally noted, and who were therefore excluded from the synagogue" (Craddock, *Luke,* 77). The Pharisees were a religious group who believed in a strict observance of the law. They were shocked to note that Jesus would accept an invitation to share a meal with those who were religiously and morally outcast.

Jesus' response to the criticism of the Pharisees is that the morally reprobate and the excommunicated need him more than people whose reputations are spotless. Luke's version of the story differs from Mark's and Matthew's in the last verse, where he reports Jesus' words as, "I have come to call not the righteous but sinners *to repentance*" (Luke 5:32, emphasis added). Jesus is not willing to settle for a strategy that leaves those who have lost their way to fend for themselves. He moves toward them, risking insult and rebuff, taking a chance that they will accept a hand extended to them, assess their situation realistically, and turn around.

However, just the fact of having shared a meal with Jesus, whether at his invitation or at theirs, is not a guarantee of admission to the *basileia*. "When once the owner of the house has got up and shut the door, and you begin to stand outside and to knock at the door, saying 'Lord, open to us,' then in reply he will say to you, 'I do not know where you come from.' Then you will begin to say, 'We ate and drank with you, and you taught in our streets.' But he will say, 'I do not know where you come from'" (Luke 13:25–27).

261

Luke shows us what it looks like when one of those to whom Jesus reached out responds positively. Zacchaeus, a chief tax collector who has become rich, has some knowledge of Jesus by reputation. When Jesus finds him up in a tree where he had hoped to get a good view of Jesus and his disciples as they pass by, Jesus calls Zacchaeus to come down, and invites himself to the man's house. Onlookers are scandalized, but Luke records that Zacchaeus repents, giving half of everything he has to the poor and paying back in quadruplicate anyone whom he has cheated. The Gospel does not tell us whether Jesus confronts Zacchaeus to bring about this about-face, or what the substance of their conversation may be. Whatever the nature of their meeting, Zacchaeus does not act under coercion, but feels drawn to follow the way that Jesus leads. The pericope ends with Jesus saying, "Today salvation has come to this house, because he too is a son of Abraham. For the Son of Man came to seek out and to save the lost" (Luke 19:10).

The Gospel writers were interested not in writing Jesus' biography, but in interpreting who he was, the nature of his mission, and, in particular, recalling events in his ministry that were relevant to pressing issues in the communities of which the evangelists were a part. No doubt the inclusive meal practices of the early churches had been noticed and considered scandalous by critics of the Christian movement, perhaps even by some Christians who continued to be influenced by traditional customs that sorted people out by categories, keeping them separated, particularly when it came to the intimacy of a shared table. By including the narratives of Jesus' sharing hospitality with those shunned by mainstream society, the evangelists provide an authoritative paradigm to support the church's practice of the communal meal that does not separate those with impeccable reputations, like the pious Pharisees, from those "in need of a physician."

In Jesus' willingness to take the risk of social disapproval by seeking out the company of those who "needed a physician," he lives out the promise implicit in his baptism, in which he deliberately identified himself with those weighed down by their sins and in desperate need of turning around. Even at the risk of being misunderstood and labeled a sinner himself, he is determined to go to where the outlaws are and open to them another way.

Hospitality

As Jesus Christ welcomes us and invites us into his presence, he calls us to welcome others and be present to them. This is difficult, living as we do in a largely urban society, in which we are mostly anonymous to one another and cannot easily assess the disposition or intentions of the stranger. Certainly, ways of extending hospitality will be different depending on local context, and prudence cannot be ruled out. Nevertheless, the rule of our gospel is hospitality, and ways need to be found to exercise it.

In Richmond, Virginia, downtown churches, Catholic and Protestant, take turns providing a free noon meal each weekday to people who need one, some of them homeless, others who have work nearby, and still others who drive to the meal site because their budget is too limited to provide one for themselves. More distant congregations in the same community send representatives to a downtown jobs center early in the morning to provide brown bags filled with breakfast, so that workers can begin the day with nourishment. Churches gather around the altar/table on the Lord's Day, then pack the bags or put on aprons to prepare meals throughout the week.

Sara Miles, having experienced a profound sense of engagement with Christ in the Eucharist, felt moved to give food away to anyone who needed it. She opened a food pantry at her church, St. Gregory of Nyssa in San Francisco, working directly from the altar as the primary point from which food was distributed, and requiring no IDs, no proof of need, no forms to be filled out. Miles understood this no-questions-asked distribution of food to grow directly out of the Eucharist, in which she had experienced the hospitality of Jesus (Miles, *Take This Bread*).

"To the ancients, 'hospitality,' which was represented as providing a meal to guests or strangers, was seen as a primary form of honoring one's neighbors. To provide hospitality was, in the social code of the banquet, to offer them a place in one's social world" (Smith, *Symposium*, 245).

Genesis 18:1–8

The LORD appeared to Abraham by the oaks of Mamre, as he sat at the entrance of his tent in the heat of the day. He looked up and saw three men standing near him. When he saw them, he

263

ran to meet them. . . . He said, . . . "Let a little water be brought, and wash your feet, and rest yourselves under the tree. Let me bring a little bread, that you may refresh yourselves." . . . And Abraham hastened into the tent to Sarah, and said, "Make ready quickly three measures of choice flour, knead it, and make cakes." Abraham ran to the herd, and took a calf, tender and good, and gave it to the servant, who hastened to prepare it. Then he took curds and milk and the calf that he had prepared, and set it before them; and he stood by them under the tree while they ate. (Gen. 18:1–8)

Many societies preserve narratives about some sort of heavenly visitation in which a human being, who does not recognize the divine character of the visitor, has been put to the test. The test has to do with meeting the obligation of hospitality to the stranger. In this text, the very first verse discloses to the reader that it was "the LORD" who appeared to Abraham at midday, sitting outside his tent at Hebron, although he knew only that three men suddenly stood before him.

The story is a theophany—a manifestation of the presence of God—but God's presence is hidden in the three unnamed visitors. In the longer pericope (including vv. 9–15), the three visitors meld into a single persona as the narrator records the dialogue. "They" (v. 9) ask where Sarah is. Then, shifting into the third-person singular, "He" (v. 10) predicted that, by the time of a second visit, "your wife Sarah shall have a son." (The NRSV reads, "Then *one* said," but the Hebrew is "he said.") Then in verse 13, it is "the LORD" who asks Abraham why Sarah had laughed when she heard this prediction.

It is not clear whether "the LORD" is one of the three visitors or somehow made manifest in the three, but it is not surprising that the biblical language should make use of ambiguity in an attempt to soften this almost unthinkable encounter between the holy God and a mere mortal. Andrei Rublev, the fifteenth-century Russian artist, painted a famous icon depicting the three visitors to Abraham. The artist understood the story to be an intimation of the Holy Trinity and used various iconic conventions to project that way of reading the story from Genesis. The idea is intriguing, but such an interpretation goes further than the text strictly permits, although devotional piety may cherish it nevertheless. What can be said is that biblical characterizations of God are not always either simple

264

or straightforward, and that is as it should be, because God is always more than we can comprehend or describe. Whoever fashioned the Genesis text is, like Rublev, an artist, who uses the artistic gift to project for us an image that is greater than our imagination—a worthy subject for our contemplation.

Abraham certainly passes the test of willingness to offer hospitality to strangers, because, enlisting the help of Sarah, he hurries to prepare a meal for them. Hospitality—being present to the other—moves in both directions. Abraham and Sarah welcome a stranger into their social world, and in that meeting they encounter One whom they could not have expected to appear at their door. In the New Testament stories of the feeding of the multitudes, the roles are reversed, and it is Jesus, the incarnate Lord, who becomes the host, extending hospitality to very human beings, all of whom are hungry.

Mark 6:30–44 (and parallels)

. . . And they went away in the boat to a deserted place by themselves. Now many saw them going . . . and they hurried there . . . from all the towns and arrived ahead of them. . . . He had compassion for them . . . and he began to teach them. . . . [H]is disciples came to him and said, . . . "[S]end them away so that they may go . . . and buy something . . . to eat." But he answered them, "You give them something to eat." . . . Then he ordered them to get all the people to sit down in groups on the green grass. . . . Taking the five loaves and the two fish, he looked up to heaven, and blessed and broke the loaves, and gave them to his disciples to set before the people. . . . And all ate and were filled . . . and they took up twelve baskets full of broken pieces. . . .

2 Kings 4:42–44

A man came from Baal-shalishah, bringing food from the first fruits to the man of God: twenty loaves of barley and fresh ears of grain in his sack. Elisha said, "Give it to the people and let them eat." But his servant said, "How can I set this before a hundred people?" So he repeated, "Give it to the people and let them eat, for thus says the LORD, 'They shall eat and have some left.'" He set it before them, they ate, and had some left, according to the word of the LORD.

265

The narrative of feeding the multitudes may be found in all four Gospels, which indicates that it was important to the early Christian communities. The evangelists are not interested in an impartial biographical account of the life of Jesus. Their interest is to interpret Jesus, and the feeding stories contribute to their interpretation. The deepest significance of the stories rests in their theological commentary, and readers are invited to ponder these things, rather than to search behind the texts for a historical event that would presumably be more authoritative than the canonical narratives.

The narrative is evocative of stories from the Old Testament, one of which is about the prophet Elisha. In Elisha's day, prophets could be found along with priests at the main shrines. When a man came to the shrine with his first-fruits offering, Elisha directed him to distribute it to those who were present, and miraculously the small amount of food was sufficient to feed a hundred people, with some left over. The Gospel feeding stories both recognize that God was at work in the prophet Elisha and subtly make the point that God is similarly at work in the ministry of Jesus, but on an even larger scale.

Another evocation of the Old Testament is the use of the Greek words *erēmon topon*, translated as "deserted place." A more literal translation is "desert place" or "wilderness place," serving to set up a parallel between Jesus' feeding of the multitudes and God's provision of manna (Exod. 16) and quail for Israel in the wilderness. Mark's description of Jesus directing the disciples to organize the people "in groups of hundreds and of fifties" is reminiscent of a similar organizing of the people by Moses (e.g., Exod. 18:25). What God had done before, God can do again. Jesus is new Moses as well as new Elisha.

The interpreter may take note of some striking evocations of Psalm 23. Jesus and his disciples reach the wilderness place by boat, and it is a place of "green grass" (v. 39). Jesus has compassion for the crowds, "because they are like sheep without a shepherd" (v. 34), reminiscent of the prophet Zechariah, who said, "Therefore the people wander like sheep; they suffer for lack of a shepherd" (Zech. 10:2). Mark's version of the story, the only one that has the "shepherd" reference, points to Jesus as the shepherd, which is particularly striking since the Hebrew of Psalm 23 is "YHWH is my shepherd."

The Lord is my shepherd, I shall not want. (Ps. 23:1)	They were like sheep without a shepherd. (Mark 6:34)
He makes me lie down in green pastures. (Ps. 23:2)	Then he ordered them to get all the people to sit down . . . on the green grass. (Mark 6:39)

The climactic moment in the feeding stories is the miraculous provision of enough bread and fish for a huge number of people.

You prepare a table before me; . . . my cup overflows. (Ps. 23:5)	And all ate and were filled; and they took up twelve baskets full of broken pieces and of the fish. (Mark 6:42–43)

Jesus, intending to take his disciples on retreat, since they have been so busy tending to needs of the crowds that they have hardly had time for a meal, has taken them to a quiet place. However, the crowds calculate where they are headed and manage to be on hand awaiting their arrival. Those who are engaged in any kind of work with people, including ministers and others who work in the church, would certainly understand if Mark had reported that Jesus simply took a day off, but that was not the case. Jesus sees the desperation of the crowds and "[has] compassion for them" (v. 34). He does not see the crowds as an unwelcome interruption but understands his agenda to be shaped by whatever the day may bring.

Jesus begins to teach the people. This is the ministry providentially laid at his feet for that day. The teaching goes on long enough that the disciples become concerned that somebody needs to do something about a meal. They suggest that Jesus send the people to the nearest civilized place to buy something to eat. His response is, "You give them something to eat" (v. 37). They are disconcerted, because feeding such a crowd would be enormously expensive, and their financial resources are few. Jesus hears their dismay, and dispatches them to canvass the crowd to see what supplies may be available. They report that there are five loaves of bread and two fish.

Jesus *takes* the loaves and fish and prays over them. He *blesses* and *breaks* the loaves, and *gives* them to his disciples to be distributed to the people. Note here the typical eucharistic sequence

267

of verbs. In Psalm 23, God is both shepherd and the host at the table, feeding the people; in the Gospel accounts of the feeding of the multitudes, Jesus is the one who both answers the need for a shepherd, and feeds the people. The disciples exercise the role of *diakonia*, the work of diaconal service. Everyone has enough to eat, with some left over, as in the days of the prophet Elisha. There is enough, and there will be enough.

Mark's narrative can be read as focusing on two primary actions: Jesus engaged in teaching, and the meal. It resembles the postresurrection meal in Luke 24, in which the same two primary actions occur: Jesus opening the Scriptures on the road, and the meal at Emmaus. This sequence mirrors the shape of Christian worship as it developed in the liturgical form of Word and Sacrament.

Fred Craddock observes,

> When the church appropriated this story for liturgical use, as bread and fish symbolism and the eucharistic language (took, blessed, broke, gave) indicated it did, the liturgy was not separated from the larger ministry to other needs. The Lord's Supper was joined to a full meal in which those who had shared with those who did not. Apart from feeding the hungry, the Eucharist becomes a ritual detached from life, just as feeding the hungry, apart from the Eucharist, is not fully satisfying. (Craddock, *Luke*, 126)

It is not surprising that the early church perceived a direct connection between their Eucharists and concern for the hungry.

John 6:1–14

Like Mark, John's Gospel signals a link between Jesus and Moses, but John does it by picturing Jesus having gone up a mountain and by bringing into the text a reference to the nearness of Passover. In John, Jesus *gives thanks* for the loaves, marking a slight distinction from the Synoptics, which report him as having *blessed* the loaves, and Jesus himself distributes the bread and the fish to the people, rather than deputizing the disciples to do it. He himself takes the diaconal role.

The verbs "took" and "had given thanks" signal that we are to understand that a eucharistic action is taking place. Sloyan indicates that the passage "is eucharistic in the widest sense. It invites to thanksgiving for every gift of God. Chief among these is Jesus who has come into the world" (Sloyan, *John*, 66). He it is who distributes

268

to the people with his very hands the gifts that will nourish them, just as he offers the same hospitality to us.

When we consider the whole of John 6, beginning with the bread of life discourse that focuses on the nourishment value of Jesus' teaching, followed by the explicitly eucharistic exposition in verses 51–58, we may discern once again a sequence that focuses first on the Word, and then on the sacramental meal. This was becoming the "shape" of the liturgy for Christians in both East and West.

"I Am the Bread That Came Down from Heaven"

John 6:25–71

> "I am the living bread that came down from heaven. Whoever eats of this bread will live forever; and the bread that I will give for the life of the world is my flesh. . . . My flesh is true food and my blood is true drink." (John 6:51, 55)

John's Gospel records that the crowds whom Jesus has fed continue to pursue him even after he has left the scene. Jesus teaches them after the miracle, after the fashion of meal-symposium, rather than before the meal, as in Mark. He proceeds to make a sharp distinction between ordinary food, such as they have received at his hands, and a different sort of food. He exhorts them to work for the latter, "the food that endures for eternal life, which the Son of Man will give you. For it is on him that God the Father has set his seal" (v. 27). The "seal" refers to the Spirit, given in Jesus' baptism, an authoritative sign that in him "God is represented and made present" (Haenchen, *John 2*, 290).

Jesus continues in dialogue with people in the crowd, who ask him what they must do "to perform the works of God" (v. 28). He replies, "This is the work of God, that you believe in him whom he has sent" (v. 29). The motif of belief is of primary importance in the Gospel of John. The Fourth Gospel is written in such a way as to make explicit what is more often implicit in the Synoptics. All four evangelists write from a postresurrection point of view, but John is more likely than the others to portray Jesus speaking of himself during his ministry in terms that have become familiar to the postresurrection church.

269

John refers to the feeding miracle as a "sign," in line with other actions reported as signs in his Gospel. The sign indicates that "This is indeed the prophet who is to come into the world" (v. 14), recalling Moses' having said, "The LORD your God will raise up for you a prophet like me from among your own people; you shall heed such a prophet" (Deut. 18:15; also see vv. 18–22). Believers will know how to interpret the sign, but people who are only interested in free food will not. It is unfortunate that when the circumstances of the moment cause us to focus on whatever problem is immediately at hand, we can become so fixed on it that we lose track of other important things. Contemporary society tends to be impatient with the need to look at the larger picture, with the result that our vision is narrowed to whatever is demanding our attention right now. Those in the crowd who are able to imagine how their hunger might be satisfied in ways beyond their need of the moment are more likely to recognize Jesus' gift of bread (a "sign") as a signal that God is in it, addressing some larger purpose, and calling them to participate in it.

Jesus' dialogue partners, as sketched by John, seldom understand what he is talking about, even though his meaning is clear to the insiders, the postresurrection believers. In this text, Jesus calls the people in the crowds to believe "in him whom [God] has sent" (v. 29), making use once again of "sent" language, so familiar in the fourth Gospel.

John pictures the crowd as pressing Jesus for some sign that will justify their believing in him. After all, they declare, quoting the book of Exodus, that their ancestors were given manna to eat in the wilderness—"bread from heaven" (v. 31). The crowd believes that Jesus is talking about ordinary bread. In midrashic style, Jesus probes these words, reminding them that it was not Moses who provided bread from heaven, but the Father. "For the bread of God is that which comes down from heaven and gives life to the world" (v. 33). Upon hearing this, they say, no doubt imagining a constant supply of food, "Sir, give us this bread always" (v. 34). In Jewish teaching, bread serves as a symbol for the Torah: "He humbled you by letting you hunger, then by feeding you with manna, with which neither you nor your ancestors were acquainted, in order to make you understand that one does not live by bread alone, but by every word that comes from the mouth of the Lord" (Deut. 8:3).

In John, bread represents Jesus' teaching. The feeding miracle "was a sign of [Jesus'] power to give life through the bread of his teaching" (Brown, *John*, 264).

At this point, Jesus says for the first time, "I am the bread of life" (v. 35). It is one of several "I am" statements in the Gospel of John, and the evangelist uses the Greek *egō eimi* ("I am") to send a subtle signal to those who know the Jewish Scriptures. In Moses' encounter with God at the burning bush, God revealed his identity to Moses: "I am the God of your father, the God of Abraham, the God of Isaac, and the God of Jacob" (Exod. 3:6). Moses pressed for a specific name, in case the people asked him the name of the God he had encountered: "'What shall I say to them?' God said to Moses, 'I AM WHO I AM.' He said further, 'Thus you shall say to the Israelites, 'I AM has sent me to you'" (Exod. 3:13–14). John employs the "I am" statements intentionally, clearly linking Jesus to the God revealed to Moses.

"Whoever comes to me will never be hungry" (v. 35). While the later church may have intuited what Jesus intended by these words, it should not be surprising if the words seemed puzzling to those who were reported to have been present on the scene. Describing himself as having "come down from heaven" (v. 38), he links the gift of eternal life with believing in the Son (v. 40). The phrase "comes down from heaven" evokes the gift of manna, "bread from heaven," nourishment provided by God. The phrase, used seven times in John 6, found a place in the Nicene Creed: "For us and our salvation he came down from heaven."

When Jesus says again, "I am the bread that came down from heaven," they complain. (Note the similarity with Exod. 16:2–4, which records the people of Israel *complaining* about the lack of food in the wilderness.) People speaking for the skeptics know Jesus' parents, and familiarity with his Galilean family makes them skeptical: "How can he now say, 'I have come down from heaven'?" (v. 42). In an echo of Jesus' encounter with Nicodemus in the "born from above" narrative in John 3, Jesus declares, "No one can come to me unless drawn by the Father who sent me" (v. 44).

Jesus contrasts himself with the manna in the wilderness. The manna nourished the people and sustained them for a time, but they were hungry again the next day, and eventually, like all mortals, they died. By contrast, "whoever eats of this bread will live

271

forever; and the bread that I will give for the life of the world is my flesh" (v. 51). Raymond Brown cites the church fathers as having contrasted Jesus' words with respect to the bread of life with the forbidden fruit in Genesis, which God warns must not be eaten, "or you shall die" (Gen. 3:3). Jesus says, "This is the bread that comes down from heaven, so that one may eat of it and not die" (v. 50). Drawing on Jewish sources from a later period, Brown comments further:

> We have evidence in later Jewish documents of a popular expectation that in the final days God would again provide manna—an expectation connected with the hopes of a second Exodus. . . . The Midrash Rabbah on Eccles. 1:9 says: "As the first redeemer caused manna to descend . . . so will the latter redeemer cause manna to descend." . . . The homiletic Midrash Tanhuma (*Beshallah* 21:66) is of particular interest when it speaks of the manna in a sapiential way: "It has been prepared for the righteous in the age to come. Everyone *who believes* is worthy and eats of it." (Brown, *John 1*, 265)

A common expectation of the time was that the Messiah would come on Passover. John has set the multiplication miracle and the subsequent teaching at a time when "Passover . . . was near" (6:4). John is juxtaposing Jesus' talk about a new kind of manna now "come down from heaven" with the Passover context in order that those who pay attention may make the connections and believe.

Most interpreters understand verses 25–51a as having to do primarily with believing in the revelation given in Jesus, with an interpretation of the Eucharist providing a sort of continuo embedded in it. Quoting Scripture, Jesus says, "It is written in the prophets, 'And they shall all be taught by God'" (v. 45). It is a call for faith in Jesus, come down from heaven, whose teaching is bread for the spiritually hungry. God reaches out to draw people to Godself, and when those who hear God's call in and through Jesus believe, they have "eternal life" (v. 47). "Eternal life" is not just living on and on for eternity. Eternal life is a quality of life that takes root in the believer even now. Many have attempted to describe it, including Diogenes Allen, who writes,

> Eternal life is a life utterly free of the burdens we now bear. It is free of failure, guilt, and sorrow; it is free of rivalry, gossip, and boasting; it is free of envy, jealousy, and strife; it is free of

boredom, depression, and addiction; it is free of unfaithfulness, deceit, and fraud; it is free of foolishness, violence, destruction, and war. Eternal life is a life filled with the love, peace, and joy that come from above. (Allen, *Theology for a Troubled Believer*, 132)

If that sounds too good to be true, at least for most of us as we attempt to make our way in this world, then let it be taken both as a promissory note and also as a state of being that does in fact touch us, lift us, and transform us and gain a foothold in us now and then, as we await the consummation of all things.

John 6:51b–58 marks a shift, bringing into the foreground eucharistic themes that are already present in verses 35–50 but in the background. It may be that these verses belonged originally to the Last Supper scene and were recast to expand the Bread of Life discourse that now precedes them. Jesus says, "I am the living bread that came down from heaven. Whoever eats of this bread will live forever; and the bread that I will give for the life of the world is my flesh" (v. 51). The saying both refers to the incarnation and alludes to the cross: "came down from heaven,"/"I will give for the life of the world." Verse 51 appears to be John's version of the words of institution, which he has not included elsewhere in his Gospel, paralleling the Synoptics' "This is my body, which is given for you" (Luke 22:19). Brown notes that in neither Hebrew nor Aramaic is there a word for "body," so that John's use of "flesh" may be nearer to the original eucharistic language of Jesus.

In response to critics, Jesus escalates his realistic speech, saying, "Unless you eat the flesh of the Son of Man and drink his blood, you have no life in you" (v. 53). This sort of language would have been shocking to Jews, for whom the law forbade the drinking of blood (e.g., Lev. 3:17), and it is jarring for many twenty-first-century people. The references to "flesh" and "blood" are not meant to separate Jesus into distinct biological or spiritual entities, but the two taken together simply indicate the whole person. What Jesus gives in the Eucharist is not a supernatural substance, but himself.

Eating and drinking bread and wine in the eucharistic meal embody something that is beyond the power of mere words to express or achieve. In the communal action of eating and drinking, we internalize the living Christ, enjoying a communion, or *koinōnia*, with him and the Father, in the Spirit.

273

The vividness of this language no doubt represents John's concern that Christians not "spiritualize" either the Eucharist or Christ himself, thus denying the reality of the incarnation. At the time of his writing, there were various gnostic and docetic communities for whom the material world was considered evil, in contrast to the spiritual world, which was ostensibly free from the contamination of the physical. That dualistic distinction reappears throughout the history of Christianity and has not disappeared today. Christian Science, for example, provides only for "spiritual communion," in which there is no physical element, either of bread or of wine. Sometimes even mainline Christians become embarrassed about the physicality of the sacraments, having been influenced more by the Neoplatonist elevation of the spiritual, with its accompanying suspicion of the body, than by classical biblical and incarnational theology. The soul/body dichotomy has so permeated Western perceptions that it contributes to the marginalization of the sacraments. Over against this "spiritualization," the church continues to testify to the incarnate Lord as it takes, gives thanks for, breaks bread, and gives it along with the cup to the faithful so that, as they consume this real, substantial nourishment, they may be nourished by the whole Christ in the eucharistic meal.

Alexander Schmemann, from the Orthodox tradition, articulates the eucharistic theology common to the early church and to the churches of the Reformation and others when he writes that, in the Eucharist, some sort of sacramental "conversion" happens,

> but this conversion remains invisible, for it is accomplished by the Holy Spirit, in the new time, and is certified only by *faith*. So also the conversion of the bread and wine into the holy body and blood of Christ is accomplished invisibly. Nothing perceptible *happens*—the bread remains bread, and the wine remains wine. For if it occurred 'palpably,' then Christianity would be a magical cult and not a religion of faith, hope, and love. (Schmemann, *Eucharist*, 222)

Even members of Jesus' circle found his teaching difficult. In fact, "because of this many of his disciples turned back and no longer went about with him" (v. 66). When Jesus asks Peter whether it is his choice to walk away, Peter responds as have many people of faith who struggle to understand deep and mysterious things.

He says, "Lord, to whom can we go? You have the words of eternal life" (v. 68). Having come to know something of God's welcoming, nourishing love and grace in Jesus Christ, how can we turn away? Even when we find matters beyond our ability to understand, what little we have understood is too dear to be abandoned. "To whom else shall we go?"

CHAPTER 9

You Have Prepared a Table

We have been invited to a wedding banquet. Food and drink will be provided in abundance, of course, but it will not be just any ordinary food, or just your everyday vintage of wine. We may not recognize all of the other guests, because some will come from a great distance, and others we will not have expected to be there. We have been invited, and there will be surprises, but it will all be good.

In a great deal of popular Christian piety, the reign/kingdom of God (*basileia*) is simply "heaven," that invisible realm to which our disembodied spirits fly one by one after death. However much we may cherish that image of heavenly reunion, the biblical images of God's reign/kingdom sketch a far bigger picture of our ultimate hope—one extending, in fact, to the whole cosmos.

The Christian faith is the story of God's redemptive action for the whole creation, and the resurrection of the Lord is God's promise of a transfigured creation: "For the creation waits with eager longing for the revealing of the children of God" (Rom. 8:19). The Bible projects that story on a wide screen. The *basileia* is about justice, which in history is elusive and often thwarted. Justice is not only about human systems, which can be challenged, resisted, and reformed, but also about making right what goes wrong by virtue of human exposure to the natural world and the contingencies of history. True justice for all who have been injured by every sort of injustice calls out for God's action. Human action is important and welcome and, when it has a successful outcome, to be celebrated, but it will always fall short of a true healing of the whole creation.

Although eschatological themes are important in both the Old and the New Testaments, they became muted in the Western church in the Middle Ages and have been peripheral to the interests of the churches of the Reformation and most Protestants. Attention was typically focused on the past, in which the apostolic faith is rooted and to which various parties turned to find authoritative sources to resolve issues in dispute. God's future became eclipsed, overshadowed both by the tendency to look backward and by preoccupation with issues related to personal salvation. The medieval Western liturgies sometimes retained the ancient link between the Eucharist and the *basileia* in some post-Communion prayers, such as this one in the *Missale Gothicum*: "Grant us, almighty God, that as we are refreshed in time by the supper of thy Passion, so we may be worthy to be filled by the banquet in eternity" (Wainwright, *Eucharist and Eschatology*, 65). However, particularly in popular piety, the image of a cosmic redemption had faded.

Liturgical texts and hymns can serve to conserve elements of the biblical witness even when they are out of fashion, embarrassing, and purposely neglected. The Protestant focus on justification, like the medieval doctrines related to salvation, paid so much attention to how salvation became realized in the individual Christian's life that the *basileia*, while not entirely forgotten, attracted no more scrupulous reconsideration than it had before the Reformation. What remained was just "heaven." However, there are some notable exceptions, for example, the eighteenth-century eucharistic hymns of John and Charles Wesley. Like the post-Communion prayer from the *Missale Gothicum* in the medieval period, they helped to preserve the eschatological vision until such time as the church might be ready to reconsider that from which it had largely turned away. For example:

> To heaven the mystic banquet leads;
>   Let us to heaven ascend,
> And bear this joy upon our heads
>   Till it in glory end.
> Till all who truly join in this,
>   The marriage supper share,
> Enter into their Master's bliss,
>   And feast for ever there.
> (Wainwright, *Eucharist and Eschatology*, 71)

278

Postmillennial preaching was commonplace in the United States for the better part of the nineteenth century, working from the presumption that Christ's return would follow a thousand years of social progress, to which congregations were earnestly exhorted. The accent on the here and now, while commendable in many ways, eventually eroded any eschatological vision and tamed it almost beyond recognition, with the *basileia* becoming an image for the benevolent social order that Christians were exhorted to build. For the most part, eschatology was left to the few who had a taste for it, usually of a sectarian bent. By the late twentieth century, a good deal of what passes for eschatology had become both bizarre and mean spirited, as, for example, the Left Behind series of novels (Tim LaHaye and Jerry B. Jenkins, authors).

The accent on bringing the reign/kingdom of God by human effort had fueled social reform movements but did not square well with a close reading of biblical texts. Perhaps emboldened by the rise of higher criticism, scholars, particularly beginning in the late nineteenth century, began to take the risk of turning their attention to biblical eschatology, and issues relating to it became much debated. Had Jesus promised that his return was imminent, only to be proven wrong? Had the eschatological promises already been realized in some way quite different from a final consummation? Should the eschatological materials in the Bible be understood simply as a longing for an idealized future, or as themes to be abandoned, no longer serviceable in today's world? Seminary students have been introduced to eschatological issues and debates, but the ordinary life of mainstream congregations is mostly untouched by them. While some evangelical or fundamentalist churches are obsessed with the Parousia (coming of the Lord), mainline Christians continue to be uneasy with it, not wanting to risk being mistaken for those whose approach smacks of fanaticism. "But, if something powerful and true about the way God is to be hoped in was lost[,] then it is necessary to see how it can be thought, prayed and lived through today. If God is the hope of the whole world, then both God's nature and the world's need to be conceived in ways that take the strange reality of the future more seriously" (Ford and Hardy, *Living*, 84).

In recent decades, the churches have at least begun to rediscover the Bible's eschatological vision and to struggle to find ways

279

to express it faithfully and positively. Liturgical and musical texts have held the image of the heavenly banquet in trust for us, and their prototypes may be discovered as early as the New Testament writings. Christian hope for the Parousia found liturgical expression in a short, exclamatory prayer found in the New Testament in both Aramaic and Greek versions. The Parousia was understood to be the inaugural moment of the longed-for *basileia*, in which God would publicly demonstrate the divine sovereignty in the whole created order.

1 Corinthians 16:22; Revelation 22:20

marana tha	*erchou, kyrie Iēsou*
Our Lord, come! (1 Cor. 16:20)	Come, Lord Jesus! (Rev. 22:20)

It is not certain whether the original Aramaic was "marana tha" or "maran atha." If it should be the latter, the translation may be the same, but it could also mean "Our Lord *has* come," which has the character of an affirmation or creedal statement of faith. In the eucharistic prayer, either or both understandings can be appropriate. Doxologically, we praise God that the Lord *has* come, and we pray that he *will* come to us sacramentally in the Eucharist and, at last, in his eschatological glory.

When set side by side with the Greek version in the book of Revelation, the grammar of 1 Corinthians 16:20 suggests that *maranatha* was used as an imperative; in other words, it served as a prayer for Christ's Parousia, as well as a petition for his presence in the eucharistic celebration. This understanding is supported by the use of *maranatha* in the *Didache* (an early-second-century church manual), in which it appears in a section that describes prayer at the Eucharist. In what may have been a dialogue between the presider and the assembly, the language used at the conclusion of the rite is this:

> Let Grace come and let this world pass away.
> Hosanna to the God of David!
> If anyone is holy, let him come. If not, let him repent.
> Our Lord, come!
> Amen.
>
> (*Didache* 10:6; in Richardson, ed.,
> *Early Christian Fathers*, 176)

Ancient eucharistic liturgies did not continue the early use of *maranatha* but, rather, substituted for it in places it had earlier occupied, "Blessed is he who comes in the name of the Lord!" (Ps. 118:26; Matt. 21:9), traditionally called the Benedictus Qui Venit, which is commonly sung (or said) at the end of the Sanctus in traditional and contemporary eucharistic prayers:

> Holy, holy, holy Lord, God of power and might,
> heaven and earth are full of your glory.
> Hosanna in the highest.
> Blessed is he who comes in the name of the Lord.
> Hosanna in the highest.
>
> (*UMBW*, 37)

Both *maranatha* and the Benedictus Qui Venit function liturgically in a similar way; they do not distinguish between prayer that the Lord may become present now, in the eucharistic action, and prayer that the Lord may come in the Parousia. The likelihood is that this both/and is intentional.

> The first coming of Christ in fulfillment of the Old Testament promise was itself a renewed promise which awaits an even greater fulfillment at the final coming. . . . The *Benedictus qui venit* found its place in eucharistic liturgies for the good reason that it can suggest, in a usefully ambiguous way, the present coming of the one who has come and who is still to come. To this extent it may be considered the legitimate replacement of *Maranatha*. (Wainwright, *Eucharist and Eschatology*, 89)

Eucharistic prayers from the early centuries, still in use in the Orthodox tradition, express gratitude not only for God's redemption in past events, but for future redemption. While we are accustomed to thinking of gratitude as directed toward something past, it can also be directed toward something yet to be. We, whose faith is rooted in the past events of Christ's incarnation, death, resurrection, and ascension, are also grateful for his present and continuing intercession for us, and our thanksgiving extends as well to his future Parousia, toward which we lean in hope. An example of gratitude that remembers forward as well as backward is from *The Divine Liturgy of St. John Chrysostom*, which may date from as early as the late third century: "Remembering, therefore, this

281

command of the Savior, and all that came to pass for our sake, the cross, the tomb, the resurrection on the third day, the ascension into heaven, the enthronement at the right hand of the Father, and the second, glorious coming . . ." (Jasper and Cuming, *Prayers of the Eucharist*, 71).

The newer eucharistic prayers found in the service books of most denominations recover these eschatological themes that have been preserved for us by the Eastern church. At the same time, contemporary eucharistic prayers, in contrast to the ancient ones, tend to highlight both the human life and ministry of Jesus in their narrative sections and the human consequences that we may expect from the Lord's Parousia as we pray for the *basileia*. For example, the one prepared for the International Consultation on English in the Liturgy includes this petition: "May his coming in glory find us ever watchful in prayer, strong in truth and love, and faithful in the breaking of the bread. Then, at last, all peoples will be free, all divisions healed, and with our whole creation, we will sing your praise, through your Son, Jesus Christ" (*BCW*, 145).

The biblical vision of God's ultimate future is one that looks for an ingathering of people from every point on the compass who come to a table where God will provide food and drink, nourishment not for the day only, but for eternal life. The meal that is prefigured by the church's Eucharist will be one marked by an abundance of wine, sufficient to make the heart glad, as on a day when the royal monarch comes or the doors of the wedding banquet open.

Peoples of the Earth Parade to the Banquet

Both the Old and New Testaments include representations of the eschatological hope set in the framework of a banquet, a meal with an abundance of food, and these vivid images influenced the development of the church's understanding of the Christian Eucharist.

1 Chronicles 12:38–40

All these, warriors arrayed in battle order, came to Hebron with full intent to make David king over all Israel; likewise all the rest of Israel were of a single mind to make David king. They were there with David for three days, eating and drinking, for their kindred had provided for them. And also their neighbors, from as far away as Issachar and Zebulun and Naphtali, came bringing food on donkeys, camels, mules, and oxen—abundant provisions of meal, cakes of figs, clusters of raisins, wine, oil, oxen, and sheep, for there was joy in Israel. (1 Chr. 12:38–40)

When Saul was dead, "they anointed David king over Israel" (1 Chr. 11:3). The text above is a description of David's coronation banquet, which, according to Dennis Smith, exhibits strong messianic overtones: "Here the warriors gather and celebrate with their new king, the prototype of the Messiah. The [tribes] come bearing gifts in tribute and "there was joy in Israel" (v. 40). This description reflects the form of the banquet of the end-time" (Smith, *Symposium*, 168).

Later, when David had put up a tent for the ark of God, and the ark had been brought into it, the king made offerings and then blessed the people: "And he distributed to every person in Israel—man and woman alike—to each a loaf of bread, a portion of meat, and a cake of raisins" (1 Chr. 16:3). Near the end of David's life, he led the assembled people in blessing God, and once again there was a huge feast: "And they ate and drank before the LORD on that day with great joy" (1 Chr. 29:22).

These festive meals, characterized by astonishing abundance, are especially joyful because they are celebrated in the presence of David, the anointed king. David, of course, established the dynasty from which it was expected the Messiah would come. Where the messianic king was, there was rejoicing, and the rejoicing took tangible expression in a festive meal, marked by abundance.

The prophet Isaiah frames another vision of the messianic banquet:

> On this mountain the LORD of hosts will make for all peoples
> a feast of rich food, a feast of well-aged wines,
> of rich food filled with marrow, of well-aged wines strained clear.
> (Isa. 25:6)

Death will be swallowed up forever. God will wipe away all the tears accumulated through the ages.

> It will be said on that day,
> Lo, this is our God; we have waited for him, so that he might
> save us. . . .
> Let us be glad and rejoice in his salvation.
> (Isa. 25:9)

283

Isaiah visualizes a parade of the nations. The mountain that will serve as the venue for a great feast for all peoples is Mount Zion. The scene is set after desolating judgment upon the whole earth, including Israel:

And it shall be, as with the people, so with the priest;
    as with the slave, so with his master;
    as with the maid, so with her mistress;
  as with the buyer, so with the seller;
    as with the lender, so with the borrower;
    as with the creditor, so with the debtor.
The earth shall be utterly laid waste . . .
    for the Lord has spoken this word.

(Isa. 24:2–3)

In Isaiah, the eschatological feast follows a time of judgment. As long as human history continues, sin will manage to flourish, appropriately accompanied by divine judgment. Judgment is not necessarily deferred until some indefinite future, but may be in process everywhere and always, wherever there are human beings. Times of suffering are not over for many people in the world, and even those who enjoy a relatively high standard of living are not free from suffering. The daily news brings reports of the deaths of innocent people by suicide bombings, death squads, drone strikes, landmines, rogue armies, assassins' bullets, school and workplace shootings, as well as random violence. The more clearly we are able to imagine what justice might look like, the more distressed we are to see justice despised, ignored, and violated. Corruption in high places, favors bought and paid for in legislatures and courts, and vicious calumnies are not rare, even in countries with an educated populace or ruled by constitutional law. It is the rule for the voices of the poor to be stifled and those of the rich and powerful to be magnified. Gender, race, and social and geographical location in most cases determine a person's destiny more than her or his own gifts and capabilities.

Any who are tuned in to the harsh realities of the world will turn with relief and hope to the words of the prophet who foresees that God has a word for us on the other side of judgment. God, whose mercy is at work in, through, and beyond judgment, will proclaim sovereignty over the whole earth. That fulfilled sovereignty will be such as to call for a huge party, an enormous banquet where there will be more than enough food and wine for everyone. The time of mourning will be over, replaced by the time of rejoicing. God's grace is at least as persistent as God's judgment, and appears over and over throughout history, but the eschatological banquet is Grace with a capital G, the ultimate act of grace, God's last word.

Human beings bear the responsibility and the burden of the sins with which we disfigure God's good creation. Judgment and grace are two sides of the same coin. Judgment is not about getting even, but is a form of God's resolute intention to make things right, whether by standing in our way when we are the problem, or exposing wickedness for what it is. God judges because God cannot be indifferent or impartial in the face of cruelty and injustice. An indifferent God cannot be a gracious God. God takes no pleasure in judgment, but judgment is necessary for healing—indeed, how can there be salvation without judgment?

But how do we recognize God's judgment? Is it possible to distinguish it from the plagues of suffering that we inflict upon ourselves? Or is it possible that judgment is hidden in and indistinguishable from some of the human-generated suffering, recognizable only to the discerning eye of faith? If we trust that God's judgment is at work, even though we cannot with certainty identify it as such, we may nevertheless take it seriously. One way of doing that is to restrain oneself from automatically discounting the dissenting voices, reflexively resisting the critics who point out wrongs and injustices in which we may be complicit, or from which we may benefit. If we take the biblical prophets seriously, we will position ourselves in such a way as to be able to recognize a prophetic voice when we hear one, even when it offends us and even when it costs us something. Judgment, like grace, is not just for other people or other communities. It is also for us, for our church, our nation, our tribe.

The postjudgment image of a parade of the nations, gathering for a festive meal, continues in Isaiah 55:

Come, buy wine and milk
    without money and without price. . . .
Listen carefully to me, and eat what is good,
    and delight yourselves in rich food. . . .
I will make with you an everlasting covenant,
    my steadfast, sure love for David.
See, I made him a witness to the peoples. . . .

See, you shall call nations that you do not know,
and nations that do not know you shall run to you,
because of the Lord your God, the Holy One of Israel.
(Isa. 55:1c, 2c, 3b–5)

The experience of Babylonian exile had seemed to discredit confidence that God would continue to honor the covenant established with the house of David. But (Second) Isaiah announced that the ruin of the house of David had not caused God's plan to fail. Rather, the covenant would now be extended to all of those who are obedient to God's word and commandment. The call to be "a witness to the peoples" had been David's calling, but now it will be the vocation of the whole community of the faithful.

Luke 13:22–30

And, at the last and glorious day, who will be welcomed at the heavenly banquet? Will they be those who have successfully managed to keep the commandments? Are they identifiable by nationality or ethnicity? As Jesus itinerates through the towns and villages of Galilee, teaching all the while, someone asks him a difficult question: "Lord, will only a few be saved?" (Luke 13:23). This question recurs over the generations. Throughout the whole Bible, two messages stand juxtaposed over and over. On the one hand, it is urgent to repent and to obey the commandments of God. On the other, God is astonishingly gracious, reaching out to sinner and saint alike. Anyone who preaches has discovered that the text for last Sunday's sermon and the one for this Sunday's sermon seem to point in opposite directions. Human beings tend to be uncomfortable with ambiguity, and logic leads us to believe that two apparent opposites cannot both be true; so we want to know whether God has set very high standards to keep the unworthy out, or whether God's mercy may find a way in for those who do not meet those standards. The Bible, however, will not make it easy for us. The truth is: high standards plus mercy. Grace, yes, but also commandments.

In response to the questioner, Jesus makes the case for high standards. It is not wise for anybody to imagine that one can be indifferent to the call to pay attention to God's commandments while blithely presuming that their indifference won't matter in the end. As Luke tells it, Jesus anticipates the protests of those who claim some kinship with him because they shared his table or occupied

286

the same geographical space he did. In response to their protest, Jesus declares that mere proximity will not be enough. Then, in a statement that must have been shocking to those who understood themselves to occupy a privileged position in the universe, Jesus says, "Then people will come from east and west, from north and south, and will eat in the kingdom of God" (v. 29; cf. Ps. 107:2–3; Isa. 25:6). He envisions a great reversal. Those who are overly confident of God's favor may find themselves outside looking in, while a parade of people from every corner of the compass will gather in God's *basileia* to sit at table at the messianic banquet.

The Gospel of Matthew places the same image in a different context. In Matthew, a Roman centurion has appealed to Jesus to heal his servant, who has become paralyzed. The centurion exhibits both faith in Jesus and reverence for him, exhibiting confidence that Jesus has the authority to act in God's stead. He does not want Jesus to endure the inconvenience of actually having to come to his house when he could effect a cure with a word: "Lord, I am not worthy to have you come under my roof" (Matt. 8:8). Jesus, impressed with this Gentile's faith, which surpasses what he has often encountered in Israel, says, "I tell you, many will come from east and west and will eat with Abraham and Isaac and Jacob in the kingdom of heaven, while the heirs of the kingdom will be thrown into the outer darkness" (Matt. 8:11).

These related passages in Luke and Matthew both anticipate a time in which the gospel will be preached beyond Israel to the Gentiles. At the same time, both point to that eschatological moment, the ultimate future, when people from all the nations will make their way to the feast that is being prepared in God's *basileia*. In this expectation, they draw both from the ministry of Jesus and from an eschatological vision already articulated in the Old Testament.

> Let the redeemed of the Lord say so,
> those he redeemed from trouble
> and gathered in from the lands,
> from the east and from the west,
> from the north and from the south.
> (Ps. 107:2–3)

The Presbyterian and UCC service books both use Luke 13:29 as an invitation to the Lord's Table: "Then people will come from east and west" (*BCW*, 68; *UCC*, 44). The intention is to draw attention to the huge scope of the eschatological banquet, in which God will be at work far beyond the borders of any one tribe or people to bring to the same table those who have been immensely distant from one another.

The God Who Feeds the Faithful

In [Third] Isaiah 65, we hear God's reply to the people's complaint that God has gone quiet (cf. Isa. 64:1: "O that you would tear open the heavens and come down"). If God has stepped back from the nation, with tragic results for them, it is because of the people's failure to respond to a gracious invitation: "I was ready to be sought out by those who did not ask, to be found by those who did not seek me. I said, 'Here I am, here I am,' to a nation that did not call on my name. I held out my hands all day long to a rebellious people" (Isa. 65:1, 2a). The people are guilty of worshiping foreign gods, engaging in superstitious practices, eating forbidden foods, and adopting an elitist and condemnatory attitude toward others. God is not impressed by their sacrifices. God will judge those who have turned away, but this judgment will not be indiscriminate:

> Therefore thus says the Lord GOD:
> My servants shall eat,
>   but you shall be hungry;
> my servants shall drink,
>   but you shall be thirsty;
> my servants shall rejoice,
>   but you shall be put to shame. . . .
> For I am about to create new heavens
>   and a new earth.
>
> (Isa. 65:13, 17a)

Although it is God who will realize this eschatological vision, human beings do not simply wait for it passively. Their part is to be servants of God, wherever they are and as they are able, not as though they could create the ultimate future entirely on their own, but neither as though they have nothing to do but stand and wait.

288   Having begun with an image of God's future involving eating, drinking, and rejoicing, the remainder of Isaiah 65 adds poetic images to help the people imagine what new heavens and a new

earth will be like: "They shall not labor in vain, or bear children for calamity" (v. 23). The prophet has projected God's promise on a broad screen, and it is a promise that the New Testament will remember and expand: "But, in accordance with his promise, we wait for new heavens and a new earth, where righteousness is at home" (2 Pet. 3:13; see Rev. 21:1).

Ezekiel 34

A text written during the Babylonian captivity expresses God's word of judgment upon "the shepherds of Israel," the kings who had failed in their responsibility to seek the welfare and protection of the people. God will displace them: "For thus says the Lord GOD: I myself will search for my sheep, and will seek them out" (Ezek. 34:11). This shepherding God says,

> I will feed them on the mountains of Israel, by the watercourses, and in all the inhabited parts of the land. I will feed them with good pasture, and the mountain heights of Israel shall be their pasture; there they shall lie down in good grazing land, and they shall feed on rich pasture on the mountains of Israel. I myself will be the shepherd of my sheep. . . . I will feed them with justice. . . .
> I will set up over them one shepherd, my servant David, and he shall feed them and be their shepherd. (Ezek 34:13b, 14, 15a, 16b, 23)

God will provide a shepherd from the messianic line of David. Of course, human beings are not sheep. However different we are from those creatures, we nevertheless resemble them in the sense that, just as the flock depends on a human sheep herder to be sure that they find food and drink, we depend on God to bring forth bread from the earth and to feed our spirits. Both the Old and New Testaments use the shepherd image to point to the Lord upon whom we depend for nourishment. After the Babylonian exile, Isaiah had written prophetically of the end of Judah's suffering and of the Lord God coming as one who "will feed his flock like a shepherd" (Isa. 40:11). In a tumultuous time, the prophet Micah spoke of a new David who would come from Bethlehem and "shall stand and feed his flock" (Mic. 5:4). In one of the "I am" passages, John's Gospel reports Jesus' promise to lay down his life for the sheep, saying, "I am the good shepherd" (John 10:11). The feeding image is found in a number of places, including Psalm 81, which

289

recalls God's tender care for Israel in the wilderness journey, thus envisioning the eschatological future by recalling redemption in the past: "I am the LORD your God, who brought you up out of the land of Egypt. Open your mouth wide and I will fill it. . . . I would feed you with the finest of the wheat, and with honey from the rock I would satisfy you" (Ps. 81:10, 16; cf. Deut. 32:13–14; Ps. 147:14).

Luke 12:35–38

> "Be dressed for action and have your lamps lit; be like those who are waiting for their master to return from the wedding banquet, so that they may open the door for him as soon as he comes and knocks. Blessed are those slaves whom the master finds alert when he comes; truly I tell you, he will fasten his belt and have them sit down to eat, and he will come and serve them. If he comes during the middle of the night, or near dawn, and finds them so, blessed are those slaves." (Luke 12:35–38)

In an apocalyptic text, Jesus shows in a good light the faithful servants who have stayed up waiting for the master of the household to return from a wedding banquet. In a remarkable reversal of the usual roles, Jesus pictures the master serving a meal to the servants! Later in his Gospel, Luke elaborates. When some of the disciples argue about which one of them is greatest, Jesus offers a counterintuitive definition of greatness: "For who is greater, the one who is at the table or the one who serves? Is it not the one at the table? But I am among you as one who serves" (Luke 22:27). This view is not limited to Luke's Gospel, as we see in John 13, when Jesus takes the servant role and washes the disciples' feet.

The master's return has clearly not taken place by the time that Luke wrote his Gospel. If Luke's fellow Christians have grown impatient, his account of Jesus' words encourages those who continue to wait expectantly without giving up. Jesus envisions the eschatological Parousia as a meal at which they will be the guests and he will be the host.

The image of the master knocking at the door occurs again in the book of Revelation, in which the Lord says, "Listen! I am standing at the door, knocking; if you hear my voice and open the door, I will come in to you and eat with you, and you with me" (Rev. 3:20).

John the seer has been delivering God's message to the church in Laodicea, a prosperous community in Asia Minor, not far from Colossae. The Lord is not happy with the Laodicean church, which is described as "lukewarm" (Rev. 3:16). The Christians there have an inflated view of themselves that stands in need of correction: "You do not realize that you are wretched, pitiable, poor, blind, and naked" (Rev. 3:17).

Christ speaks harshly to them, not to crush them, but because he loves them and wants them to make a new start. The Laodicean church celebrates the Eucharist, but "they do so without Christ's approval and presence. This is why Christ likens himself to someone standing outside their door and knocking" (Blount, *Revelation*, 83). If they get this pointed message, it will mean that they "hear" his voice. When they open the door to him and extend a welcome, he will come in and share a meal with them. Only at that point will they eat the Eucharist in his presence, instead of tricking themselves into thinking that they do, just as they have tricked themselves into believing that they are rich when they are poor, perceptive when they are blind, and dressed in victorious garb when they are in truth naked" (Blount, *Revelation*, 83–84)

The church in Laodicea is probably not the only church, then or now, that might be described as lukewarm. It is not unknown for churches of well-meaning people, whose desire is to present a credible message to potential members, to find that their message has evolved until it conforms so closely to conventional wisdom that it no longer carries the sharp flavor of the gospel. This happens across the spectrum, in churches that have been shaped by the church-growth movement as well as in those that are so attuned to contemporary intellectual and social trends as to lose the ability to distinguish those from the gospel. There is always a danger that the church may be lulled by a stubborn complacency. Can any of us be sure that our church might not be one of those at which Christ is outside, knocking on the door, hoping to find entrance?

If we imagine that we somehow "possess" Christ, as though he were at our disposal, safely secured within the certainties of which we are so proud, we ourselves might be categorized as "lukewarm." In other words, contrary to what we imagine, Christ may be standing at the door of our church, tapping, tapping, hoping that the door may be flung open for him. If we hear his voice and permit

291

him entry in order that he may speak to us and help us to change course, then all of our speaking and thinking and doing, all of our baptizing and our eucharistic eating and drinking will be reanimated in the power of the Spirit.

The text points to a possibility for the Laodicean church in the immediate present, but it also suggests an eschatological reference to this meal. "To the one who conquers I will give a place with me on my throne" (Rev. 3:21).

Christians pray regularly for the coming of the *eschaton*, the public exhibition of God's glory and God's sovereignty, when we pray the Lord's Prayer.

Matthew 6:9–13	*Luke 11:2–4*
Pray then in this way:	When you pray, say:
Our Father in heaven,	Father, hallowed be your name.
hallowed be your name.	Your kingdom come.
Your kingdom come.	Give us each day our daily
Your will be done,	bread.
on earth as it is in heaven.	And forgive us our sins,
Give us this day our daily bread.	for we ourselves forgive
And forgive us our debts,	everyone indebted to us.
as we also have forgiven our	And do not bring us to the
debtors.	time of trial.
And do not bring us to the time of	
trial,	
but rescue us from the evil one.	

For many centuries, the Lord's Prayer has directly followed the eucharistic prayer in classical liturgies. Two characteristics of the Lord's Prayer may have served to suggest this traditional link: (1) the prayer that the kingdom might come; (2) the petition "Give us this/each day our *epiousion* [translated as 'daily'] bread."

When we understand the Eucharist itself as a meal that anticipates God's feeding of the faithful in the eschatological age, it is particularly fitting that the Lord's Prayer, with its petition for the kingdom, should be included as the capstone of the eucharistic prayer.

The Greek word *epiousios* is rare in secular Greek, although it occurs at least once, and it is used in the New Testament only in the Lord's Prayer. Interpreters ancient and modern have debated the etymology of the word and its possible meaning, with no firm consensus. Notes in the *New Oxford Annotated Bible* offer an alternative translation, namely, "our bread for tomorrow." Various students have believed that it means "necessary for existence" or "for the current day" or "for the following day." Others understand it to mean "bread for the future" (Arndt and Gingrich, 296–97). Wainwright cites Jerome's version of the petition: "The bread which thou wilt give us in thy kingdom, give us today" (Wainwright, *Eucharist and Eschatology*, 40).

Following Lohmeyer, Wainright's opinion is that

> the bread for which we pray is *at one and the same time* both earthly bread to meet the hunger and need of the present day, and also the future bread which will satisfy the elect in the eschatological kingdom and is already given to us in anticipation— just as Jesus' meals with his disciples and with sinners as well as his miraculous feedings of the crowds were, in sign and reality, present experiences of the future messianic meal at which those who now hunger will be satisfied. (Wainwright, *Eucharist and Eschatology*, 41–42)

A person of faith never reaches a point where there is no longer a need to be fed. Whether one has been a disciple for a month or for many decades, the appetite for "spiritual food" and "spiritual drink" (1 Cor. 10:4) never diminishes. It does not seem as though a surplus ever builds up to a point where it does not require to be replenished. The bumps and obstacles of everyday life constantly pose a threat to faith, and some may be experienced as severe shocks. This is as true for clergy, church officers, and others whose daily work has to do with holy things as it is for laity. Thoughtful persons of ordinary sensibilities are aware of the possibility of the loss of faith. We have seen it in others, and are aware of similar vulnerabilities in ourselves. Every Christian, of whatever experience in the faith or seniority in the church, requires regular sustenance.

When the risen Lord appeared to some of the disciples by the lake, he repeatedly asked Simon Peter whether his love was genuine. When Peter assured him that he did indeed love him, the Lord replied, "Feed my lambs" (John 21:15). We may not easily think of ourselves as "lambs," and yet we remain as vulnerable as lambs and equally in need of frequent food and drink. Augustine, John Calvin, and others have used the image of "mother" to describe the church, and it is fitting, because we, the "lambs," are dependent on her, as the steward of God's mysteries, to nourish us, whether with milk or with solid food (1 Cor. 3:1–2; Heb. 5:12–14). In John 21, Peter, charged with feeding Christ's lambs, stands in for the church in her role as mother to all the faithful. The mother/shepherd/caretaker tends orphaned lambs as well as others who need help in finding nourishment.

God provides that nourishment for us, whether as the bread from heaven manifested in the Word preached and taught, or as the sacramental meal, in which the risen Christ becomes present to us in bread and wine shared in thanksgiving. That food is sufficient to sustain us and build us up in faith as we strain forward in expectation of the table spread for us in the *basileia*: bread to strengthen the human heart and wine to gladden it. We strain forward because faith that sustains us only for today falls short. Whatever our own destinies, those who trust the biblical God need to be strengthened in the certainty that the God of the past and the present is also the God of the future. The God of the exodus and of Easter is Lord of everything that is yet to be, and all will be well. That confidence is the food that God gives and that we eat and drink in the Eucharist, in anticipation of a day when the glory of the Lord shall be revealed not just to those who have faith but publicly, to all flesh.

The Wine of the *Basileia*
(Dominion/Kingdom of God)

Matthew 26:29; Mark 14:25; Luke 22:18, 30

I tell you, I will never again drink of this fruit of the vine until that day when I drink it new with you in my Father's kingdom.	Truly, I tell you, I will never again drink of the fruit of the vine until that day when I drink it new in the kingdom of God.	[F]or I tell you that from now on I will not drink of the fruit of the vine until the kingdom of God comes . . . You are those who have stood by me in my trials; and I confer on you, just as my Father has conferred on me, a kingdom, so that you eat and drink at my table in my kingdom, and you will sit on thrones judging the twelve tribes of Israel.

In biblical times, wine was a staple drink for virtually everyone, although still precious enough to be an essential for a festive occasion. Sometimes biblical references to wine are absolutely straightforward, having to do with a drink, whether as part of the goodness of life or as a pitfall, but sometimes the references to wine, a cup, or a vine play a symbolic role. The institution narratives in the Synoptic Gospels all link wine with the *basileia*, and Luke makes use of "throne" language, anticipating Revelation 3:21, which is explicitly eschatological. Elsewhere in the Bible, one may discern an eschatological dimension in language about wine, cups, or the vines that support the fruit from which wine is made. For example, wine is a festive drink, a gift of God "to gladden the human heart" (Ps. 104:15), which can both suggest a simple observation of its power to make social relations a bit smoother and happier and offer a characterization of the joy of the *basileia*. The prophet Isaiah describes Israel metaphorically as a vineyard: "The vineyard of the LORD of hosts is the house of Israel, and the people of Judah are his pleasant planting" (Isa. 5:7). In John's Gospel, Jesus identifies himself, in one of the "I am" passages, as "the true vine" (John 15:1). In an extended metaphor, Jesus compares the disciples to the branches of the vine: "Those who abide in me and I in them bear much fruit, because apart from me you can do nothing" (John 15:5). Where the vine is, it is possible to perceive the reign of God, whose loving-kindness overflows for us, always more than expected, never exhausted.

An abundance of wine was understood to be a sign of messianic days. The prophet Joel, writing about the Day of the Lord, prophesies that "in that day the mountains shall drip sweet wine, the hills shall flow with milk, and all the stream beds of Judah shall flow with water" (Joel 3:18). Amos uses the same image: "The time is surely coming, says the LORD, when . . . the mountains shall drip sweet wine, and all the hills shall flow with it" (Amos 9:13; also see Jer. 31:12).

Matthew and Luke both record a saying about the need to put new wine into fresh wineskins (Matt. 9:17; Luke 5:38). In both pericopes, the question has arisen as to why Jesus and his disciples do not engage in the spiritual discipline of fasting. Jesus' response would have been puzzling to his immediate audience, but makes sense to those for whom Matthew and Luke wrote their Gospels. He says, "The wedding guests cannot mourn as long as the bridegroom is with them, can they? The days will come when the bridegroom is taken away from them, and then they will fast" (Matt. 9:15). Jesus follows up with two images: an unshrunk piece of cloth and new wine. The new wine is the wine of the *basileia*. If new wine is put into old wineskins, it will cause them to burst, because the *basileia* is too dynamic to be contained within the old forms. Where Jesus is present, the *basileia* is present, and the presence of the *basileia* calls for the kind of rejoicing that resembles a wedding banquet, rather than for fasting.

The story of the wedding at Cana in Galilee also uses wine as a symbol for the *basileia* (John 2:1–11). Jesus turns an astonishing amount of water into wine. The servants fill with water six large jars ordinarily used for Jewish rites of purification. Just as the stories of the multiplication of the loaves point to messianic abundance (twelve baskets left over), so does the Cana story.

Both water and wine are useful, serving similar and yet different purposes. The same water that may be used for washing also quenches thirst, but wine is a festive drink, particularly appropriate for a celebration. The steward (headwaiter or master of ceremonies) unknowingly comments to the bridegroom about the excellent quality of the water transformed into wine, contrasting it with the wine that has been provided the guests by ordinary means: "But you have kept the good wine until now" (John 2:10).

What Jesus has brought to the wedding reception is something new that has roots in something old. His gift is to make manifest something precious that has been held in store for revealing "now." The meaning of the old religious institutions, customs, and feasts becomes richer in his presence. That which is new is Jesus himself, and he himself is the good wine, that is, the manifestation of the kingdom, brought into the present moment for the joy and delight of those who are able to discern it. The miracle at Cana is "the first of his signs . . . and revealed his glory" (John 2:11). This revealing is evocative of Old Testament references to the revelation of God's glory as a sign of the eschatological age (e.g., Ps. 102:16: "For the LORD will build up Zion; he will appear in his glory"). The miracle is the first of a series of signs that will be comprehensible only once the whole sweep of Jesus' story has played out, but even this sign, the Gospel tells us, is sufficient for his disciples to discern his glory and believe in him. The very quantity of the water turned to wine is a sign of the lavishness of God's provision for us in Christ and his

296

gospel, sufficient for now and overflowing in the *basileia*. Even now, in the midst of the ambiguities of human life, the Christ we meet in Word and Sacrament is able to make the heart glad.

The Wedding Banquet

"On this mountain the LORD of hosts will make for all peoples a feast of rich food, a feast of well-aged wines" (Isa. 25:6). Old Testament images of a feast as a symbol for the life of the eschatological age influence New Testament descriptions of meals, particularly in metaphorical use of the wedding banquet. One that makes the comparison quite explicit is this: "Once more Jesus spoke to them in parables, saying: 'The kingdom of heaven may be compared to a king who gave a wedding banquet for his son'" (Matt. 22:1).

Jesus has been invited to a banquet by a leader of the Pharisees. Having already noticed how the guests seek out the places of honor, he uses the occasion to teach that one ought rather to choose the less prestigious places. He follows up with an instruction that, when giving a banquet, one ought to invite those who cannot pay you back, "for you will be repaid at the resurrection of the righteous" (Luke 14:14).

Picking up on the eschatological reference, "one of the dinner guests . . . said to him, 'Blessed is anyone who will eat bread in the kingdom of God!'" perhaps presuming that those seated at the Pharisee's table would certainly be included in that blessed company. But Jesus says to him, "Someone gave a great dinner and invited many" (Luke 14:15–16), and then proceeds to tell how that worked out. The familiar story tells how the invited guests repeatedly rebuff the host's emissaries (the prophets?) and ends with the host's indignant statement that "none of those who were invited will taste my dinner" (Luke 14:24).

It is safe to presume that those who had been invited, and had early on indicated that they would accept the invitation, were devout people, as were the guests at the Pharisee's dinner. They knew the Scriptures, were scrupulously observant of the law, honored the prophets, and anticipated the messianic age. It would be comfortable to imagine that it was only those Pharisees back then who, though they had the Scriptures, the rites, the teachings, and

297

the rules that ought to have made clear to them how to listen for a Word from God, did not hear it. Of course, we are not exempt. We also have the Scriptures, the rites, the teachings, the rules that, when we take them seriously, should enable us to hear our own names when they are being called, but we are distracted by many things. We are busy with honorable things, secular and "religious," but that very focus on our duty can easily crowd out of mind the urgent call to be disciples. There are sermons to be crafted, lessons to be prepared, meetings to attend, the sick to be visited, troubled persons to be counseled, budgets to be balanced, but in the busyness of it all, it is easy to lose track of that one voice that we desperately need to hear, both for our own sakes and for the sakes of those to whom our busyness is ostensibly devoted.

The parable makes its point without our having to turn it into a law of its own: that the Jews' invitation has been canceled, while the Gentiles will inherit the *basileia*. No. The parable is not about religious or ethnic identity. Rather, it contrasts, on the one hand, those who have had every opportunity to hear, study, consider, and embrace God's gracious invitation, but instead respond with indifference, taking for granted that they occupy a privileged position and, on the other hand, those guests rounded up at the last minute, who would be astonished to hear that God wanted them to feast at the royal table.

Over and over the Bible has set before us images of a feast, a banquet table, of bread and wine and rich foods, of food for the hungry, joy for the broken. This is, of course, picture language. It tells the truth and tells it profoundly, but not literally. It is not possible using only discursive, rational, literal language to say anything about the *basileia* that is comprehensible within the three-dimensional world that we occupy. When we literalize it, the image turns wooden and is spoiled. On the other hand, when we imagine that we can do without the picture language, we are misled. The truth of the *basileia* is a mystery embedded in human language and images, with all its limitations and its promise. However, even in an era of skepticism, it continues to exhibit power to kindle a heartfelt passion (see Luke 24:32). The church needs to hear about the *basileia* from the pulpit as well as to pray for it. The times call for deeper immersion in the challenging images of Scripture as those who preach search for and cultivate the language of astonishment. Thomas G. Long has written,

Vibrant Christian preaching depends upon the recovery of its eschatological voice, an eschatology that avoids literalism while insisting that the full disclosure of God is not fully contained in the present tense. As Duke Ellington once said, "There are two types of music, good and bad, and you can tell them apart by listening." Just so, there are two types of eschatology, and you can tell them apart by living them out. The first kind of eschatology depends upon a literalistic grip on biblical images and results in a gospel that is intellectually implausible. . . . The second kind . . . allows the eschatological affirmations that "Christ is risen!" and "Jesus is Lord!" to exercise tension upon the present tense, generating both judgment and promise, creating the possibility of ethical action in the world sustained by hope. (Long, *Preaching from Memory*, 123)

Matthew 25:1–10

"Then the kingdom of heaven will be like this. Ten bridesmaids took their lamps and went to meet the bridegroom. Five of them were foolish, and five were wise. . . . And while they went to buy [oil for their lamps], the bridegroom came, and those who were ready went with him into the wedding banquet; and the door was shut." (Matt. 25:1, 2, 10)

This parable is attached to the preceding apocalyptic discourse and makes use of familiar eschatological images, sometimes allegorically, in a description of the *basileia*. Both bridegroom and wedding banquet are used as messianic and eschatological images here and elsewhere.

Half of the ten bridesmaids are portrayed as foolish and half as wise. The foolish seem to presume that there is no need to make a contingency plan in case the bridegroom should not arrive on schedule, while those who are wise clearly understand that things frequently do not work out as imagined. Understood allegorically, the bridesmaids are Christians of Matthew's time, who have been looking for the anticipated Parousia, the return of the Lord. However, the timing of the event is turning out not to be what many Christians have expected, as indicated by the statement that the bridegroom has been delayed.

299

Those who have made too facile presumptions about the timing of the Parousia find themselves in an awkward position, and they turn to the five wise bridesmaids, hoping to borrow more oil so that they will have enough to see them through to the fateful moment. Those who have taken care to prepare for contingencies think it not prudent to share their supply. Much later than expected, the bridegroom/Parousia arrives, and those whose lamps continue to burn escort him into the wedding banquet. Those who have not allowed for the possibility of delay plead to be admitted. "Lord, lord, open to us" (v. 11), they beg, which recalls Jesus having said, on another occasion, "Not everyone who says to me, 'Lord, Lord,' will enter the kingdom of heaven" (Matt. 7:21).

The parable is intended to serve as a warning that we do not know everything we need to know about the Parousia or the timing of it, and yet it is important to persevere in confident, hopeful expectation: "Keep awake, therefore, for you know neither the day nor the hour" (v. 13).

Since the contemporary mainline church devotes so little attention to the cosmic scope of redemption, as promised in Scripture, this parable may not seem to have much to do with either our personal piety or the ongoing life of the church. The customary focus tends to be *either* toward a heavenly reward to which we are admitted one by one at the end of each mortal life *or* toward doing good works in the hope of contributing to the building of the kingdom.

Contemporary mainline churches tend to advocate taking an active role in shaping the world, so that it more nearly resembles the kingdom of God. As commendable and as biblical as that action surely is, there is a case for *both/and*. The biblical images of the *basileia* are vivid and powerful enough to stir our longing to see them realized in our own times and places, even if imperfectly. Perhaps it is beyond our power to shape a world in which it is certain that every infant will live more than a few days and everyone of every age will live a full lifetime (Isa. 65:20), but it is in our power to distribute health care more justly and to reduce poverty and crime. No amount of animal husbandry is likely to realize the vision of a world in which the wolf and the lamb feed together, and the lion becomes a vegetarian (Isa. 65:25), but it is possible to imagine a world that is not tolerant of violence and looks for ways to heal the social frustrations and the physical and mental conditions that contribute to them. We may not be able to imagine a world in which anxiety about where the next meal is coming from will disappear everywhere and altogether, but it is conceivable that we may be able

300

to learn to see how our own interests are better served by economic strategies that look beyond the old familiar "winner takes all."

The biblical images of the wedding banquet, where everyone has a place at the table, encourage us to imagine what could be. So, yes—the God of the Bible has not called us to sit on our hands, passively waiting for God to make it better. At the same time, we might do well to entertain the questions, What sort of banquet host is God? Is God up to creating a new heaven and a new earth? Capable of wringing ultimate justice out of injustices? Competent to spread a table for those who come from the four corners of the compass, where the high and the low, the wise and the simple, the articulate and those whose voices are seldom heard may eat and drink together, not in uneasy proximity, but rejoicing? Is God strong enough to heal the painful estrangements that disfigure all of life? Is God big enough to have the last word? Adequately equipped to lead us and the whole creation to a redemption that is cosmic in scope? The God who led Israel through the sea with unmoistened foot, and raised from the dead the Lord Jesus, may indeed be able to keep each and every promise!

It is, indeed, both/and. We are called to be obedient and given vivid examples of what obedience looks like in acts of service and compassion. And we are called to keep awake, to be alert, to be watchful for what God will do in God's own time, far beyond what we ourselves are able to do. We have been invited to a wedding banquet!

J. S. Bach's Cantata in D Major, "Gottes Zeit ist Die Allerbeste Zeit" (BWV 106) reads, in English, "God's time is the very best time." These words resonate with the wedding parable, when in God's time, those who are waiting with lit lamps will go in and enjoy the wedding feast together: "The bridegroom came, and those who were ready went with him into the wedding banquet" (Matt. 25:10).

God's time—quite distinct from the schedules we work out in our own minds—is indeed the very best time.

Revelation 19:5–9

> And from the throne came a voice saying,
>   "Praise our God,
>   all you his servants,
>   and all who fear him,
>   small and great."

301

Then I heard what seemed to be the voice of a great multitude, like
the sound of many waters and like the sound of mighty thunder
peals, crying out,
  "Hallelujah!
  For the Lord our God
    the Almighty reigns.
  Let us rejoice and exult
    and give him the glory,
  for the marriage of the Lamb has come,
    and his bride has made herself ready;
      to her it has been granted to be clothed
        with fine linen, bright and pure"—
  for the fine linen is the righteous deeds of the saints.
And the angel said to me, "Write this: Blessed are those who are
    invited to the marriage supper of the Lamb." And he said
    to me, "These are true words of God."
                                                      (Rev. 19:5–9)

In the Sermon on the Mount, Jesus pronounces ultimate blessings
upon those who have been reviled and persecuted and slandered,
and says, "Rejoice and be glad, for your reward is great in heaven"
(Matt. 5:12). Here we have the seer John's vision of what that heavenly rejoicing might look like. The "great multitude" whose voices
are raised are all those who love and serve God, both the small and
the great. In Revelation 17 and 18, God has destroyed Babylon/
Rome and has begun to establish the divine rule on earth. John uses
liturgical language of which Handel made use in his great choral
work *Messiah*. The great chorus of witnesses cries out in praise of
God, who has demonstrated heavenly rule in the vanquishing of the
earthly kingdoms that threatened God and God's servants.

It is easy, in any era, to identify enemies who seem to be hostile to God and opposed to the Gospel. If we are not careful, the
book of Revelation can be read in a Manichean sense, in which we
read every contemporary conflict as one between Christ and the
antichrist. Are there sharp disagreements in the church over one
issue or another, each side quoting Scripture with absolute confidence? It is easy to denounce and demonize our opponents. Is
there conflict in society over economics, cultural changes, the role
of government? Conflict between nations, religious communities,
races? Rich and poor? How easy to believe, quite sincerely, that our

opponents are utterly evil, worthy only of destruction! It is exactly when we are so persuaded that we need to be most careful.

Most of the conflict in the world is not between an unmixed "good" and an unmixed "evil." If it were, it would perhaps not be so difficult for people of goodwill to choose the "right" side, the side of truth and justice! God certainly calls us to live in the world as those who know that Christ is Lord, even if neighbors and opponents do not know it and may not be persuaded, particularly when we try to push them to believe it or require them at least to pretend that they do. Living in such a way as to witness—with or without words—to the sovereignty of God and of the Lamb calls for us to be discerning as we evaluate political, social, and religious movements and the conflicts related to them. In *False Presence of the Kingdom*, the French theologian Jacques Ellul warns against identifying any political movement with God's kingdom. To grant such status to any human project leads inevitably to idolatry, the result of which will always be bitter disappointment.

To live in this world requires coming to grips with complexity, with the certainty that no one person or group or movement will always be right in all things every time. To bear witness to God and to the Lamb requires engaging in a constant process of discernment that is seasoned not only with prayer, but also with study and with patient dialogue as we consult with the whole church, insofar as possible, that we may be equipped to serve God faithfully in the hard decisions required of us as disciples and citizens and global neighbors. Our daily prayer may be, "Do not bring us to the time of trial" (Matt. 6:13a); but we also pray, if we should be brought to a time of trial, that we be found faithful: "Rescue us from the evil one" (6:13b). Martyrdom of the ultimate sort is probably not likely for many of us, but we will all face moments, alone or together, when our witness (Gk. *martyreō*) counts.

John indicates that in heaven a great celebratory moment is at hand, "for the marriage of the Lamb has come." The Lamb is Jesus, risen and exalted. The Old Testament has depicted Israel as God's bride: "Thus says the LORD: I remember the devotion of your youth, your love as a bride, how you followed me in the wilderness" Jer. 2:2). In Revelation the "bride" represents a broader community of God's servants, "saints from every tribe and language and people and nation" (Rev. 5:9).

303

Earlier in the book, the seer has revealed that those who had been "slaughtered for the word of God and for the testimony they had given" would each be given a white robe (Rev. 6:9, 11). Now it has been granted that the bride "'be clothed with fine linen, bright and pure'—for the fine linen is the righteous deeds of the saints" (Rev. 19:8). It is God who provides the elegant clothing; that is, it is God who enables the faithful witness of God's servants.

Brian Blount points out that "John is paradoxically mixing human initiative with divine causality" (Blount, *Revelation*, 345). Indeed, human beings have faced down the opposing forces and borne witness to God's lordship.

"This righteous behavior does not, however, mean that humans can achieve salvation through their own merit. John means to make this point by implying that the witnessing he so celebrates has been enabled and empowered by God" (Blount, *Revelation*, 345).

Once again, we encounter the both/and that links human responsibility and God's action, without suggesting either that God is helpless apart from human initiative or that human initiative can be an adequate substitute for God's action. Human action and God's action are providentially and mysteriously joined together in a way that neither permits human passivity nor elevates our role in such a way that God finds it indispensable.

Human beings are not autonomous, but neither are we simply pawns whom God may move here and there on the chessboard. In the mystery of the divine/human synergy, it matters when people willingly give themselves to the service of God. Those who have been faithful will be blessed, indeed honored, by God: "Blessed are those who are invited to the marriage supper of the Lamb" (Rev. 19:9). Here again Scripture sets before us the bountiful table, the table of celebration and relief, a table prepared for those who have fought the good fight.

Horatio Bonar's hymn "Here, O Our Lord, We See You Face to Face" captures the celebratory tone of the messianic banquet as anticipated in the Eucharist:

> This is the hour of banquet and of song;
> This is the heavenly table for us spread;
> Here let us feast and, feasting, still prolong
> The fellowship of living wine and bread.

In the eucharistic feast, the "hour of banquet and of song," we enjoy proleptically the wedding feast of the Lamb, the messianic banquet, the bread and wine of the blessed *basileia,* in which the risen Lord himself will be both friend and host. From the standpoint either of one serving Communion or the communicant, the moment of standing face to face, the words spoken directly from one to another, the touch of the hand as bread is placed in the open palm, can be a profound moment of encounter. Geoffrey Wainwright cites a touching image from one of Theodore of Mopsuestia's *Catechetical Homilies*: "So now in each particle of the broken loaf [the Lord] approaches each communicant, greets him [her], manifests his own resurrection and gives the communicant the earnest of the good things to come, for the sake of which we approach this holy mystery" (Wainwright, *Eucharist and Eschatology*, 58).

Crossing Over: Eucharistic Witness at a Time of Death

In the church's treasury of resources for pastoral care, one that is too often neglected by Protestant churches is the Eucharist. All the service books provide for the Eucharist to be celebrated at funerals or memorial services, and yet the practice is still uncommon, with the exception of Episcopalians and, in some places, Lutherans.

One reason may be that for many Protestants, even those who have excellent published liturgical resources, the Lord's Supper remains a melancholy affair, in which the accent falls on Christ's death at the expense of his resurrection. This melancholy, historically rooted in the medieval Mass and the insufficiently reformed liturgies of the Reformation, persists because the actual details of conventional eucharistic practice overpower texts and rubrics. As Martha Moore-Keish points out in her excellent study *Do This in Remembrance*, an introspective and melancholic piety may be engrained in the way congregations actually do the Eucharist. Although they follow the celebratory language of the new service books, nonetheless styles of music, demeanor, bodily postures, and engrained expectations combine to mute any sense that this is "the joyful feast of the people of God." It is no wonder, then, that anyone planning a funeral would avoid a eucharistic service that has for so long been associated so strongly with death and loss, while the resurrection and eschatological themes have been muted.

Another reason that mourners may not even consider celebrating the Eucharist at a funeral is that the sacrament is inescapably material, requiring the use of bread and wine, while our culture has shaped people to see the spiritual as detached from the material. The American funeral, as Thomas Long has so ably pointed out, has undergone a process of transformation in recent years to the point that it has become more and more remote from a Christian approach to life or death (*Accompany Them with Singing*). "Spirituality" is in, while "religion" is out. The soul is in, more or less, while the body is out. For Aunt Sal, the family organizes a "celebration of life" at her favorite restaurant or the nearest "legacy center." In many cases, Aunt Sal will not be present at her own funeral, both coffins and cremated remains having been banished as in bad taste.

Yet at some level we recognize that our bodies matter. The material world matters. Bodies are in a sense sacramental, since it is in and by means of our bodies that we are known to one another. Long quotes Thomas Lynch, a funeral director and writer, who reports the rage of a bereaved mother when a member of the clergy tried to comfort her by saying that the body of her teenage daughter, dead of leukemia, was "just a shell." "I'll tell you when it's 'just a shell,'" she retorted. "For now and until I tell you otherwise, she's my daughter."

The Eucharist is the sacrament of a people gathered around the incarnate Lord—a people for whom bodies matter. The Spirit, as Scripture tells us over and over, has not disdained to become manifest to us in actions that make use of physical things like water, bread, and wine. To celebrate the Eucharist at a funeral is counter to the prevailing culture and, as such, a profound testimony to the gospel that affirms that the divine Word has become flesh.

As Long has pointed out, "a Christian funeral is a continuation and elaboration of the baptismal service" (Long, *Accompany Them with Singing*, 81). Baptism is layered with multiple meanings, but a central one is undoubtedly death and resurrection. In baptism, we die metaphorically, united with Christ in his death, in anticipation of being united with him in his resurrection. When our life ends, we die literally, and the fact of it highlights the baptismal hope and confidence that we shall share in his resurrection life.

306

A pastor of a Presbyterian congregation in the Southwest, unaccustomed to Communion at a funeral, was just beginning a D.Min. project that involved working with her session (board of elders) to deepen their appreciation of the Eucharist when one of the elders unexpectedly died. The elder's family requested that the Lord's Supper be celebrated at the funeral. The most typical practice in that congregation was for the elders to take the bread and cup to the people in the pews, but for the funeral they followed a practice that was used occasionally in their church, in which the communicants left the pews and came forward to receive. The other elders on the session, colleagues of the deceased, were the servers. The pastor reports that the service was transformed and that the family, the elder servers, and those present felt gathered in something like a joyful feast, a foretaste of the heavenly banquet, even as they mourned one whom they loved.

It probably helped that the way the Eucharist was celebrated that day made use of practices already introduced to the congregation, though not the ones to which they were most accustomed. The newer practices interrupted the narrative in the participants' minds about what a funeral should be and what the Lord's Supper should be, and permitted them to tune in to the witness to the resurrection made so profoundly in the liturgical texts, especially when accompanied by a procession to Communion that is so reminiscent of the pilgrim journey we all share as we move toward the heavenly banquet.

It is not necessary to belittle the ways that survivors attempt to personalize the exits of those they love, particularly when they are trying without much help to fill a vacuum left by the loss of faith or the dilution of it. Nor is there value in trying to impose upon families practices that they either cannot understand or actively resent. As always, pastoral sensitivity is a priority. However, there are, in every church, people for whom Christ and his church matter deeply. Pastoral care for them can be enhanced if ways are found to encourage them to consider the witness they want to make when their own lives end, including a celebration of the holy meal, the foretaste of the heavenly banquet.

BIBLIOGRAPHY

For Further Study

Benedict, Daniel T. *Come to the Waters: Baptism and Our Ministry of Welcoming Seekers and Making Disciples.* Nashville: Discipleship Resources, 1996.

Byars, Ronald P. *Christian Worship: Glorifying and Enjoying God.* Louisville, KY: Geneva Press, 2000.

———. *Lift Your Hearts on High: Eucharistic Prayer in the Reformed Tradition.* Louisville, KY: Westminster John Knox Press, 2005.

Davis, Thomas J. *This Is My Body: The Presence of Christ in Reformation Thought.* Grand Rapids: Baker Academic, 2008.

Jones, Cheslyn, Geoffrey Wainwright, Edward Yarnold, and Paul Bradshaw, eds. *The Study of Liturgy.* Revised edition. New York: Oxford University Press, 1992.

Neusner, Jacob. *A Short History of Judaism: Three Meals, Three Epochs.* Minneapolis: Fortress Press, 1992.

Stookey, Laurence Hull. *Baptism: Christ's Act in the Church.* Nashville: Abingdon Press, 1982.

———. *Eucharist: Christ's Feast with the Church.* Nashville: Abingdon Press, 1993.

What Do You Seek? Welcoming the Adult Inquirer. Minneapolis: Augsburg Fortress, 2000.

Yarnold, Edward. *The Awe-Inspiring Rites of Initiation: The Origins of the R.C.I.A.* 2nd edition. Collegeville, MN: Liturgical Press, 2001.

Literature Cited

Achtemeier, Paul J. *1 Peter.* Hermeneia—A Critical and Historical Commentary on the Bible. Philadelphia: Fortress Press, 1996.

African American Heritage Hymnal. Chicago: GIA Publications, 2001.

Allen, Diogenes. *Theology for a Troubled Believer: An Introduction to the Christian Faith*. Louisville, KY: Westminster John Knox Press, 2010.

Arndt, W. F., and F. W. Gingrich. *A Greek-English Lexicon of the New Testament and Other Early Christian Literature*. Chicago: University of Chicago Press, 1952.

Baptism, Eucharist and Ministry. 1st printing. Geneva: World Council of Churches, July 1982.

Benoit, André. *Le Baptême Chrétien au Second Siècle: La Théologie des Pères*. Paris: Presses Universitaires de France, 1953.

Berger, Peter. *The Heretical Imperative: Contemporary Possibilities of Religious Affirmation*. New York: Anchor Press/Doubleday, 1979.

Bibb, Bryan D. *Ritual Words and Narrative Worlds in the Book of Leviticus*. New York: T. & T. Clark, 2009.

Blount, Brian K. *Revelation: A Commentary*. New Testament Library. Louisville, KY: Westminster John Knox Press, 2009.

The Book of Common Prayer and Administration of the Sacraments and Other Rites and Ceremonies of the Church. New York: Church Hymnal Corporation and the Seabury Press, 1979.

Book of Common Worship. Louisville, KY: Westminster/John Knox Press, 1993.

Book of Common Worship: The Presbyterian Church in Canada. Board of Congregational Life, The Presbyterian Church in Canada, 1991.

Book of Worship: United Church of Christ. New York: United Church of Christ Office for Church Life and Leadership, 1986.

Bouyer, Louis. *Eucharist: Theology and Spirituality of the Eucharistic Prayer*. Notre Dame, IN: University of Notre Dame Press, 1968.

Bradshaw, Paul. *Early Christian Worship: A Basic Introduction to Ideas and Practice*. Collegeville, MN: Liturgical Press, 1996.

Brown, Raymond E. *An Introduction to the New Testament*. Anchor Bible Reference Library. New York: Doubleday, 1997.

———. *The Gospel according to John I–XII*. Anchor Bible. Garden City, NY: Doubleday & Co., 1966.

Byars, Ronald P. "Indiscriminate Baptism and Baptismal Integrity." *Reformed Liturgy and Music* 31:1. Also, www.pcusa.org/theologyandworship/issues/baptism.htm.

Calvin, John. *Institutes of the Christian Religion*. Edited by John T. McNeill. Philadelphia: Westminster Press, 1960.

Celebrate God's Presence: A Book of Services for the United Church of Canada. United Church of Canada, 2000.

Chauvet, Louis-Marie. "Are the Words of the Liturgy Worn Out?" *Worship* 84:1 (January 2010).

Childs, Brevard S. *The Book of Exodus: A Critical, Theological Commentary*. Philadelphia: Westminster Press, 1974.

———. *Memory and Tradition in Israel*. Naperville, IL: Alec R. Allenson, 1962.

Christian Initiation of Adults: Revised. Liturgy Documentary Series 4. Washington, DC: United States Catholic Conference, 1988.

Collins, Adela Yarbro. "The Origins of Christian Baptism." In *Living Water, Sealing Spirit: Readings on Christian Initiation*, edited by Maxwell E. Johnson. Collegeville, MN: Liturgical Press, 1995.

Common Worship: Services and Prayers for the Church of England. London: Church House Publishing, 2000.

Connell, Martin F. "On 'Chrism' and 'Anti-Christs' in 1 John 2:18–27: A Hypothesis." *Worship* 83 (May 2009).

The Constitution of the Presbyterian Church (U.S.A.): Part 1 Book of Confessions. Louisville, KY: Published by the Office of the General Assembly, 2002.

Copenhaver, Martin B. "Back to the Future: 'Retraditioning' in the Church Today." *Reflections: Yale Divinity School*. Fall 2009.

Cousar, Charles B. *Galatians*. Interpretation: A Bible Commentary for Teaching and Preaching. Louisville, KY: John Knox Press, 1982.

Craddock, Fred B. *Luke*. Interpretation: A Bible Commentary for Teaching and Preaching. Louisville, KY: John Knox Press, 1990.

Dahl, Nils. "Anamnesis: Mémoire et Commémoration dans le christianisme primitif." *Studia Theologica* 1 (1948).

Davis, Ellen F. *Wondrous Depth: Preaching the Old Testament*. Louisville, KY: Westminster John Knox Press, 2005.

Didache: Teaching of the Twelve Apostles. Translated by J. Fitzgerald. New York: John B. Alden, Publisher, 1891.

Dillard, Annie. *Teaching a Stone to Talk: Expeditions and Encounters*. San Francisco: Harper & Row, 1982.

Directory for Worship. In *The Constitution of the Presbyterian*

311

Church (U.S.A.), Part II, Book of Order. Louisville, KY: The Office of the General Assembly, 2005–2007.

Driver, Tom F. *Liberating Rites: Understanding the Transformative Power of Ritual*. Boulder, CO: Westview Press, 1991.

Ellul, Jacques. *False Presence of the Kingdom*. New York: Seabury Press, 1972.

Emerson, Ralph Waldo. "Miscellanies." In *A Documentary History of Religion in America to the Civil War*, edited by Edwin S. Gaustad. 2nd edition. Grand Rapids: Eerdmans, 1993.

Evangelical Lutheran Worship. Minneapolis: Augsburg Fortress, 2006.

Ford, David F., and Daniel W. Hardy. *Living in Praise: Worshipping and Knowing God*. Grand Rapids: Baker Academic, 1984, 2005.

Frei, Hans W. *Theology and Narrative: Selected Essays*. Edited by George Hunsinger and William C. Placher. New York: Oxford University Press, 1993.

Gather. 2nd edition. Choir Book. Chicago: GIA Publications, 1994.

Gench, Frances Taylor. *Encounters with Jesus: Studies in the Gospel of John*. Louisville, KY: Westminster John Knox Press, 2007.

Gerrish, B. A. *Grace and Gratitude: The Eucharistic Theology of John Calvin*. Minneapolis: Fortress Press, 1993.

Grimes, Ronald L. *Ritual Criticism: Case Studies in Its Practice, Essays on Its Theory*. Columbia: University of South Carolina Press, 1990.

Haenchen, Ernst. *John 1*. Hermeneia—A Critical and Historical Commentary on the Bible. Philadelphia: Fortress Press, 1984.

———. *John 2*. Hermeneia—A Critical and Historical Commentary on the Bible. Philadelphia: Fortress Press, 1984.

Hanson, Paul D. *Isaiah 40–66*. Interpretation: A Bible Commentary for Teaching and Preaching. Louisville, KY: John Knox Press, 1995.

Hare, Douglas R. *Matthew*. Interpretation: A Bible Commentary for Teaching and Preaching. Louisville, KY: John Knox Press, 1993.

Hartman, Lars. *"Into the Name of the Lord Jesus": Baptism in the Early Church*. Edinburgh: T. & T. Clark, 1997.

Hauerwas, Stanley, and William H. Willimon. *Resident Aliens: Life in the Christian Colony*. Nashville: Abingdon Press, 1989.

Hays, Richard B. *First Corinthians*. Interpretation: A Bible Commentary for Teaching and Preaching. Louisville, KY: John Knox Press, 1997.

Hutson, James H. *Religion and the New Republic*. Lanham, MD: Rowman & Littlefield Publishers, 1999.

The Hymnal 1982: According to the Use of the Episcopal Church. New York: Church Publishing Inc., 1985.

Invitation to Christ: A Guide to Sacramental Practices. Louisville, KY: Office of Theology and Worship, Presbyterian Church (U.S.A.), 2006.

Jasper, R. C. D., and G. J. Cuming. *Prayers of the Eucharist: Early and Reformed*. Collegeville, MN: Liturgical Press, 1990.

Jefferson, Thomas. *The Jefferson Bible: The Life and Morals of Jesus of Nazareth*. Boston: Beacon Press, 2001.

Johnson, Maxwell E. "The Archaic Nature of the Sanctus, Institution Narrative, and Epiclesis of the Logos in the Anaphora Ascribed to Sarapion of Thmuis." In Paul F. Bradshaw, ed., *Essays on Early Eastern Eucharistic Prayers*. Collegeville, MN: Liturgical Press, 1997.

————. *The Rites of Christian Initiation: Their Evolution and Interpretation*. Collegeville, MN: Liturgical Press, 1999.

Jungmann, Joseph A. *The Mass of the Roman Rite: Its Origins and Development*. New York: Benziger Brothers, 1959.

Kaminsky, Joel. *Yet I Loved Jacob: Reclaiming the Biblical Concept of Election*. Nashville: Abingdon Press, 2007.

Lamott, Anne. *Traveling Mercies: Some Thoughts on Faith*. New York: Anchor Books, 1999.

Lathrop, Gordon W. *Central Things: Worship in Word and Sacrament*. Minneapolis: Augsburg Fortress, 2005.

————. *Holy People: A Liturgical Ecclesiology*. Minneapolis: Fortress Press, 1999.

————. *Holy Things: A Liturgical Theology*. Minneapolis: Fortress Press, 1993.

————. "The Reforming Gospels: A Liturgical Theologian Looks Again at Eucharistic Origins." *Worship* 83.9 (May 2009).

————. "Worship in the Twenty-first Century: Contextually Relevant and Catholic." *Currents in Theology and Mission* (August 1999).

Long, Thomas G. *Accompany Them with Singing—The Christian Funeral*. Louisville, KY: Westminster John Knox Press, 2009.

———. *Preaching from Memory to Hope*. Louisville, KY: Westminster John Knox Press, 2009.

Luther, Martin. *Commentary on the Epistle to the Galatians*. 5th printing. Grand Rapids: Zondervan Publishing House, 1962.

———. *Sindflutgebet* (Flood Prayer). http://ematthaei.blogspot .com/2006/08/luthers-flood-prayer_11.html (accessed October 11, 2010).

Martos, Joseph. *Doors to the Sacred: A Historical Introduction to Sacraments in the Catholic Church*. Revised and updated edition. Liguori, MO: Liguori/Triumph, 2001.

Marx, Karl. *Critique of Hegel's Philosophy of Right* (1843). Edited by Joseph O'Malley. Cambridge: Cambridge University Press, 1970.

McKenzie, Alyce M. *Matthew*. Interpretation Bible Studies. Louisville, KY: Geneva Press, 1998.

Meeks, Wayne A. *The First Urban Christians: The Social World of the Apostle Paul*. New Haven, CT: Yale University Press, 1983.

Meyer, Paul W. *The Word in This World: Essays in New Testament Exegesis and Theology*. Edited by John T. Carroll. New Testament Library. Louisville, KY: Westminster John Knox Press, 2004.

Miles, Sara. *Take This Bread: A Radical Conversion*. New York: Ballantine Books, 2008.

Milgrom, Jacob. *Leviticus: A Book of Ritual and Ethics*. Minneapolis: Fortress Press, 2004.

Miller, Patrick D. *The Ten Commandments*. Interpretation: Resources for the Use of Scripture in the Church. Louisville, KY: Westminster John Knox Press, 2009.

Moore-Keish, Martha L. *Do This in Remembrance of Me: A Ritual Approach to Reformed Eucharistic Theology*. Grand Rapids: Eerdmans, 2008.

The New Oxford Annotated Bible. Augmented 3rd edition. New York: Oxford University Press, 2007.

Nichols, J. Randall. "Worship as Anti-Structure: The Contribution of Victor Turner." *Theology Today* 41:4 (January 1985).

O'Day, Gail R., and Susan E. Hylen. *John*. Louisville, KY: Westminster John Knox Press, 2006.

Old, Hughes Oliphant. *The Shaping of the Reformed Baptismal Rite in the Sixteenth Century*. Grand Rapids: Eerdmans, 1992.

O'Rourke, Meghan. "Good Grief: Is There a Better Way to Be Bereaved?" *The New Yorker*. February 1, 2010.

Postman, Neil, and Andrew Postman. *Amusing Ourselves to Death: Public Discourse in the Age of Show Business*. New York: Viking Press, 1985.

The Presbyterian Hymnal. Louisville, KY: Westminster/John Knox Press, 1990.

Propp, William H. *Exodus 1–18*. The Anchor Bible. New York: Doubleday, 1998.

The Revised Common Lectionary: Consultation on Common Texts. Nashville: Abingdon Press, 1992.

Richardson, Cyril C., ed. *Early Christian Fathers*. New York: Collier Books/Macmillan Publishing Co., 1970.

Ricoeur, Paul. *The Symbolism of Evil*. New York: Harper & Row, 1967.

The Rites of the Catholic Church as Revised by the Second Vatican Council, vol. 1. Collegeville, MN: Liturgical Press, 1990.

Schmemann, Alexander. *The Eucharist: Sacrament of the Kingdom*. Crestwood, NY: St. Vladimir's Seminary Press, 1987.

———. *Liturgy and Tradition: Theological Reflections of Alexander Schmemann*. Edited by Thomas Fisch. Crestwood, NY: St. Vladimir's Seminary Press, 2003.

———. *Of Water and the Spirit: A Liturgical Study of Baptism*. Crestwood, NY: St. Vladimir's Seminary Press, 1974.

Searle, Mark. "Infant Baptism Reconsidered." In *Living Water, Sealing Spirit: Readings on Christian Initiation*, edited by Maxwell E. Johnson. Collegeville, MN: Liturgical Press, 1995.

Sloyan, Gerard. *John*. Interpretation: A Bible Commentary for Teaching and Preaching. Atlanta: John Knox Press, 1988.

Smith, Dennis E. *From Symposium to Eucharist: The Banquet in the Early Christian World*. Minneapolis: Fortress Press, 2003.

Spinks, Bryan D. "Calvin's Baptismal Theology and the Making of the Strasbourg and Genevan Baptismal Liturgies 1540–1542." *Scottish Journal of Theology* 48:1 (1995).

———. *Early and Medieval Rituals and Theologies of Baptism: From the New Testament to the Council of Trent*. Burlington, VT: Ashgate Publishing Co., 2006.

———. *Reformation and Modern Rituals and Theologies of Baptism: From Luther to Contemporary Practices*. Burlington, VT: Ashgate Publishing Co., 2006.

Stookey, Laurence Hull. *Calendar: Christ's Time for the Church.* Nashville: Abingdon Press, 1996.

Talley, Thomas J., "From *Berakah* to *Eucharistia*: A Reopening Question." In *Living Bread, Saving Cup: Readings on the Eucharist,* edited by R. Kevin Seasoltz. Collegeville, MN: Liturgical Press, 1982.

Thompson, Bard. *Liturgies of the Western Church.* Philadelphia: Fortress Press, 1961.

Thompson, Marianne Meye. "Reflections on Worship in the Gospel of John." *Princeton Seminary Bulletin* 19:3, new series 1998.

Thurian, Max. *The Eucharistic Memorial.* Part 1. Richmond, VA: John Knox Press, 1962.

Tillich, Paul. *The Dynamics of Faith.* New York: HarperOne, 2001.

The United Methodist Book of Worship. Nashville: United Methodist Publishing House, 1992.

von Allmen, J. J. *Worship: Its Theology and Practice.* New York: Oxford University Press, 1965.

von Rad, Gerhard. *Deuteronomy: A Commentary.* Old Testament Library. Philadelphia: Westminster Press, 1966.

———. *Genesis: A Commentary.* Old Testament Library. Philadelphia: Westminster Press, 1961.

Wainwright, Geoffrey. *Eucharist and Eschatology.* Akron, OH: OSL Publications, 2002.

Willimon, William H. *Acts.* Interpretation: A Bible Commentary for Teaching and Preaching. Atlanta: John Knox Press, 1988.

Winkler, Gabriele. "The Original Meaning of the Prebaptismal Anointing and Its Implications." In *Living Water, Sealing Spirit: Readings on Christian Initiation,* edited by Maxwell E. Johnson. Collegeville, MN: Liturgical Press, 1995.

Wright, N. T. *The Resurrection of the Son of God.* Minneapolis: Fortress Press, 2003.

Zimmerli, Walther. *Ezekiel: A Commentary on the Book of the Prophet Ezekiel,* vol. 2. Trans. by James D. Martin. Hermeneia: A Critical and Historical Commentary on the Bible. Philadelphia: Fortress Press, 1983.

SCRIPTURE INDEX

317

SUBJECT INDEX

327

333

337

345